THE KEY CONCEPTS

GLOBALIZATION

THOMAS HYLLAND ERIKSEN

BLOOMSBURY

Globalization

KEY CONCEPTS SERIES

ISSN 1747–6550

The series aims to cover the core disciplines and the key cross-disciplinary ideas across the Humanities and Social Sciences. Each book isolates the key concepts to map out the theoretical terrain across a specific subject or idea. Designed specifically for student readers, each book in the series includes boxed case material, summary chapter bullet points, annotated guides to further reading, and questions for essays and class discussion.

Design: The Key Concepts
Mark Westgarth and Eleanor Quince

Fashion: The Key Concepts
Jennifer Craik

Film: The Key Concepts
Nitzan Ben-Shaul

Food: The Key Concepts
Warren Belasco

Globalization: The Key Concepts (1st Edition)
Thomas Hylland Eriksen

Technoculture: The Key Concepts
Debra Benita Shaw

The Body: The Key Concepts
Lisa Blackman

New Media: The Key Concepts
Nicholas Gane and David Beer

Photography: The Key Concepts (1st Edition)
David Bate

Photography: The Key Concepts (2nd Edition)
David Bate

Globalization

The Key Concepts

Second Edition

THOMAS HYLLAND ERIKSEN

BLOOMSBURY

LONDON • NEW DELHI • NEW YORK • SYDNEY

Bloomsbury Academic

An imprint of Bloomsbury Publishing Plc

50 Bedford Square
London
WC1B 3DP
UK

1385 Broadway
New York
NY 10018
USA

www.bloomsbury.com

Bloomsbury is a registered trade mark of Bloomsbury Publishing Plc

First edition published in 2007

This second edition published in 2014

British Library Cataloguing-in-Publication Data
A catalogue record for this book is available from the British Library.

ISBN: HB: 978-0-85785-727-9
PB: 978-0-85785-742-2
ePDF: 978-0-85785-581-7
ePub: 978-0-85785-765-1

Library of Congress Cataloging-in-Publication Data

Eriksen, Thomas Hylland.
Globalization : the key concepts / Thomas Hylland Eriksen. — Second edition.
pages cm.
Includes bibliographical references and index.
ISBN 978-0-85785-742-2 (pbk.)
ISBN 978-0-85785-727-9 (hardback)
ISBN 978-0-85785-765-1 (epub)
1. Anthropology. 2. Globalization.
3. Globalization—Social aspects. 4. Culture and globalization. I. Title.
GN27.E69 2014
306—dc23 2013042234

Typeset by Apex CoVantage, LLC, Madison, WI, USA

Contents

Preface

"**M**y office desk is large and sturdy, ergonomically adjusted to suit a person of my height and constructed by world-class Swedish engineers from the finest mock hardwood and real steel. With the flick of a switch, it can be raised (if I want to stand while working to save my back) or lowered (if I were to lend my office to a shorter person). Yet, lately it has been groaning audibly. The reason is simple: The desk is burdened not just by the usual pile of half-read books and exam papers; it carries the additional weight of a good-sized library on globalization, sorted roughly into about a dozen wavering stacks. These books and articles, which comprise only a small fraction of the total number of volumes dealing with globalization and transnationalism since around 1990 (as well as a few older ones), form the bulk of the source material used to write this book—one is reminded of the old pun about a scholar being a library's means to create another library—together with countless journal articles, newspaper clippings, downloaded texts, and a reasonable collection of personal observations jotted down on scraps of paper. Even to begin to summarize the contents of each book and every important article would be a hopeless, endless (and rather boring) job. And then there are all the other texts, which I haven't read and probably never will. I am reminded of my countryman Tor Åge Bringsvaerd's short story about the man who collected the first of September, 1973 (1988). Of course, although if he was at it for years, he went insane long before he was finished."

This is how the preface for the first (2007) edition of this book began. As I began to take notes for it in February 2006, pondering where to begin to tackle the in every way huge topic of globalization, an event in the outside world came to my rescue, as is so often the case with us academics. I had just been reading two very different books about globalization. The American journalist Thomas L. Friedman, in his ambitious *The World Is Flat* (2005: 7), described an increasingly integrated world market where "the playing field had been leveled" in the sense that Indian, Chinese, North Atlantic, and other companies were competing with few impediments: His integrated world was a place where capitalism had won and where the fittest would survive, like it or not. Worrying about the future of the American job market, Friedman noted the emergence of China as a rising power in the global economy, and he spoke about the Internet and global financial markets as guarantors for global economic growth.

The other book was James Lovelock's *The Revenge of Gaia* (2006), a deeply pessimistic book about climate change and environmental destruction, where the author argued that the Earth's self-regulating mechanisms were beginning to falter in the face of massive human energy use, with unforeseeable but doubtless enormous consequences. A different take on globalization from Friedman's upbeat assessment of global capitalism, Lovelock's book indicated an important way in which globalization creates universal vulnerability.

Thinking about these books and how to compare them, I glanced at my morning paper only to be met by a picture from a heated demonstration in a Middle Eastern city. The reason for this demonstration, and subsequent acts of arson, consumer boycott, rioting, and a brief diplomatic crisis, was the publication, some months earlier, of twelve cartoons depicting the Prophet Mohammad in a leading Danish newspaper. Few of the cartoons could be described as offensive in their content, but there is a general ban against depictions of the Prophet in Sunni Islam, and many Muslims outside (and not least inside) Denmark felt that their dissemination was a deliberate act of humiliation. Regardless of his motivation for commissioning the cartoons, the Danish editor could not have anticipated the reactions, fanning out across the Muslim world and, through its repercussions, damaging relations between Denmark and several Muslim countries.

Reflecting on the implications of the cartoon controversy for our attempts to understand globalization, it occurred to me that the affair had demonstrated that not only are political, economic, cultural, and ecological issues globalized these days, but so are emotional ones, in this case, the feeling of humiliation and offense. One can no longer publish a critique of Islam (or Judaism, or Hinduism, or Orthodox Christianity) intended for a local readership assured that it will not be read and possibly misunderstood anywhere else. Not all messages travel freely and swiftly in a globalized world, but all have the potential to do so.

We live in a shrunken world, a world of contacts, frictions, comparisons, communication, and movements, which are sometimes unrestricted by distance. At the same time, and partly for that very reason, boundary making of various kinds has gained a new and heightened significance through attempts to stem and regulate such flows, and besides, many human activities continue to take place without any consequences beyond the local. The aim of this book is to outline some of the main dimensions of globalization, to highlight its dual (local/nonlocal) character, and to indicate some ways in which they are being studied and critiqued. Far from being a comprehensive overview of the area, this book is an attempt to open more doors than it closes and to point the reader in directions that I have myself found fruitful.

The best part of a decade after the completion of the first edition of this book, changes and new developments in the world have made a fairly comprehensive revision and updating necessary. Let me just mention a few things. The rise of China as a world economic power, evident already then, is now making its influence felt in all parts of the global system. The political upheavals in North Africa and the Middle East ("the Arab Spring," as it was known in the beginning), starting just before Christmas 2010, have created a new political configuration in that part of the world, fueled to a great extent by transnational communication technologies. Climate change, again a major source of anxiety a decade ago, is currently a chief preoccupation across the world as it continues to spread uncertainty and perceived changes in many places. Finally, the financial crises of the early twenty-first century, from the subprime crisis starting in the United States in 2008 to the Euro crisis, which has sent ripples throughout the world since 2010, are a constant reminder of the volatility and unpredictability of the world economy, as are the increasingly well-organized reactions against global neoliberalism, sometimes spoken of as the new social movements and epitomized in recent years through the Occupy movement centered in the United States.

Yet, the speed of change, and its direction, varies. Not everything has changed equally or even perceptibly. For example, countries like Cuba and North Korea remain, in different ways, partly disconnected from the world of neoliberal globalization. The then emerging regional powers of Brazil, South Africa, and India remain emerging as I write, and the global military hegemony of the United States remains unchallenged.

Not many people have been directly involved with this book, but those who have—two anonymous referees and Berg's Tristan Palmer in the first edition, five external readers as well as Bloomsbury's Sophie Hodgson and Louise Butler for the second edition—have helped me improve, sharpen, and professionalize the text, and for this I am grateful. Kristin Opsahl Alvarez tracked down and copied a vast number of relevant articles for the first edition—thanks, Kristin! Of more enduring, if less direct, significance, is my association with the Transnational Flows group at the University of Oslo (2001–2004), directed by Marianne E. Lien, my collaboration on the comparative anthropology of human security with colleagues at the Free University of Amsterdam (2003–2006), under the leadership of Oscar Salemink, and my enduring participation in various intellectual projects over the years with Oscar Hemer and Malmö University College. Since late 2012, I have directed a comparative project on the crises of globalization, "Overheating," and the regular conversations and seminars taking place in the research group continuously produce new insights. Many others could have been mentioned, but one will have to do: It was Eduardo Archetti who put me on the track many years ago, and until his premature death in June 2005, we discussed the topics featured in this book (and many other things) so incessantly that I still feel him peering over my shoulder, eager to offer his views and criticisms, as I try to write about globalization.

Oslo, autumn 2013

Introduction

A Shrinking Planet

Although the term globalization is recent and came into widespread use only in the early 1990s, the phenomena to which it refers are older, since transnational connections have existed far longer. However, global consciousness, the awareness of being part of global networks, is recent as a mass phenomenon. Globalization refers to transnational connectedness and encompasses important economic, political, cultural, and environmental dimensions. It creates new opportunities and constraints, possibilities and vulnerabilities. In most parts of the world, there is a continuous tension between globalizing and localizing tendencies, and this relationship constitutes the central dialectic of globalization.

The very popularity of the word globalization signals a need for caution. Although the first usage of the word can be traced back to the early 1960s (Steger 2009), it was scarcely used before the late 1980s, even in academic circles. Today, you can hardly open a newspaper without encountering the term. It may easily appear to be a fashionable label used to designate phenomena one has the vaguest ideas about but that somehow represent newness and a new stage in the history of modernity. Globalization has rapidly become a basket concept, which seems to include anything from climate change to terrorism and petty market trade in the Global South. Yet to discard the concept of globalization on such grounds would be foolish. There is a real need for a common, generic term to describe the manifold, ambiguous, complex ways in which the world is, and increasingly so, interconnected. However, used by itself, the word globalization is empty or at least fuzzy. Before moving to some substantial areas of globalization research in the subsequent chapters of this book, it is therefore necessary to do some sorting and sifting, to delimit some fields of enquiry, and to propose a theoretical approach.

Globalization in Earlier Times

The fact that the term globalization is new does not mean that various parts of the world have not been interconnected before—nor that people were not thinking and theorizing about global interconnectedness in earlier periods. Perhaps the philosopher G.W.F. Hegel (1770–1831) was the first theorist of globalization proper, since he did not merely talk of connections between disparate areas and places but about the emerging consciousness about such connections. Through his famous concept of the world-spirit (*Weltgeist*), an abstract entity immanent in all peoples but unevenly developed, Hegel saw the possibility of imagining all of humanity as a kind of community. However, Hegel's older contemporary Immanuel Kant (1724–1804) had already developed, chiefly in his late essay on eternal peace (Kant 2001 [1795]), an idea of cosmopolitanism that demanded equitable and respectful dialogue between the peoples of the world, regardless of their differences. In these philosophical reflections, we see the incipient notion of a global conversation, which, in the view of many, is being realized now, not least thanks to the technologically induced shrinking of the world in contemporary times. The philosophies of Kant and Hegel were developed in the same period as modern nationalism, and as will later become clear, the ideology of nationalism, although it is often contrasted with and seen as an enemy of globalization, shares many of its characteristics.

The nineteenth century was an era of colonial expansion, scientific discovery, and industrialization in the North, and accompanying these processes were new forms of thought, new models of the world. Karl Marx's political philosophy was certainly global in its scope and ambitions, and nineteenth-century cultural historians in the West tended to include all of humanity in their vast treatises, which often had an evolutionist bent, placing the author's own society at the top of a developmental ladder. Thanks to industrial development, colonial expansion, and technological change (the steamboat first appeared in the 1780s but became widespread only in the 1830s), the growth in international trade was formidable in that century. Another important nineteenth-century invention, the telegraph (1839), made it possible for the first time in human history to move a message independently of an object physically carrying it. With the opening of the first functioning transatlantic cable in 1866, messages could be sent from London to New York in a matter of minutes. It goes without saying that such innovations changed the perception of space and distance. In terms of speed of communication, New York was now closer to the London telegraph office than any suburb only a few miles away.

Technological development in both main forms of communication technology— that transmitting messages and that transporting physical objects—continued in the twentieth century with the invention of the airplane, the radio, and so on. In the 1920s, the Marxist theorist Leon Trotsky argued that socialism in one country was impossible since the world was too interconnected for separate development at the national level to be feasible, and he agitated in favor of a world revolution. The Second World War was, despite its name, the first truly global war that involved fighting in, and troops from, all continents (the First World War was mainly European).

In the first postwar decades, global interconnectedness continued to intensify. The number of transnational companies grew from about seven thousand in 1970 to about eighty thousand in 2013, as did the number of transnational NGOs (nongovernmental organizations)—from about one thousand in 1914 to more than forty thousand in 2013.

The United Nations grew from relatively modest beginnings in 1945 into an immense conglomerate of suborganizations with offices in nearly all countries. International travel became easier, cheaper, and more widespread. In the 1960s, the Canadian media theorist Marshall McLuhan coined the term "global village" to designate the new mass media situation, where television in particular, in his view, would create shared frames of reference and mutual knowledge between people across the globe (McLuhan 1994 [1964]). In this period, global change—economic, environmental, political—became the subject of many new scholarly books. Many used the term development, intimating that the poor countries would eventually catch up with the rich ones (e.g., Rostow 1960). Others, especially voices from the political left and/or the Third World, preferred to use the word imperialism, suggesting that the rich countries were actively exploiting the poor ones and preventing them from developing (e.g., Amin 1980; Frank 1975). The term Westernization, usually used in a derogatory way, became common. Around this time, the historical sociologist Immanuel Wallerstein developed his influential world-system theory (1974–79), which traced the development of the contemporary world system to the intercontinental trade beginning in the fifteenth century. In Wallerstein's view, a permanent international division of labor subsequently developed, dividing the globe into the core (the rich countries), the periphery (the poor countries), and the semiperiphery (countries like Russia, Brazil, and China). Elaborating on world-system theory, Christopher Chase-Dunn and Thomas Hall (1997) take a longer view than Wallerstein, describing the development of transnational systems in a perspective spanning ten thousand years and showing that a multicentered world was finally becoming integrated at the outset of the nineteenth century, in the sense that all major centers were by then in regular contact. Focusing on cultural processes as well as economic ones, the anthropologist Eric Wolf's *Europe and the People Without History* (1982) marked a decisive departure from anthropology's tendency to study ostensibly isolated, small groups. The book, which analyzes imperialism from the perspective of the conquered, showed that most indigenous peoples "stopped being indigenous a long time ago" (Lewellen 2002: 14) and explores the process of colonialization as it was perceived and experienced not by the colonizers but by the colonized.

Globalization Today: A Compressed World

Various parts of the world were interconnected, and there was considerable awareness of this, long before the recent coinage of the term globalization. The Hellenistic Empire, founded through the conquests of Alexander the Great (323–30 B.C.E.), and the Roman Empire (ca. 30 B.C.E.–476 C.E.) are the best known examples of expansive transnational networks from European antiquity, but Chinese, Mongols, and other steppe peoples connected groups across the Eurasian continent and beyond, the most famous trade route being the Silk Road. As the centuries went by, trade, conquests, cultural borrowings, and migration increasingly brought people across the world in contact with each other, directly or indirectly. The late nineteenth century, when the

British Empire was a realm where "the sun never set," marked a high point in early modern globalization.

Yet, it can be argued that there is something new to the present world, that is to say the world that began with the end of the Cold War in 1989–91, which goes a long way to explain the meteoric rise of public interest in globalization and transnational phenomena more generally. Three factors, roughly coinciding in time, may be mentioned here:

● The end of the *Cold War* itself entailed a broadening and deepening of global integration. The global two-bloc system, which had lasted since the 1940s, had made it difficult to think of geopolitics, transnational communication, and international trade in terms not dictated by the opposition between the United States and the Soviet Union and their respective allies. With the dissolution of this conflict, the world seemed to have been left with a one-bloc system (notwithstanding the continued existence of a few states, such as North Korea, which continue to stay largely aloof). The world appeared to have become a single marketplace.

● The *Internet*, which had existed in embryonic form since the late 1960s, began to grow exponentially around 1990. Throughout the 1990s, media buzzwords were about bandwidths, websites, portals, the new economy, and its business opportunities. The World Wide Web was introduced in 1992–93, around the same time as many academics and businesspeople grew accustomed to using e-mail for their daily correspondence. Cell phones became ubiquitous in the rich countries and the middle classes of the poorer ones. The impact of this double delocalization—the physical letter replaced by e-mail, the fixed landline replaced by the wireless mobile—on the everyday life of millions of people has been considerable, but it remains undertheorized.

● *Identity politics*—nationalist, ethnic, religious, territorial—were at the forefront of the international agenda, both from above (states demanding homogeneity or engaging in ethnic cleansing) and from below (minorities demanding equal rights or secession). The Salman Rushdie affair, itself an excellent example of the globalization of ideas, began with the issuing of a fatwa by Iran's ayatollah, Khomeini, following the publication of Rushdie's allegedly blasphemous novel *The Satanic Verses* (1988). It soon became apparent that Rushdie could move freely nowhere in the world since the fatwa had global implications. Only two years later, Yugoslavia dissolved, with ensuing civil wars based on ethnic differences. In the same period, debates about immigration and multiculturalism came to dominate political discourse in several Western countries, while the Hindu nationalists of the BJP (Bharatiya Janata Party, or "Indian People's Party") came to power in India.

These three dimensions of globalization—increased trade and transnational economic activity; faster and denser communication networks; and increased tensions between (and within) cultural groups due to intensified mutual exposure—do not suggest that the world has been fundamentally transformed after the late 1980s, but that the driving forces of both economic, political, and cultural dynamics are transnational—and that this is now widely acknowledged. As a pioneering theorist of contemporary globalization, Roland Robertson succinctly puts it: "Globalization as a concept refers *both* to the compression of the world *and* the intensification of consciousness about the world as a whole" (1992: 8, emphasis mine).

The compression of the world, in all of its forms, brings us closer to each other for better and for worse. The consciousness about these connections gives a sense of both opportunities and of vulnerability. This dual aspect of globalization—increased interconnectedness and increased awareness of it—can be studied from a myriad of empirical vantage points. It would be perfectly feasible, within the compass of globalization studies, to write a dissertation on, say, European and American reactions to the Asian bird flu in 2006. The impact of, and local perceptions of, globalization among the small, until very recently illiterate and stateless peoples in Melanesia, has long been a subject in anthropology (see Martin 2013 for a recent, excellent treatment). Human geographers write about the displacement of people in India as a result of climate change. Sociologists study the growth of slums in Africa. Anthropologists and others try to figure out the effects of the phenomenal rise of the Chinese export economy and its implications, locally as well as in China itself. Thousands write about migration, again from a variety of perspectives. Others are concerned with the distribution of economic power in the global economy, or the distribution of symbolic or definitional power in the global media world; some write about standardization of goods and services as an outcome of the globalization of the economy; others write about the spread of certain consumer preferences, yet others about the global tourist industry and the commodification of cultural identity; others again study international law, with human rights as a main dimension of globalization, or the *antiglobalization* or *alterglobalization* movement, which opposes the inequalities and power disparities created through processes of economic globalization. Just to mention a few subject areas. As far as academic disciplines are concerned, globalization is a central topic in sociology, political science, cultural history, geography, anthropology, media studies, education, law, cultural studies, and so on. The examples in this book, I should emphasize, are meant to indicate variations over a (large) theme and do not claim to be representative in a statistical sense.

What Globalization is Not

Before outlining some central analytical dimensions of globalization, it seems pertinent to mention a few notions often associated with globalization, either simplistically or wrongly:

- *Globalization is really very recent and began only in the 1980s.* This view betrays the beholder's poor knowledge of history. World-systems have existed earlier in the sense that people all over the world have participated, often involuntarily, in political and economic systems of a huge, often intercontinental scale. The European colonial era is the most obvious instance, but one might argue that the Roman Empire, encompassing as it did most of the known world (for Europeans), or the Aztec Empire, shared many of the characteristics of today's globalization (Friedman 1994). Indeed, Nayan Chanda (2007) begins his compelling narrative about the "traders, preachers, adventurers and warriors" who shaped globalization, with the exodus from Africa and pays considerable attention—rightly so—to the mobilities of people, goods, plants, and ideas during colonialism. However, the inhabitants of earlier world-systems were rarely aware of each other beyond their own experience, or only dimly so through the presence of rare objects from afar and tall stories told by travelers. As a form of human consciousness, globalization is new as a mass phenomenon. The labor market situation in Oslo has been known to thousands of Pakistani villagers for decades, and reggae music in Melanesia, advertising in Central Africa, and the rhetoric of the political opposition in South Korea all indicate the existence of a global *discourse*, a shared (but not uniform) communication system. In this cultural sense, globalization is recent as a mass phenomenon, and the number of people who are unaware of the existence of television, chewing gum, and basic human rights is decreasing every year.

- *Globalization is just a new word for economic imperialism or cultural Westernization.* This view reduces the vast range of transnational processes to certain economic ones. Although it is tautologically true that rich countries are dominant, the situation is not static. Not only China, but India, South Korea, and other formerly poor countries are emerging as equal players, and regional powers such as South Africa and Brazil are both exploited and exploiters in the global economy. However, the main problem with this view is its neglect of the noneconomic dimensions of globalization. The direction of transnational flows is not unilateral: Some things flow from north to south, others from south to north, and there is also considerable movement between east and west and within the south. The millions of pirated CDs and DVDs sold in Mexico have been imported, illegally or semilegally, from China (Aguiar 2012). The violent uprising in Mali, beginning in spring 2012, was ideologically inspired by ideas originating in the Arab peninsula. The largest group of Somali refugees lives in neighboring Kenya. And the main groups of labor migrants in South Africa come from other African countries, notably Zimbabwe and Nigeria. Westernization is not a good synonym for globalization.

- *Globalization means homogenization.* This view is always simplistic and usually misleading. First, the participation in global, or transnational, processes often entails a vitalization of local cultural expressions, be it African art, Caribbean popular music, or Indian novels, which depend on an overseas market for their survival. Second, large segments of our everyday lives are hardly touched by globalization. Although Taiwanese, like people from the North Atlantic, wear jeans and fiddle with touch phones while eating burgers and drinking Cokes, they do not thereby become Europeans or Americans. However, as will be argued in a later chapter, it is true that similarities between discrete societies develop as an integral dimension of globalization.

- *Globalization is opposed to human rights.* On the contrary, the global spread of human rights is one of the most spectacularly successful forms of globalization witnessed in the world. It is true, of course, that transnational companies operating in poor countries do not necessarily recognize workers' rights, but it is only thanks to the globalization of political ideas that local communities and organizations can argue effectively against them and canvas for support from transnational NGOs and governments overseas.

- *Globalization is a threat to local identities.* At the very best, this is a truth with serious modifications. Since tendencies towards globalization (understood as the dissolution of boundaries) usually lead to strong, localizing counterreactions favoring local food, local customs, and so on, some theorists have followed Robertson's (1992) lead in talking about *glocalization* as a more accurate term for what is going on. Local identities are usually strengthened by globalization because people begin to emphasize their uniqueness overtly only when it appears to be threatened. The emergence of identity politics, which explicitly aims to protect and strengthen local identities, is a reaction to perceived dominance from the outside and dissolving boundaries. On the other hand, it is evidently true that local power is often weakened as a result of globalization. It nonetheless remains indisputable that globalization does not create global persons; people continue to live in particular places with a unique mix of the old and the new, the near and the distant, change and continuity, and these places do not become identical overnight, or indeed ever.

Globalizers and Skeptics

Not everybody who writes about the contemporary world agrees that it has entered a distinctively global era. Some, in fact, argue that the extent of global integration was just as comprehensive, and in some ways more encompassing, in the belle epoque of 1890–1914 than it is today. Others claim that the nation-state remains, even today, "the pre-eminent power container of our era" (Giddens 1985: back cover; he would later revise his position, cf. Giddens 1999). Yet others point out that a large number of people, and huge swathes of social and cultural life, are relatively untouched by transnational processes. It may be useful, following David Held and Anthony McGrew (2000: 38; see also Steger 2009), to distinguish between *globalizers* and *skeptics*, to highlight some of the debates and the positions taken by different scholars.

According to the skeptics (see, e.g., Gray 2005; Hirst and Thompson 1999), we are witnessing a process of *internationalization* and *regionalization* rather than the emergence of one integrated world of rapid communication, transnational networks, and global financial capital, which is the view of globalizers. Skeptics argue further that the nation-state remains the most important political entity, while globalizers claim that state sovereignty is on the wane and that multilateralism and transnational politics are replacing it. While skeptics have identified the development of regional economic blocs like NAFTA (North American Free Trade Agreement) and the EU, globalizers see the world economy as "a single playing-field" (Friedman 2005: 7) with diminishing obstacles to truly global competition. Skeptics see a continuation of the classic North-South divide in terms of prosperity and power, while globalizers argue that inequalities are chiefly growing within and not between societies. While skeptics believe in the continued or indeed increasing power of national identities and cultures, globalizers describe hybridities and cosmopolitan orientations as an outcome of intensified interaction.

The skeptics do not deny that massive changes are taking place, but they emphasize continuities with the modern world of the nation-state at the levels of politics, economy, and identity, while globalizers are concerned to show that the world is going through a series of qualitative changes.

There is no reason to take an unequivocal position here. Few are simply globalizers (or even *hyperglobalizers*) or skeptics, and both positions can often shed light on the issues. For example, the extent of global solidarity in environmental and human rights questions is no doubt enhanced by extensive travel and global communication and media, and this lends credibility to the view that cosmopolitanism and cultural hybridity (mixing) results from increased interconnectedness. Yet at the same time, identity politics based on religion, ethnicity, or nationality aimed to strengthen social and cultural boundaries is also on the rise. Both phenomena coexist side by side and are possible responses to the opportunity space created by intensified transnational contacts. There can be no effects of say, global capitalism, the Internet, or politicized Islam, that are not mediated by human understandings and experiences, and they vary. Most empirical generalizations about globalization are therefore false. At the same time, it is possible to delineate a framework for global or transnational processes, objective changes, or features of the world that people everywhere have to relate to, but they do so in different ways.

A related debate concerns the moral, or normative, dimension of globalization: Is it chiefly good or is it mostly bad? This is an even more impossible dichotomy to relate to than the (hyper-)globalizer versus the skeptical one. Neoliberal capitalism, characterized by the deregulation of markets and a strong emphasis on free trade (in theory if not always in practice), has its winners and losers; it produces wealth as well as poverty. Neoliberalism also necessarily leads to local reactions from persons, groups, and communities who resist its flattening and homogenizing tendencies, insisting on basing their economy on local needs and skills rather than global markets (see Hann and Hart 2011). Indeed, already in the 1940s, the economic historian Karl Polanyi (1957 [1944]) saw what he described as a "double movement" between global standardization and local autonomy in the economy. Migration regimes, whether restrictive or liberal, create both opportunities and constraints. Even global climate change, virtually unequivocally seen as perilous, creates new opportunities—for example, for farmers in cold regions. The effects of globalization are, thus, not good or bad but complex and influence people's lives differently in different societies and different groups in the same society.

Overheating as a Metaphor

A number of key features of contemporary globalization can be captured through the metaphor of overheating. In physics, heat and speed are synonyms, and the present globalized world is one of intensified tensions and frictions linked with an increase in the speed of change. One need only count the present number of transatlantic flights or the number of transpacific telephone connections to realize that the webs of connectedness are hotter, faster, and denser than in any previous period, with repercussions virtually everywhere. There are areas in rural West Africa that until a decade ago had no paved roads but that now experience traffic jams; there are villages in New Guinea that had existed for millennia in relative isolation until the 1970s but whose inhabitants are now wage earners, voters, and students—and there are millions of Indians who logged on to Facebook for the first time last year.

Overheating is a way of talking about accelerated change. It is the kind of change that can be depicted as exponential growth. The rise of the Brazilian economy, the growth of Chinese cities, the increase in the number of cruise ship passengers, e-mail servers, television channels, or transnational remittances—these are just some examples of global processes that have accelerated in the last few decades and are, in ways that are still not fully known or understood, transforming the planet.

The first subject area that comes to most people's minds when the term overheating is mentioned is climate change, which will be discussed in a later chapter. Although the average global temperature has only risen by 0.8 degree Celsius (1.44 degrees Fahrenheit) since the early twentieth century, the amount of CO_2 has grown far more significantly, and many climate researchers believe that an exponential growth in temperature change is imminent. However, overheating also fits developments in the financial economy, where pundits and dealers occasionally speak literally about overheated markets, economic meltdown, and the need to cool down the economy. This is a way of describing a situation where too many transactions are taking place at the same time, leading to a loss of overview and unpredictable outcomes. Moreover, in the realm of identity politics, to mention a third example, the metaphor also often seems appropriate. Violent clashes, hateful exchanges, and mutually exclusive claims to scarce resources, which are all too common in this twenty-first-century world, all result from perceived frictions, which in turn are the outcome of increased contact.

An overheated world is one of frictions and tensions, simply because there are more of us, with more activities, projects, opportunities, and technologies than ever before in history. We are now 7 billion; a century ago, there were only 1.7 billion of us. In research on traffic, it is sometimes pointed out that there essentially exist only three kinds of traffic—free flow (when there is scarcely anybody else on the highway), synchronized flow (when you have to take others into consideration), and traffic jams. We may think of the contemporary world as one characterized mostly by synchronized flows at a high speed, where the occasional crash is, perhaps, inevitable.

Dimensions of Globalization

Whether we look at global capitalism, trends in consumer tastes, transnational migration and identity politics, or online communication, the globalizing processes of the early twenty-first century have a few salient characteristics in common. These features are dealt with in detail in the main chapters of this book, and I shall only briefly mention them here:

- *Disembedding*, including delocalization. Globalization implies that distance is becoming irrelevant, relative, or at the very least less important. Ideas, songs, books, investment capital, labor, and fashions travel faster than ever, and even if they stay put, their location can be less important than it would have been formerly. This aspect of globalization is driven by technological and economic changes, but it has cultural and political implications. Disembedding, however, also includes all manners through which social life becomes abstracted from its local, spatially fixed context.

- *Speed.* The speed of transport and communication has increased throughout the twentieth century, and this acceleration continues. It has been said that there are no delays any more in an era of instantaneous communication over cell phones, Internet servers, and television satellites. Although this is surely an exaggeration—delays exist, even if only as unintended consequences— speed is an important feature of globalization. Anything from inexpensive plane tickets to cheap calls contribute to integrating the world, and the exponential growth in the numbers of Internet users since the early 1990s indicates that distance no longer means separation. However, acceleration is uneven, and relative slowness may be just as significant as relative speed. Different parts of societies and cultural worlds change at different speeds, and there are places and countries where change takes place at a different, more sluggish rate than elsewhere.

- *Standardization*. Continuing the processes of standardization begun by nationalism and national economies, globalization entails comparability and shared standards where there were formerly none. The rapid increase in the use of English as a foreign language is suggestive of this development, as is the worldwide spread of similar hotels and shopping centers, as well as the growing web of international agreements and industry standards.

- *Connections*. The networks connecting people across continents are becoming denser, faster, and wider every year. Mutual dependence and transnational connections lead to a need for more international agreements and a refashioning of foreign policies and create both fields of opportunities, constraints, and new forms of power.

- *Mobility*. The entire world is on the move, or so it might sometimes seem. Migration, business travel, international conferences, and not least tourism have been growing steadily for decades, with a number of important implications for local communities, politics, and economies.

- *Mixing*. Although *cultural crossroads*, where people of different origins met, are as ancient as urban life, their number, size, and diversity is growing every day. Both frictions and mutual influence result. Additionally, at the level of culture, the instantaneous exchange of messages characteristic of the information era leads to probably more cultural mixing than ever before in human history. However, cultural mixing does not necessarily lead to the breakdown of boundaries between identities.

- *Risk*. Globalization entails the weakening, and sometimes obliteration, of boundaries. Flows of anything from money to refugees are intensified in this era. This means that territorial polities have difficulties protecting themselves against unwanted flows. Typical globalized risks include AIDS and other epidemics, transnational terrorism, and climate change, but there is also increased attention to ecological disruptions caused by invasive species, like the Caribbean cane toad in Australia or the Burmese python in Florida. Most of these risks cannot be combated efficiently by single nation-states, and on a more general note, it has often been pointed out that the planet as a whole lacks efficient political instruments able to deal with and govern the technology- and economy-driven processes of globalization.

- *Identity politics*. Politics founded not in ideology or quests for universal rights but in the maintenance and strengthening of particular collective identities are related to globalization in two main ways. First, identity politics, whether nationalist, ethnic, religious, or regionalist, are direct responses to globalizing processes, which seem to threaten the local and unique by introducing new, often standardizing or universalistic values, ideas, and practices. Second, identity politics in itself has a universalistic dimension in that the grammar, or rhetoric, used to promote the rights of particular groups has important similarities across the world.

- *Alterglobalization.* Reactions to global neoliberalism were initially described in the media and by analysts as antiglobalization, which is a simplistic and misleading term (see Graeber 2001). The new social movements, ranging from ATTAC in France to the Occupy movement in the United States, the Slum Dweller Alliance in Mumbai, and *los indignados* in Spain, are not opposed to global connectedness as such but reject the narrowly profit-seeking neoliberalist version of globalization, which they see as dehumanizing and oppressive. What these diverse organizations have in common is resistance to the disembedding tendencies of globalization, and they may be described collectively as reembedding movements. In fact, all the key features of globalization mentioned above have their countervailing forces opposing them and positing alternatives. The fragmented, fleeting social world made possible through disembedding processes is counteracted through strong networks of moral commitment, concerns with local power and community integration, and a "human economy" embedded in social life as an alternative to neoliberal capitalism operating at a global level (Hart 2013: 1).

Moreover, acceleration is counteracted through social movements promoting slowness in many guises, standardization through uniquely fashioned one-of-a-kind goods and services, transnational interconnectedness through localism and nationalism, movement through quests for stability and continuity, mixing through concerns with cultural purity, and vulnerability through attempts at self-determination and relative isolation.

Globalization is not a unidirectional process. It has no end and no intrinsic purpose, and it is neither uncontested, unambiguous, nor ubiquitous. If we want to get the whole picture, it must include both benefactors and victims, both the active globalizers and those who are merely globalized, both those who are caught up in the whirlwind of global processes and those who are excluded. Huge, atrocious slums mushrooming all over the poor parts of the world are products of transnational economic processes (Davis 2006), but they are generally seen as the debris of the global economy—the people living there cursorily defined as problems not resources.

Ways of Looking at Globalization

A few further distinctions should also be made initially. The examples in this book deal with economic, political, cultural, aesthetic, and environmental aspects of globalization, but the boundaries drawn between such domains are largely artificial and will be dispensed with when they are not needed. It should also be kept in mind that different threads, or domains, in transnational processes do not necessarily move in the same directions, at the same levels of intensity, or at the same speed. This means that all societies are unequally affected by different tendencies. Such disjunctures or discrepancies will be explored further.

Globalization can take place, and can be studied, from *above* or from *below*. A problematic but necessary distinction, this dichotomy refers to the state, to major international organizations, and to powerful business enterprises on the one hand and to interpersonal relationships on the other hand. I shall show that the interpersonal globalization from below is far more encompassing and more important in shaping the world than often assumed.

A distinction between *objective* and *subjective* globalization, also not unproblematic, must also be made initially. Objective globalization means that something is being incorporated into a global, or wide-ranging, transnational system without necessarily being aware of it, whereas subjective globalization amounts to the acknowledgement of such processes taking place (which they may or may not; citizens often blame globalization for changes wrought locally).

Finally, and this is a main point in this book, globalization does not entail the production of *global uniformity*, or homogeneity. Rather, it can be seen as a way of organizing *heterogeneity*. The similarities dealt with, for example, in the chapter on standardization are formal and abstract and do not necessarily lead to homogeneity at the level of *content* or experience. The local continues to thrive, although it must increasingly be seen as *glocal*—that is, enmeshed in transnational processes.

The growth of urban slums throughout the Global South is an indirect result of economic globalization, just as the relative disconnectedness from the Internet in Africa is a significant fact alongside the growth in text messages in China, from zero to eighteen billion a month in less than ten years. The networked capitalist world is a framework, or scaffolding, for almost any serious inquiry into cultural and social dynamics, and it is characterized by an intensification of processes of change, which makes it, in important ways, volatile and unpredictable.

Seven Key Debates about Globalization

Research on globalization is sprawling and multidisciplinary. It is not the ambition of this book to sum it up or even to do justice to the vast scope of globalization studies (most of which have been published since 1990). That would plainly have been impossible. Yet, it may be kept in mind that much of the research, and indeed much of the public debate in most countries, about globalization is concerned with a few central questions:

- First, a chiefly academic question: Is globalization new or old? I have already commented briefly on this. The answer has to be sphinx-like: it depends on your definition. Sprawling, but well-integrated political systems with thriving trade, internal migration, standardized measures, and a common high culture have existed in several continents well before the modern era. However, there are so many characteristic features of our present age—even if we limit it to the post-Cold War era—that it merits treatment on its own terms. One of the leading theorists of the information society, Manuel Castells, mentions in a lengthy footnote towards the end of his monumental *The Information Age* that students have sometimes asked him what is new about the world he describes. His answer deserves to be quoted in full:

> Why is this a new world? . . . Chips and computers are new; ubiquitous, mobile telecommunications are new, genetic engineering is new; electronically integrated, global financial markets working in real time are new; an inter-linked capitalist economy embracing the whole planet, and not only some of its segments, is new; a majority of the urban labor force in knowledge and information processing in advanced economies is new; a majority of urban population in the planet is new; the demise of the Soviet Empire, the fading away of communism, and the end of the Cold War are new; the rise of the Asian Pacific as an equal partner in the global economy is new; the widespread challenge to patriarchalism is new; the universal consciousness on ecological preservation is new; and the emergence of a network society, based on a space of flows, and on timeless time, is historically new. (Castells 1998: 336)

● A few years later, he could have added the advent of deterritorialized warfare and humanly induced climate change to the list. Be this as it may, Castells adds that it does not really matter whether all this is new or not; his point is that this is our world, and therefore we should study it.

● A second question raised in the debates over globalization, academic and nonacademic, concerns the relationship of globalization to neoliberal economics—that is, the view that free trade will eventually lead to prosperity everywhere and that states should encumber the economy as little as possible. Severely criticized (see, e.g., Gray 1998; Klein 1998; Rodrik 2011; Soros 2002; Stiglitz 2002;, among very many others) for not delivering the goods—many countries that have complied with measures imposed by international agencies like the World Bank and the IMF (International Monetary Fund) have experienced a steep decline in de facto standards of living—neoliberalism is often associated with, indeed sometimes treated as a synonym for, globalization (Kiely 2005). Here it must be said that such a usage narrows the concept too much. The global spread of human rights ideas is no less a feature of globalization than the global financial market; the vaccination programs of the WHO (World Health Organization) are no less global than the moneylending of the World Bank, and the small-scale lending programs initiated by 2006 Nobel Peace Laureate Mohammad Yunus and his Bangladeshi Grameen Bank have spread to other countries; one could go on. Global governance (see Held et al. 2005; Scholte 2011) is sometimes posited as an alternative to an anarchic market economy, which is, in any case, imperfect insofar as poor countries rarely get full market access in the rich ones. Globalization is form not content; it can be filled with neoliberal market economics, but this is not the whole story.

- A third, related debate concerns the relationship between globalization and democracy. Many scholars, politicians, and commentators are concerned about the loss of political power experienced by nation-states when so much economic power is diverted to the transnational arenas (see, e.g., Sassen 1998; Rodrik 2011). Clearly, there are some real issues to be tackled here: The institutions of the nation-state arguably lose some of their clout when capital and wealth are disembedded and become transnational. Yet, the spread of democratic ideas, institutions, and practices are also part of the global process. In other words, one cannot say that globalization is either favorable or detrimental to democracy; it is necessary to be more specific.

- A fourth, important debate deals with the relationship between poor and rich countries: Do the poor become poorer and the rich richer as a result of economic globalization? Again, there can be no simple, unequivocal answer. Who benefits in the long (or for that matter short) run from the globalization of economies? The answer is far from clear. Some countries mired in poverty, notably in Africa, are among the least globalized in terms of integration into the world economy. Their exports are modest, and foreign investment is considered risky and therefore is rare. Some rich countries, not least in Western Europe, begin to notice the competition from poorer countries (notably China and central-eastern Europe) as an unpleasant experience. In other cases, it can be argued that current trade regimes, such as the ones negotiated by the WTO (World Trade Organization), help rich countries to continue exploiting poor ones by buying cheap unprocessed goods from them and selling them expensive industrial products back. This would fit with the dependency theory developed by Andre Gunder Frank, Samir Amin, and other Marxist scholars, as well as its close relative, Immanuel Wallerstein's world-system theory (see Amin et al. 1982). However, this description fits the older neocolonial trade regime better than the current one, where China is fast making inroads into markets in Asia and Africa with its inexpensive industrial goods and willingness to invest in industrial enterprises. As argued by Daniel Cohen (2006), the poorest countries are not so much exploited as neglected by transnational investors. It has been proved conclusively that inequalities have grown in most of the world since the 1980s, but it is unclear whether this is a result of globalization or of domestic policies aiming to deregulate markets and encourage investment.

● A fifth, no less important, theme is that of cultural dynamics: Does globalization lead to homogenization or to heterogenization—do we become more similar or more different due to the increased transnational movement and communication? In one sense, we become more similar. Individualism, which we here take to mean the belief that individuals have rights and responsibilities regardless of their place in wider social configurations, is a central feature of global modernity. It is also easy to argue that similarities in consumer preferences among the world's middle classes indicate flattening, or homogenization. Yet, at the same time, local adaptations of universal or nearly universal phenomena show that global modernities always have local expressions and that the assumed similarities may either conceal real differences in meaning or that they may be superficial with no deep bearing on people's existential condition. Again, the question is phrased too simplistically to have a meaningful yes/no answer.

● Related to this problematic is a sixth area of debate—namely, that to do with identity politics. Does globalization, through increasingly exposing us to each other's lives, lead to enhanced solidarity, tolerance, and sympathy with people elsewhere, or, rather, does it lead to ferocious counterreactions in the form of stubborn identity politics—nationalism, religious fundamentalism, racism, and so on? This question has, perhaps, a short answer. Globalization does makes it easier for us to understand each other across cultural divides, but it also creates tensions between groups that were formerly isolated from each other, and it creates a need to demarcate uniqueness and sometimes historical rootedness. The more similar we become, the more different from each other we try to be. Strong group identities may serve several purposes—economic, political, existential—in a world otherwise full of movement and turmoil. Divisive and exclusionary identity politics are a trueborn child of globalization, but so is transnational solidarity.

● Finally, an important question concerns how European (or Western, or North Atlantic) globalization is. The conventional view is that globalization is largely fuelled by the economic, technological, and political developments of Western Europe. Those who take the long view may begin with the Renaissance, the Italian city-states, and the European conquests of the fifteenth and sixteenth centuries; those who write about the present may emphasize transnational corporations, computer technology, and the dynamics of capitalism. However, other perspectives may be useful and indeed necessary. If we look at history, the powerhouses of transnational economies have been located in many places. Andre Gunder Frank (1998), a long-standing collaborator with Wallerstein, increasingly saw the latter's world-system theory as overly Eurocentric and showed, in one of his last books, that large-scale transnational markets were flourishing in Asia before and during the European expansionist period, centered on China and parts of India, and leading to both migration waves and cultural exchange. Only with the last period of European colonialization in the nineteenth century did that continent become truly dominant in the world economy, according to Frank. Non-Eurocentric histories of the world, such as Felipe Fernandez-Armesto's *Millennium* (1995; cf. also Fernandez-Armesto 2000; Goody 2010; Morris 2010), also tend to emphasize important interconnections in the past outside Europe. If a Martian were to visit the Earth in the year 1300, Fernandez-Armesto (1995) says, the Martian would not be able to predict the rise of Europe as the center of global power. There were thriving civilizations in Mesoamerica, in the Andes, in West Africa, in the Arab world, in India, and in China, easily surpassing stagnant European societies in transnational trade, cultural achievements, and political might. As pointed out by Jack Goody (2010), if it is true that Asia is currently about to achieve dominance in the global economy, that would only entail a new spin on the historical oscillations between Eastern and Western hegemony.

If we restrict ourselves to the present, the picture is also less straightforward than a superficial look might suggest. In popular culture as well as literature, major achievements of global significance come from outside the West; Indian films (Bollywood movies) are popular in many countries, as are Mexican and Brazilian soap operas, Argentine tango, and Japanese manga comics. Major alternatives to Western ideologies, such as political Islam, are expanding, and China and India, which combined have 40 percent of the world's population, have economic growth rates far surpassing those of the North Atlantic countries. The division of the world into core, periphery, and semiperiphery, thus, is a model that needs to be tested and does not always yield the expected results.

* * *

We shall return to these and other debates as we go along. Before we move on, I should point out that unlike many introductions to globalization, this book does not suggest what to study in the sense of providing a catalogue of substantial topics deemed particularly important by the author. Rather, it suggests where to look and, to some extent, how to look for it. The dimensions of globalization presented in the chapters that follow—my key concepts—can be mined for insights through immersion into diverse empirical fields. In the following chapters, I will outline the main characteristics of globalization: It *standardizes*, *modernizes*, *deterritorializes*, and, by dialectical negation, *localizes* people, since it is only after having been globalized that people may become obsessed with the uniqueness of their locality. I emphasize that although globalization is driven by powerful economic and technological forces, it takes place between people; the transnational webs of the world depend on interpersonal trust, and people often use the opportunities offered by globalizing processes in unexpected ways.

Globalization creates a shared grammar for talking about differences and inequalities. Humans everywhere are increasingly entering the same playing field, yet they do not participate in equal ways, and thus frictions and conflicts are an integral part of globalizing processes. This, too, will be evident in the chapters that follow.

- Globalization entails both the intensification of transnational connectedness and the awareness of such an intensification.
- Globalization is largely driven by technological and economic processes, but it is multidimensional and not unidirectional.
- Globalization entails both processes of homogenization and processes of heterogenization: it makes us more similar and more different at the same time.
- Globalization is a wider concept than Westernization or neoimperialism and includes processes that move from south to north as well as the opposite.
- Although globalization is old in the sense that transnational or even global systems have existed for centuries—indeed for millennia—contemporary globalization has distinctive traits due to enhanced communication technology and the global spread of capitalism.

Questions

- Discuss differences and similarities between contemporary globalization and the colonial world-system of the nineteenth century.
- In what sense does the author claim that the post-Cold War world entails a new phase of globalization? Do you agree?
- How can identity politics be said to be an outcome of globalization?
- What is the difference between globalization and Westernization?
- What is meant by glocalization?
- What does the author mean by overheating?

Further Reading

Chanda, Nayan (2007) *Bound Together: How Traders, Preachers, Adventurers, and Warriors Shaped Globalization.* New Haven, CT: Yale University Press. An entertaining and erudite account of globalization, which takes the long perspective of several thousand years, with a consistent focus on the individuals that made the globally connected world come about, and their motivations—from missionary zeal to personal greed.

Robertson, Roland (1992) *Globalization: Social Theory and Global Culture.* London: Sage. A collection of highly influential essays by one of the architects of current globalization theory, the book discusses conceptualizations of the global, the history of the global system, and introduces the term glocalization to overcome the artificial dichotomy of the global and the local.

Wolf, Eric (1982) *Europe and the People without History.* Berkeley: University of California Press. A history of the last five hundred years, written from the perspective of the colonized peoples, offering an alternative and challenging view of the processes of globalization, so often seen from a Western perspective.

1

Disembedding

Disembedding is the most abstract of the key terms of globalization, and this stands to reason, since it in fact refers to the historical movement towards a more abstract world. When something is disembedded, it is moved from a concrete, tangible, local context to an abstract or virtual state. Money is disembedded value; clock time is disembedded time; writing is disembedded language. For globalization to integrate people all over the world into a shared system of communication, production, and exchange, some disembedding common denominators are necessary.

In August, 1989, I visited San Juan, Puerto Rico. I was in the middle of anthropological fieldwork in Trinidad and took a break in order to familiarize myself a little with the wider Caribbean region. At the airport, I was on my way to an exchange office when I came across an ATM with a VISA symbol up front. Tentatively sticking the card into the machine and typing my PIN code, I was uncertain as to what to expect, but after a few seconds, the machine duly presented the required greenbacks and—even more impressively—a receipt, which told me my exact (meager) bank balance. My money no longer had a physical form; it had been moved to cyberspace (a term coined five years earlier in William Gibson's novel *Neuromancer*, 1984). The money had been *disembedded*, removed from a tangible, physical context.

As a rule, anything that can be accessed anywhere is disembedded. It could be a clip on YouTube, an international agreement, a stock exchange rate, or a soccer game (provided its main audience watches it on TV and not at the stadium). One main contemporary form of disembedding is *deterritorialization*, which takes place when something is "lifted out of" its physical location (Giddens 1990: 21). Before we delve more deeply into the concept and its implications for the real world, let us consider a famous example of deterritorialized warfare.

When, in September 2001, the then U.S. president George W. Bush announced his "war on terror," it may have been the first time in history that an actual war was proclaimed on a nonterritorial entity. Unlike metaphorical wars on drugs or wars on poverty, this was meant to be a war fought with real weapons and real soldiers. The only problem was that it initially appeared to be uncertain where to deploy them, since terrorism was potentially anywhere. The ostensible goal of the war was not to conquer another country or to defend one's boundaries against a foreign invasion but to eradicate terrorism—that is, a nonterritorial entity.

The cause of the declaration of war was the terrorist attack on the United States, where three civilian airplanes were hijacked by terrorists belonging to the militant Muslim al-Qaeda organization and flown into the World Trade Center and the Pentagon. A fourth plane, with an uncertain destination, crashed en route. Rather than seeing this as a large-scale crime, the U.S. government defined the event as the beginning of a war. However, it was not to be a war between territorially defined units, such as nation-states. Several of the hijackers lived and studied in the United States. Most of them were of Saudi origins, but they were not acting on orders from the Saudi state. The organization on whose behalf they acted seemed to have its headquarters in Afghanistan, but the members were scattered—some living in North America, some in Europe, some in Pakistan, and so on.

The nation-state has unambiguous boundaries; it is defined in Benedict Anderson's famous terms as being imagined as "inherently limited and sovereign" (1991 [1983]: 6). Wars are fought by the military, whose mission it is to protect the external borders of the country. A nation-state thus has a clearly defined inside and outside. The events of September 11 were a shocking reminder that the boundaries of a nation-state are far from absolute. Nations are effectively being deterritorialized in a number of ways through migration, economic investments, and a number of other processes, and the war on terror illustrates that this is now also the case with war. America's enemies can in fact be anywhere in the world and operate from any site, since American interests are global.

A few days after the September 11 events, a thought-provoking photo was reproduced in newspapers worldwide. It depicted military guards watching over the entrances to New York's Grand Central Station. The image was a reminder of two features of globalization: The boundary between police and military becomes blurred even in democracies where the military is not normally visible in the streets and suggests a partial collapse of the boundary between inside and outside. (This blurring of the inside/outside boundary is also evident in the military patrolling of EU borders along the northwest African coast and the military's role in typical transit areas, such as the Canary Islands. The division of labor between police and military is negotiable and uncertain in these regions.) Second, this image is suggestive of vulnerability in a world society where everything travels more easily than before, including weapons and the people carrying them.

The war on terror is instructive as a lesson in the form of a disembedding characteristic of the global era, where the disembedding mechanisms of modernity, which create abstract common denominators and thus conditions for global communication and comparability, are used transnationally. A main form of disembedding is deterritorialization—that is, processes whereby distance becomes irrelevant.

Globalization and Distance

A minimal definition of globalization could delimit it simply as all the contemporary processes that make distance irrelevant. A major body of work in globalization studies is, accordingly, concerned with disembedding (Giddens 1990) and its effects on social life and the organization of society.

Disembedding entails the "lifting out" of phenomena (things, people, ideas . . .) from their original context. Writing, it could thus be said, disembeds language just as an ATM disembeds money, and the wristwatch disembeds time. This concept (and its close relatives) draws attention to the *relativization of space* engendered by development in communication technologies and the worldwide spread of capitalism. In the early nineteenth century, newspapers in North America reported from the Napoleonic wars in Europe weeks and sometimes months after the event. News had to be transported, erratically and unpredictably, by sail ship. Travel, even in the relatively developed Western Europe, was slow, cumbersome, and risky. Most goods were, for practical reasons, produced in physical proximity to the markets. With the development of global financial networks, transnational investment capital, consumption mediated by money in all or nearly all societies, and not least the fast and cheap means of transportation typified in the container ship, goods can travel, and often do travel, far from their site of production. When it doesn't matter where something was made or done, it has been disembedded.

However, disembedding has a deeper and more comprehensive meaning; it does not merely, or even primarily, refer to the shrinking of the globe as a result of communication technology and global capitalism. Anthony Giddens defines disembedding as "the 'lifting out' of social relations from local contexts of interaction and their restructuring across indefinite spans of time-space" (1990: 21). Put in everyday language, it could be described as a gradual movement from the concrete and tangible to the abstract and virtual. Think of the global financial system as an example. Values registered on a stock exchange, or the value of a particular currency, are somehow related to tangible goods and services but in an abstract and general way.

Disembedding processes are associated with modernity and are indeed a central feature of it. Some important disembedding processes evolved in premodern times, but the central argument of this chapter is that global modernity, or the globalization of modernity if one prefers, can be described as a series of disembedding processes with a transnational and potentially global reach.

Towards a More Abstract World

The most important disembedding revolution of premodern times was arguably the invention of writing. Through writing, and especially phonetic writing (alphabets rather than pictographic systems, such as hieroglyphs), utterances were separated from the utterer and could, for the first time in human history, travel independently of a given person. The utterance became a permanent, moveable thing. First developed in what is now Turkey and Mesopotamia, writing was invented independently in Mesoamerica and China.

Writing made it possible to develop knowledge in a cumulative way, in the sense that one had access to, and could draw directly on, what others had done. One was no longer dependent on face-to-face contact with one's teachers. They had left their thoughts and discoveries for posterity in a material, frozen form. The quantitative growth in the total knowledge of humanity presupposes the existence of writing. Thomas Aquinas (1225–74) could, working in a European monastery in the thirteenth century, spend a lifetime trying to reconcile two important sets of texts—the Bible and Aristotle's philosophy—which were already then considered ancient. Explorers travelling in the Black Sea area in the sixth century C.E. could compare their observations with Herodotus's descriptions from the fifth century B.C.E. Mathematicians and scientists could draw on Euclid's *Elements* and written works by Archimedes as points of departure when setting out to develop new insights. Writing makes it possible to stand firmly and rationally on the shoulders of deceased and remote ancestors (Goody 1977). This would also be the case in other parts of the world with writing systems; the mature versions of Chinese philosophy, Indian mathematics, and Mayan astronomy were clearly the results of long, cumulative efforts presupposing a technology capable of freezing thought.

A nonliterate society has an oral religion where several versions of the most important myths usually circulate, where the extent of the religion is limited by the reach of the spoken word, and where there is no fixed set of dogma to which the faithful must adhere. A literate society, on the contrary, usually has a written religion (often in the shape of sacred texts), with a theoretically unlimited geographic reach, with a clearly delineated set of dogma and principles, and with authorized, correct versions of myths and narratives. Such a religion can in principle be identical in the Arabian Peninsula and in Morocco (although it is never this simple in practice; local circumstances impinge on it, and oral traditions never die completely). The three great religions of conversion from West Asia (the Abrahamic religions) have all these characteristics, which they do not share with a single traditional African religion. (In real life, nonetheless, oral and literate cultures mix in one and the same societies. The orally transmitted little traditions live side by side with the fixed great traditions; the former, often dismissed as superstitions or heresies, have proved remarkably resilient over the centuries, even in societies dominated by powerful, literate traditions.)

A nonliterate society, further, has a judicial system based on custom and tradition, while a literate society has a legislative system based on written laws. Morality in the nonliterate society depends on interpersonal relations—it is embedded in tangible relationships between individuals—while morality in the literate society in theory is legalistic—that is, embedded in the written legislation. Even the relationship between parents and children is regulated by written law in our kind of society.

In a nonliterate society, knowledge is transmitted from mouth to ear, and the inhabitants are forced to train their memory. The total reservoir of knowledge, which is available at any particular point in time, is embodied in those members of society who happen to be alive. When an old person dies in a small, nonliterate society, the net loss of knowledge can be considerable.

Most nonliterate societies are organized on the basis of kinship, while literate societies tend to be state societies where an abstract ideology of community, such as nationalism, functions as a kind of metaphorical kinship. In certain nonstate societies, the "religions of the Book" (Christianity, Islam, and Judaism) have historically worked in a similar way, creating a disembedded, or abstract, community encompassing persons who will never physically meet.

At a political level, the general tendency is that nonliterate societies are either decentralized and egalitarian, or chiefdoms where political office is inherited. Literate societies, on the other hand, are strongly centralized and tend to have a professional administration where office is, in principle, accorded following a formal set of rules. In general, literate societies are much larger, both in geographic size and in population, than nonliterate ones. And while the inhabitants of nonliterate societies tell myths about who they are and where they come from, literate societies have history to fill the same functions, based on archives and other written sources (Lévi-Strauss 1966 [1962]).

Writing, in this way, has been an essential tool in the transition from what we could call a *concrete society* based on intimate, personal relationships, memory, local religion, and orally transmitted myths, to an *abstract society* based on formal legislation, archives, a book religion, and written history. I shall mention four other innovations in communication technology, which, together with writing, indicate the extent of disembedding in the social life of modern societies.

Abstract Time and Temperature

The mechanical clock was developed in the European medieval age, partly due to a perceived need to synchronize prayer times in the monasteries. (The calls of the Muslim *muezzin* and the Christian church bells are contemporary reminders of this initial function of timing technology.) Calendars are older and were developed independently in many more societies than writing. In general, however, calendars in nonmodern societies were not a technical aid to help societies make five-year plans and individuals to keep track of their daily schedules and deadlines but were rather linked with the seasons, ritual cycles, astronomy, and the agricultural year. The clock is more accurate and more minute (literally) than the calendar. It measures time as well as cutting it into quantifiable segments. In spite of its initially religious function, the clock rapidly spread to coordinate other fields of activity as well. The Dutch thinker Hugo Grotius (1583–1645) formulated a moral maxim, which illustrates this. Grotius is widely known for his contributions to political philosophy, but he is also sometimes mentioned as the first postclassic European to defend a moral principle completely divorced from religion: "Punctuality is a virtue!" ("Time is money" is a later refinement of this principle, sometimes attributed to Benjamin Franklin.)

In the same way as writing externalizes language, clocks externalize time. Time becomes something existing independently of human experience, something objective and measurable. This was definitely not the case in traditional societies, where inhabitants live within an event-driven time structure in their everyday existence. Events regulate the passage of time, not the other way around. If a traveler, or an ethnographer, to an African village wonders when a certain event will take place, the answer may be: "When everything is ready." Not, in other words, "at a quarter to five." But today, there are no clear-cut distinctions. Even in societies where clocks and timetables have made their entry long ago, it may well be that they are not directly connected to people's everyday life. A colleague who carried out anthropological fieldwork in the Javanese countryside told me that one day, he needed to take a train to the nearest town. So he asked a man when the train was due. The man looked at him with the proverbial puzzled expression and pointed to the tracks: "The train comes from that direction, then it stops here, and after a little while it continues in the other direction." End of account.

Clock time turns time into an autonomous entity, something that exists independently of events. An hour may exist (in our minds) in an abstract way; it is an empty entity that can be filled with anything. Hence, it is common to speak of clock time as empty, quantified time. It is chopped up into in accurately measured pieces, like meters and deciliters. These entities are presupposed to be identical for everybody, anywhere and anytime. Living in our kind of society sometimes gives us the feeling that we were somehow obliged to sign a contract the moment we were born, committing us to lifelong faith in clock-and-calendar time.

Mechanical time measurement turns time into an exact, objective, and abstract entity, a straitjacket for the flows and ebbs of experienced time perhaps—for this kind of time will always pass at varying speed; as everybody knows, five minutes can last anything from a moment to an eternity. The philosopher who has developed the most systematic assault on this quantitative time tyranny is, doubtless, Henri Bergson (1859–1941). In his doctoral thesis from 1889, *Sur les données immédiates de la conscience* ("On the immediate givens of consciousness"), rendered in English as *Time and Free Will*, he severely criticizes the quantitative, empty time that regulates us from the outside, instead of letting the tasks at hand fill the time from within.

The clock also has the potential to synchronize everybody who has been brought within its charmed circle. Everyone who reads this is in agreement regarding what it means when we say that it is, say, 8:15 P.M. Everybody knows when to turn on the television to watch a particular program, and they do it simultaneously, independently of each other. If the program has already begun when one turns it on, it is not because the TV channel fails to meet its commitments, but because something is wrong with the viewer's timepiece. Coordination of complex production in factories and office environments would also, naturally, have been unthinkable without the clock, as would anything from public transport to cinema shows.

The thermometer does the same to temperature as the clock does to time. Under thermometer-driven regimes, it is not acceptable to state merely that it feels cold when one can walk over to the thermometer and obtain the exact number of degrees. If it shows more than 20 degrees Celsius (68 degrees Fahrenheit), it is not the air temperature, as it were, but oneself that is to blame.

Money as a Means of Communication

An even more consequential kind of technology than the thermometer is another invention that pulls adherents and victims in the same direction—namely, money. In traditional societies, the concept of both language and time exist but writing and clocks do not. Similarly, money-like instruments exist in many kinds of societies, but our kind of money, general-purpose money, is recent and historically culture bound. It does roughly the same thing to payment, value measurements, and exchange as clocks and writing do to time and language, respectively. They make the transaction abstract and impose a standardized grid onto a large area (ultimately the whole world). They place individual, mundane transactions under an invisible umbrella of abstraction.

Shell money, gold coins, and other compact valuables are known from a wide range of traditional societies. They may, perhaps, be used as *value standards* to make different goods comparable—a bag of grain equals half a gold coin; a goat equals half a gold coin; ergo, a sack of grain can be bartered with a goat. They may be used as *means of exchange*; I can buy two goats with a gold coin. They may even be used as *means of payment*; I have killed my neighbor, and I have to pay the widow and children three gold coins in compensation. However, modern money is a much more powerful technology than anything comparable to what we know from traditional societies. Above all, it is universal in its field of applicability. It may be that Lennon and McCartney were correct in their view that love is not a marketable commodity ("Can't Buy Me Love"—although it is easy to find cynical sociologists who argue the contrary), but in general, one single kind of money functions as a universal means of payment and exchange, and as a value standard. West African cowries had no value outside a limited area, and even there, only certain commodities and services could be purchased with them. General-purpose money is legal tender in an entire state of millions of inhabitants, and if we belong to a country with a convertible currency, that money is valid worldwide. Regarded as information technology, money has truly contributed to the creation of one world, albeit a world into which only people of means are integrated. Money makes wages and purchasing power all over the world comparable, makes it possible to exchange a ton of taro from New Guinea with electronics from Taiwan, and it is a necessary medium for the world economy to be possible at all. Whereas transaction and trade in many societies depended on trust and personal relationships between seller and buyer, the abstract and universal money we are familiar with imply an externalization of economic transactions. As long as there is agreement over the economic value of the colored bits of paper, I need not know either my debtors or my creditors personally. With the recent move of money into cyberspace, which entails that the same plastic card can be used for economic transactions nearly anywhere in the world, it becomes even more abstract.

Abstract Music

A final example is musical notation. All or nearly all societies we know possess some kind of music, but notation was only invented a couple of times—namely, in Europe (ninth century C.E.) and China/Japan (tenth century C.E.). However, it was only in Europe that an expressed aim of notation from the very beginning was to create an entirely symbolic language for communicating musical content—the Chinese/Japanese system was based on pictographs proper to the written language. In the beginning, the rudimentary notes marked only ascent and descent of tone level. Eventually, they became more accurate, and in the eleventh century, Guido of Arezzo introduced the staff, which made it possible to mark specified intervals. In the same period, the notation system was standardized, and symbolic markers depicting tone duration were also introduced. At the beginning of the sixteenth century, the system with which we are familiar was largely in place.

Several aspects of musical notation are relevant in the present context. First, written music does the same to music as script does to language; it liberates music from the performer and makes it possible to store music independently of people as well as makes it possible for individual players to learn a piece without personal contact with another performer. Only those aspects of music that can be depicted in writing are copied with a high degree of fidelity across the generations. Just as there is an indefinite residue in speech that is not transmitted through texts, the same could be said of music (feeling and, until quite recently, absolute tempo, are two such aspects). Second, notes freeze music, just as history freezes myths and clocks attempt to fix the variable flow of time. In several European countries, folk music that had evolved gradually for centuries was suddenly transcribed and preserved in frozen form during national romanticism; as a result, it is played today note by note as it was played, say, in the mid-nineteenth century (Sinding-Larsen 1991). Third, notation lays the conditions for another kind of complexity than what would otherwise have been possible. Tellingly, notation was developed in the same period as polyphony, a musical innovation that appeared only in Europe. Neither the mathematical regularity of Bach's fugues nor the very large number of voices in Beethoven's symphonies would have been possible without an accurate system of notation. The standard tone A440 (a pure A is a wave with the frequency 440) was finally defined in 1939, after having fluctuated for hundreds of years. It is the equivalent in music to the gold standard, Greenwich Mean Time, and the meter rod in Paris. A shared, abstract standard is assumed to be valid for all persons at all times.

Printing and Factories

The transitions from kinship to national identity, from custom to legislation, from cowrie money or similar to general-purpose money, from local religions to written religions of conversion, from person-dependent morality to universalistic morality, from memory to archives, from myths to history, and from event-driven time to clock time, all point in the same direction: from a small-scale society based on concrete social relations and practical knowledge to a large-scale society based on an abstract legislative system and abstract knowledge founded in logic and science.

Two further historical changes, with important implications for both thought and ways of life, need mentioning as conditions for widespread disembedding: printing and the industrial revolution.

Before the era of print—Johann Gutenberg lived from about 1400 to 1468—literacy existed in many societies, but it was not particularly widespread. There were several causes for this; among other things, the fact that a book could be as costly as a small farm. Both in Europe and Asia, books were written by hand, largely by monks, but also by professional copyists. Then Gutenberg invented his printing press with movable type, frequently seen as the single most important invention of the last two thousand years, and suddenly, books became relatively inexpensive. This happened from 1455 and onwards, to be exact; this was the year Gutenberg printed the famous forty-two-line Bible. That is to say, books did not become really cheap yet. Gutenberg's Bible cost thirty guilders, and the annual salary for a manual worker in his home area was ten guilders. During the following decades, the new technology spread rapidly to cover the central parts of Europe, and books became increasingly inexpensive. The first printing shop had already been founded in England by William Caxton in 1476. Caxton was a printer, editor, book salesman, and publisher (a common combination as late as the nineteenth century), and he contributed in no small degree to standardizing English orthography and syntax. Printing entailed standardization in other countries as well, in addition to facilitating access to books written in native languages, at the expense of Latin. The market was suddenly much larger than the small elite of Latin scholars. Printing was a decisive factor for the emergence of new science, philosophy, and literature in early modern times. It was crucial for both mass education and the creation of civil society in European cities and led to consequences Gutenberg could never have foreseen. His main ambitions seem to have been to print Bibles and pay his debts.

The features of printing that are most relevant here are its contribution to the spectacular growth in information and its standardizing effects on language and thought. Cheap, printed books contributed to the standardization of both language and worldviews. An identical message, clothed in identical linguistic garb, could now be broadcast to the entire middle class from Augsburg to Bremen. Thus, a national public sphere could emerge for the first time, consisting of equals who were preoccupied with the same writers, the same political and theological questions, the same philosophical, geographic, and scientific novelties. Printing was so important for the development of democracy and nationalism that Benedict Anderson gave the leading role to print capitalism in his historical drama about the rise of nationalism, *Imagined Communities* (1991 [1983]). Without this formidable system of production and distribution, it is difficult to see how a person in Marseilles could even dream of having a morally committed feeling of community with a person in Lille. Seen as a technological device for creating abstract communities—that is, solidarity and empathy between people who will never meet in the flesh—print capitalism is king. An underlying question for us is, naturally: if print capitalism bequeathed nationalism and democracy, what lies in store for us after a period similarly dominated by the Internet and digital satellite television?

It took a long time for literacy to become truly widespread even after the rise of printing technology. In Shakespeare's time, perhaps 10 percent of the population in England and Wales was literate. No country has an illiteracy rate even approaching this today. Even women in conservative, patriarchal societies have a higher literacy rate than the male inhabitants of Shakespeare's England.

It was printing coupled with universal primary education and mass media, like newspapers and magazines (including books published in monthly installments), that truly pulled the minds of ordinary men and women into the new, abstract society. This society consisted of an enormous number of persons who were all cogs in a giant machine, and eventually, they could easily be replaced by others in the productive process. Their knowledge and skills were not unique but standardized and therefore comparable to others' knowledge and skills. With the harnessing of fossil fuels and the subsequent industrial revolution from the late eighteenth century onwards, this possibility was turned into practice for the first time.

Disembedded Nations

Disembedding means the lifting out of social relations from their local embed-dedness. Thinking along these lines, and looking at identification and belonging, one may imagine the development of state-sponsored virtual nations on the Internet, ensuring the continued loyalty and identification of citizens or ex-citizens living abroad. In terms of economics and strategic interests, such an enlarging of the national interest makes perfect sense. The Chilean government discovered this potential in the early 2000s. During the military dictatorship (1973–90), roughly a million Chileans left the country, and the majority did not return after the reintroduction of democracy. There are people registered as Chileans in 110 countries around the world, even if many lost their citizenship after fleeing from the Pinochet dictatorship. In the early 2000s, the government actively sought to reintegrate overseas Chileans and their descendants, not by encouraging their return, but by enhancing their sense of Chileanness, which might in turn benefit the state through investments and Chilean activities scattered around the globe. Chile was officially made up of thirteen regions, but increasingly, a fourteenth region, called the region of *el exterior* or *el reencuentro* (the reunion) was mentioned in official and unofficial contexts. Initiatives were even taken to allow Chilean artists living abroad to apply for government funding.

Another, more common way of using the Internet to enhance national identities that lack a territorial base is by nations lacking a state or exiles in political opposition. On the Internet (and with a growing presence on Facebook), various Tamil, Kurdish, Palestinian, Sikh, and Iranian websites bring news and host discussion forums representing and aimed towards their scattered, deterritorialized constituencies, thereby encouraging and strengthening strong collective identities among people who would otherwise have been isolated from each other (Eriksen 2007b).

The use of the Internet by states in order to stimulate and kindle national loyalty among nationals living in diasporas is by now very widespread. Since most debates about immigration in the receiving countries deal with integration, this kind of measure is bound to be perceived as a fragmenting force in the host countries. Yet, what is interesting here is the fact that disembedding mechanisms have the potential of making political boundaries congruent with cultural ones, as Ernest Gellner puts it in *Nations and Nationalism* (1983)—even when both kinds of boundaries are thoroughly deterritorialized.

Nationalism as a Template for Globalization

Nationalism, often seen as an obstacle to globalization, is a product of the same forces that are shaping the latter (see Sassen 2006). Historically, an important part played by nationalist ideologies in contemporary nation-states has consisted in integrating an ever larger number of people culturally, politically, and economically. The French could not be meaningfully described as a people before the French Revolution, which brought the Ile-de-France (Parisian) language, notions of liberal political rights, uniform primary education, and not least, the self-consciousness of being French, to remote areas—first to the local bourgeoisies, later (in some cases much later) to the bulk of the population. Similar large-scale processes took place in all European countries during the nineteenth century, and the modern state, as well as nationalist ideology, is historically and logically linked with the spread of literacy (Eriksen 2010; Goody 1977), the quantification of time, and the growth of industrial capitalism. The model of the nation-state as the supreme political unit has spread throughout the twentieth century. Not least due to the increasing importance of international relations (trade, warfare, etc.), the nation-state has played an extremely important part in the making of the contemporary world. Social integration on a large scale through the imposition of a uniform system of education, the introduction of universal contractual wage work, standardization of language, and so forth, is accordingly the explicit aim of nationalists in the parts of the world often spoken of as developing countries. It may be possible to achieve some of these aims by contrasting the nation with a different nation or a minority residing in the state, which is then depicted as inferior or threatening. This strategy for cohesion is extremely widespread and is not a peculiar characteristic of the nation-state as such: similar ideologies and practices are found in kinship-based societies and among urban minorities alike. Insofar as enemy projections are dealt with in the present context, they are regarded as means to achieve internal, national cohesion, since international conflicts are not considered.

Nationalism as a mode of social organization represents a qualitative leap from earlier forms of integration. Within a nation-state, all men and women are citizens, and they participate in a system of relationships where they depend upon, and contribute to, the existence of a vast number of individuals whom they will never know personally. The main social distinction appears as that between insiders and outsiders—between citizens and noncitizens. The total system appears abstract and impenetrable to the citizen, who must nevertheless trust that it serves his needs. The seeming contradiction between the individual's immediate concerns and the large-scale machinations of the nation-state is bridged through nationalist ideology proposing to accord each individual citizen particular value. The ideology simultaneously depicts the nation metaphorically as an enormous system of blood relatives or as a religious community and as a benefactor satisfying immediate needs (education, jobs, health, security, etc.). Through this kind of ideological technique, nationalism can serve to open and close former boundaries of social systems. Some become brothers metaphorically; others, whose membership in the nation (and consequently, loyalty) is debatable, become outsiders. Unlike the situation in premodern societies, nationalism communicates mainly through abstract media (written laws, newspapers, mass meetings, etc.), whereas kinship ideology is communicated in face-to-face interaction. The former presupposes the latter as a metaphoric model (Eriksen 2010; see also Smith 1991).

Nationalism is ideally based on abstract norms, not on personal loyalty. Viewed as a popular ideology, nationalism is inextricably intertwined with the destiny of the nation-state. Where the nation-state is ideologically successful, its inhabitants become nationalists—that is, their identities and ways of life gradually grow compatible with the demands of the nation-state and support its growth. Where nationalism fails to convince, the state may use violence or the threat of violence to prevent fission. The monopoly on the use of legitimate violence is, together with its monopoly of taxation, one of the most important characteristics of the modern state; however, violence is usually seen as a last resort. More common are political strategies aiming to integrate hitherto distinctive categories of people culturally. Since national boundaries change historically, and since nations can be seen as shifting collectivities of people conceiving of their culture and history as shared, this is an ongoing process. Ethnic groups can vanish through annihilation, or more commonly, through assimilation. They may also continue to exist and may pose a threat to the dominant nationalism in two main ways, either as agents of subversion (they do, after all, represent alternative cultural idioms and values—this was how the Jews of Nazi Germany were depicted) or as agents of fission (which was evidently the case with Baltic nationalists before 1991).

Nationalist strategies are truly successful only when the state simultaneously increases its sphere of influence and responds credibly to popular demands, thereby stimulating national sentiment from below. It is tautologically true that if the nation-state and its agencies can satisfy perceived needs in ways acknowledged by the citizens, then its inhabitants become nationalists. The main threats to national integration are therefore alternative social relationships, which can also satisfy perceived needs. There are potential conflicts between the nation-state and nonstate modes of organization, which may follow normative principles incompatible with those represented by the state. This kind of conflict is evident in every country in the world, and it can be studied as ideological conflict, provided ideology is not seen merely as a system of ideas but as sets of practices guided by such ideas. Typical examples are African countries, where *tribalism*, or organization along ethnic lines, is perceived as a threat (by the nation-state) or as an alternative (by the citizens) to the universalist rhetoric and practices of nationalism. From the citizen's point of view, nationalism may or may not be a viable alternative to kinship or ethnic ideology (or there may be two nationalisms to choose between—e.g., an Ethiopian and a Somali one, in eastern Ethiopia)—and she will choose the option best suited to satisfy her needs, be they of a metaphysical, economic, or political nature. The success or failure of attempts at national integration must therefore be studied not only at the level of political strategies or systemic imperatives, but it must equally be understood at the level of the everyday life-world. In a word, the ideological struggles and the intrastate conflicts, as well as the context-specific options for the good life, shape and are simultaneously rooted in the immediate experiences of its citizens, and the analysis must begin there.

Other Disembedding Mechanisms

In the realm of production, the *labor contract* of the capitalist enterprise is a disembedding instrument separating the labor power of the individual from the entire person. Under a labor contract, workers were and are, at least in principle, free to quit, and their obligations to the employer are limited to their working hours. Other examples could have been mentioned. The point is that modern societies are characterized by a particular kind of complexity, where the lives of individuals are compartmentalized (Berger et al. 1973) into separate roles or functions and thereby become replaceable with each other in particular domains. This is not the only possible way of making a society work. Indian caste society and traditional Australian worldviews are two spectacular examples of social and cultural complexity, respectively. Nonetheless, modernity is today in a uniquely important position; it is hegemonic on the verge of becoming universal, and due to its disembedding and compartmentalizing functions, it lays the foundations for global networking. It synchronizes and standardizes an enormous number of persons, all of them little cogs in a great machinery. It draws on a shared mechanical time-structure, a global medium for economic transactions (money), technologies of production and destruction based on a shared theoretical science and easily transferable knowledge. Modernity coordinates the movements and thoughts of an enormous number of people in ways that were both unknown and unthinkable in nonmodern societies. It divorces its resources from particular individuals by externalizing time, language, economy, memory, morality, and knowledge. And it enables a nearly infinite social complexity in a world where boundaries are increasingly relative and negotiable.

Many react critically to particular aspects of disembedding, seeing it as dehumanizing or alienating, oppressive or inauthentic—or they are simply unable to reap its profits—for example, by being excluded from the formal labor market. They are engaged in various forms of reembedding, witnessed, for example, in the informal sector in the economy (based on trust and interpersonal relationships) or in local identity politics (emphasizing the virtues of that which is locally embedded).

So far, I have considered some of the main conditions of modernity, chiefly in its guise as the modern nation-state. However, with the replication and diffusion of technologies and modes of organization across boundaries, what emerged during the twentieth century, and particularly in its second half, was a world-system of nation-states based on many of the same premises. Thus, given these emerging similarities across the globe, contemporary globalization became feasible. It would neither be economically profitable nor culturally possible to create enduring reciprocal ties between nonstate, nonliterate tribal groups and the economic machinery of the industrialized countries, but with the increasingly transnational disembedding of communication, trade, and production, such ties have become both viable and widespread.

Giddens (1990) distinguishes between two kinds of disembedding mechanisms: the creation of *symbolic tokens* and the establishment of *expert systems*. A typical symbolic token is money, which travels independently of persons and goods (and is increasingly located to the abstract realm of cyberspace); a typical expert system is economic science, assumed to be context-independent and valid everywhere.

As mentioned, the increasing dominance of disembedding mechanisms and their growing spatial range can fruitfully be seen as a movement from the concrete to the abstract, from the interpersonal to the institutional, and from the local to the global. The next two chapters, on acceleration and on standardization, present features of globalization that are closely related to disembedding.

Disembedded Friendship

American colleges and universities have a long tradition of publishing an annual face book, including names and mug shots of all students. A kind of directory, the intention of these face books was to make it easier for sophomore students to get acquainted with others. During the 1990s, face books were increasingly turned into online catalogues, and in 2004, the Harvard student Mark Zuckerberg used material from Harvard face books, some of it acquired by hacking into the protected areas of houses at Harvard, to create a more comprehensive catalogue, including a comment field. In spite of legal difficulties with the Harvard administration, the site became an instant success. During the following year, the network was expanded to include other universities as well as high schools, the user interface was developed beyond that of commenting on photos, and in September 2006, Facebook as we know it today was opened to the general public. By autumn 2013—less than seven years after its launch—Facebook had more than a billion users worldwide.

Modeled on face-to-face social relationships, but lifted out into the virtual world of cyberspace, Facebook can be described as an ongoing, deterritorialized conversation between people who sometimes know each other outside of Facebook, who are sometimes aware of each other outside of Facebook, and who sometimes know each other only through their online presence. The range of subjects dealt with on Facebook parallels the breadth of social and cultural life itself. A typical newsfeed on my own account would include a few photos of cute animals and children celebrating their birthdays, a few political cartoons, news from environmental organizations and the gas industry in Australia (where I am doing research), comments on recent news in Norway and the European Union, a few links to YouTube clips, and a handful of links to academic articles. I know less than half of my Facebook friends personally, but I know something about them (such as their occupation, musical tastes, or authorship).

What is peculiar about Facebook in this context is not only the fact that it is totally disembedded and deterritorialized but that it is chiefly being used for reembedding by sharing personal experiences, spontaneous thoughts, and judgments with friends, physical and virtual. Of course, Web 2.0 (where the social media play an important part) encompasses far more than Facebook—Twitter (for microblogging), Instagram (for photo sharing), and LinkedIn (for professional networking) are interesting in their own right—but Facebook is the most powerful and widely used medium of this kind. The reason may be that it offers possibilities to share the whole range of human emotions with like-minded (or not) people anytime, anywhere; or it may be, as Daniel Miller says, "the desire by nearly everyone on our planet to be on the same network as everyone else" (2011: 217).

Neoliberal Economics and Disembedding

The term neoliberalism is often used to describe a particular kind of disembedded economic ideology and practice characteristic of the late twentieth and early twenty-first centuries. It is commonly agreed that it began in earnest with the policies of deregulation and privatization instigated in the United States and the United Kingdom around 1980, under Ronald Reagan and Margaret Thatcher's respective leaderships. The structural adjustment programs implemented by the IMF (International Monetary Fund) in the so-called developing world in the 1980s and 1990s conformed to the same principles, cutting down public expenditure and encouraging the development of competitive markets wherever possible. This set of policies, believed to lead to a healthy economic development, is generally known as the Washington Consensus, as it was the outcome of an agreement between the IMF, the World Bank, and the

U.S. Treasury Department. The influential geographer and social theorist David Harvey defines neoliberalism as follows:

> Neoliberalism is . . . a theory of political economic practices that proposes that human well-being can best be advanced by liberating individual entrepreneurial freedoms and skills within an institutional framework characterized by strong private property rights, free markets, and free trade. The role of the state is to create and preserve an institutional framework appropriate to such practices. (2005: 2)

Neoliberal policies have in the subsequent decades been pursued by governments in most parts of the world, fully or partly privatizing formerly public enterprises, such as railways and postal services, and encouraging an unhampered market economy (although restrictions are usually placed on imports in the form of tariffs).

The neoliberal view is that the removal of hindrances to competition (such as import tariffs, strong trade unions, inefficient and bureaucratic state institutions, unprofitable activities) will eventually lead to prosperity and economic growth through the workings of the market principle. Such a view of the economy is, for better or worse, a disembedding vision since it sees the economy as lifted out of social relations, following its own logic and its own dynamic, driven by anonymous market forces.

Neoliberalism has been criticized from many quarters. Some have simply argued that it did not deliver the goods and that deregulation and slimming of the public sector sent countries like Argentina into a prolonged crisis. Others have pointed out that neoliberalism did not so much lead to increased prosperity as to increased inequality (Harvey 2005). Yet, others see the economy as a socially embedded kind of activity, which cannot and should not be viewed as an abstract and virtual thing (Hart et al. 2010). Others have warned against the instability of a financially driven world economy; the concept "casino capitalism," previously coined by the international relationist Susan Strange in 1986, was frequently used during the financial crisis beginning in 2008. Finally, some critics of neoliberalism argue that a deregulated global market cannot coexist with national democracies (Rodrik 2011). The reason is that national politicians would have minimal space for maneuvering and few effective tools for social planning in a deregulated world economy where the local fortunes depend on global processes.

In spite of these and other objections and criticisms of neoliberalist ideology and practice, privatization, deregulation, and calls for marketization are still widespread around the world. The disembedded market economy is a key feature of contemporary globalization, although—as will be made increasingly clear in later chapters—it encounters resistance, and alternatives to it are being developed.

The Gated Community as a Form of Disembedding

Segregation in cities has been studied widely by urban sociologists, anthropologists, and not least geographers. The term gated community, often used in literature, describes an urban area, which is guarded, usually by a private security company, and closed off, usually physically, from the surrounding city. The people inhabiting the gated community are economically privileged and have closed off their local area in order to control their interaction with the surroundings, seen as threatening and dangerous. Naturally, the gated community is a feature of cities that are strongly class-divided. Inhabitants of the gated community have their own infrastructure, wholly or partially; they send their children to private schools and buy imported goods in expensive shops. In an analysis of the development of a gated community, or fortified enclave, in Managua, Nicaragua, Dennis Rodgers (2004: 123) describes them as "disconnected worlds that are the antithesis of public space, in that they constitute a withdrawal from the fabric of the city, leading to its fragmentation." The social form of the gated community leads to the exclusion of others from formerly shared spaces and limits the interaction between the enclave's inhabitants and outsiders. It definitely contributes to a fragmentation of the city and also has consequences for the political life in that the very notion of a shared public space is challenged. Inhabitants of gated communities consume pretty much in the same way as middle- or upper-class citizens in rich countries; they watch cable television and communicate online from home. Their integration into the world economy is indisputable—many work in international agencies or transnational companies—but their level of participation in the domestic public sphere is debatable and often very insignificant. The spread of gated communities throughout the poorer countries—Rio de Janeiro, Nairobi, Johannesburg, Santiago de Chile, Guatemala City, and so on—suggests not only a disembedding of an urban form from its physical location but also the emergence of a global middle class, transnationally integrated through shared ideas, practices, and lifestyles, but with a weakening tie towards the local and domestic.

This example suggests a development that is complementary to and signifies the opposite of the example of the fourteenth Chilean province: while the Internet and increased transnational interaction can serve to reintegrate diaspora Chileans into the imagined community of the nation, the growth of gated communities in third-world cities signifies the detachment of groups, which are physically located to the nation-state, from it.

Critics of Disembedding

An especially grim interpretation of disembedding processes sees them as resulting in fragmentation, alienation, and anonymity, ultimately removing every trace of the local and particular. In an original essay on *non-places*, the anthropologist Marc Augé (1992) describes a condition he labels *supermodernity* (*la surmodernité*), which continuously produces uprootedness and alienation because it obliterates and neglects historically rooted places imbued with particularity. Augé's non-places are frictionless and lack resistance. They communicate through a rudimentary pidgin language devoid of particular experiences. He writes that we live in a world where one is:

born in a clinic and dies in a hospital, where transitional points—luxurious or dehumanising—proliferate (hotel chains and temporary shacks, holiday resorts, refugee camps, slums soon to be demolished or which are in a condition of permanent decay), where a network develops which is tied together by means of transportation which are also dwellings, where the routine user of shopping centres, ATMs and credit cards carries out his transactions without a word, a world where everything encourages lonely individuality, the transition, the provisional and temporary. (1992: 100–101, my translation)

In the abstract, generalized world described by Augé, the local and peculiar is lost. Augé's countryman Paul Virilio (1996, 2000) goes even further, in seeing disembedding processes as heralding the death of civil society. In Virilio's view, a main cause of social fragmentation and alienation is contemporary communication technology. Whereas some of the disembedding communication technologies, notably the book and the newspaper, were important for the creation of civil societies by creating shared frames of reference for people who would never meet physically (Anderson 1991 [1983]), the contemporary, transnational, and instantaneous communication technologies (such as the Internet) dissolve it in Virilio's view. He describes a world where people no longer need to—or even want to—meet their neighbors, where they are entertained and informed online, and where communication with others is also increasingly online, deterritorialized, disembedded, and detached from ongoing social life. As a result, Virilio fears that the everyday conversation about society, the little compromises and conversions taking place in discussions about anything from sports to politics, fade away because the organization of society no longer creates conditions for such interactions.

There is in the social sciences a long tradition of criticizing modern societies, and not least the features we have described as disembedding processes, for alienating people, and reducing the conditions for existential security, intimacy, self-reliance, and autonomy. Most of the leading pioneers of social theory, including Marx, Durkheim, and Tönnies, contrasted the abstract, large-scale, industrial societies of their own day with the concrete, small-scale, agricultural societies that had preceded them. Some of their arguments can be refound in contemporary debates about globalization, which is in a certain sense just modernity writ large, or, in the words of Arjun Appadurai (1996), simply "modernity at large." However, the era of global modernity is in important ways different from the modernity defined and described by the sociological classics. Notably, the economy and communications have become increasingly globalized—or deterritorialized—without a similar development in politics. The "democratic deficit" of globalization is a much debated topic (cf. Held et al. 2005), and in the view of the critics, the national public, and political spheres are being marginalized. Some call for a strengthening of national power, while others argue in favor of transnational governance through international organizations and regional entities, like the European Union. Yet, others have faith in the potential of grassroots movements—that is, organizations from below, as alternative ways of influencing both local and transnational politics.

Through presenting some of the disembedding mechanisms of modernity at some length, this chapter has shown how contemporary globalization is a development presupposing the implementation and dissemination of a series of disembedding processes, which have created abstract societies, now increasingly transnational in their ongoingness.

- Disembedding can be defined as "the 'lifting out' of social relations from local contexts of interaction and their restructuring across indefinite spans of time-space."
- Disembedding refers to a main trajectory of globalization—namely, the increasingly abstract character of communication and objects, whereby their origin becomes obscured and their currency more and more widespread.
- Writing (often in the form of printing), money, clock time, and standardized measurements are some of the most important disembedding mechanisms in modern society.
- The disembedding mechanisms of contemporary global or transnational systems rely on electronic information and communication technology (ICT) for their efficacy.
- Critics of contemporary disembedding see the "lifting out" of social relations as a recipe for alienation and fragmentation.

Questions

- In which ways does disembedding occur as deterritorialization? Give some examples and discuss the consequences.
- Mention three main forms of deterritorialization that are integral to modernity, and indicate how they are necessary conditions for contemporary globalization.
- In what way does the author see musical notation as connected to globalization? Do you agree?
- How can nationalism be said to be a product of the same forces that are shaping globalization?
- What are some of the main differences between contemporary globalization and the modernity of the nation-state?

Further Reading

Bauman, Zygmunt (1999) *Globalization—The Human Consequences*. New York: Columbia University Press. Written by the famous Polish-English social theorist known for his theoretical analyses of modernity and postmodernity, this book describes new forms of inequality, surveillance, and risk resulting from tighter integration.

Gellner, Ernest (1990) *Plough, Sword, Book*. Chicago: University of Chicago Press. There are many books trying to explain the transition from tribal to modern society, and this is among the very best. The author looks at familiar dimensions, such as technological changes and population growth, but he also places great emphasis on writing and scientific thought.

Giddens, Anthony (1999) *Runaway World: How Globalization is Reshaping our Lives*. London: Routledge. This is a compact and informal book, based on a lecture series, highlighting some important aspects of disembedding and global modernity but emphasizing the positive aspects of globalization, such as human rights, the spread of feminism, and cosmopolitan ideas.

2

Speed

As a result of the need for instantaneous responses, particularly because of the speed implied by the telephone, telex, fax, electronic signals and so on, the future increasingly appears to dissolve into an extended present.

—JOHN URRY, *SOCIOLOGY BEYOND SOCIETIES*, 128

Acceleration is an important dimension of globalization. Faster transportation and communication have been preconditions for the current globally interconnected world. As production and consumption have sped up, capitalism has continued to grow and to conquer new markets, which are thereby incorporated into global networks of communication and exchange. The most spectacular kind of acceleration witnessed in recent years is arguably that taking place in instantaneous communication. The number of people online in the world has grown spectacularly and continues to do so. At the same time, acceleration takes place unevenly, both between societies and regions and within groups and societies. Different parts of a culture change at different speeds, and there are groups, activities, and places that hardly change at all, forcibly or through neglect or active exclusion.

As I sat by my desk in relative peace and quiet a fine spring morning some years ago, I was interrupted by three simultaneous and identical e-mails marked with red tags (Priority: High!), followed by a physical visit by our secretary, who actually walked around in the corridor, knocking on doors and warning the occupants of imminent danger. (After we got e-mail in the early 1990s, we hardly saw our secretary any more, and so we immediately understood that the situation had to be very serious.)

It soon became clear that the reason for this unusual and dramatic behavior was neither a fire on the ground floor, a general strike, an attempted coup d'etat by the military, nor even a spontaneous wave of suicides among university employees protes-ting against the decay of our institution, but a small computer program that had settled on many of our hard disks. A virus! The virus program had arrived as an attachment to an e-mail entitled "ILOVEYOU," which contained an imploring request for the recipient to open the attached "love letter from me to you." If one did—and many did, understandably, given that they had been promised an unconditional declaration of love—a malign virus would begin deleting files, messing up data, and then moving on to other innocent computers via the victim's electronic address list. A surprising number of colleagues received the virus before lunch on that day, generally from different sources, and many got it twice or even three times.

The virus, which in a matter of hours had been nicknamed "The Love Worm," was first observed in Hong Kong late in the evening on Wednesday, May 3, 2000 (local time). When the American population began to get out of bed a little while later (and it was Wednesday morning in the United States), the virus began to move across the world with astonishing speed. Within the next couple of days, it had settled—among many other places—at the University of Gothenburg (Sweden), a weekly Oslo newspaper, and the Norwegian Institute of International Relations, and arrived from individual computers in all three places to my desktop computer on the Thursday morning. As people began to return home from work on that fateful Thursday, the leading antivirus companies had already developed remedies, which were freely available on the Web. The virus was virulent and epidemic from the very beginning (other, real-world viruses, such as that which carries bubonic plague, may be endemic for years before turning vicious), and the entire epidemic lasted less than three days. Within that span, between 60 and 80 percent of the computers in the United States were estimated to have been infected to a greater or lesser degree. On Thursday evening, CNN online reported that the Scandinavian photo agency Scanpix had lost 4,500 images, in spite of impeccable security routines.

In a couple of days, the epidemic dissemination all over the world was brought to an abrupt end, following the spread of loud warnings in virtually all the world's media. A week later, the virus makers were arrested by the Filipino police.

One cannot help but compare this epidemic with earlier major epidemics in European history. The most famous and most consequential was the Black Death (1347–51). Probably originating in the steppes of Central Asia, it had already caused mass death and political fragmentation in large parts of Eurasia for a couple of years when it finally reached Bergen in 1349, arriving in the Baltic lands only the following year. It took the plague three years to make the trip from Sicily to Riga, in spite of being extremely contagious. Except for the immediate neighboring areas (West Asia and North Africa), no other continents other than Europe were affected. Indeed, the great plague of the 530s (Keys 1999) was even more comprehensive in its reach—it started in East Africa and wrought havoc in China, Arabia, and Europe—and it moved just as fast as the plague eight hundred years later. Whatever was far away in space, in the fourteenth century as well as in the sixth, was also far removed in time. The transport and communication technologies in Europe had scarcely evolved in the intervening centuries.

Acceleration is a central feature of globalization and indeed of modernity. Everything, it seems, happens faster and faster, bringing disparate parts of the world closer to each other, leading to frictions of the kind that we may call *overheating effects*.

Time-space Compression

The concept of disembedding discussed in the last chapter refers chiefly to the reorganization of social relations by virtue of processes that render society and culture more abstract and detached from local circumstances. Although disembedding is a key feature of modernity itself, it was argued that it is also an important condition for stable transnational connections and globalization, since it makes things, people, and ideas more easily comparable and moveable than they were—and are—in societies where most of what goes on is embedded in the local.

A close relative to Anthony Giddens's concept of disembedding is David Harvey's term "time-space compression," developed in his influential book *The Condition of Postmodernity* (1989). You may envision it as the squeezing together of time and space. The forms of deterritorialization briefly discussed in the context of disembedding are also instances of time-space compression.

There are many possible theoretical approaches to our near past, and the history of modernity has kept generations of academics and students busy for more than a century. Some concentrate on the development of concepts and ideas, while others emphasize economics or politics. The analysis of the past can be approached in other ways as well. For example, it can be highly illuminating to view the history of the last two hundred years as a history of *acceleration*. Strangely, this dimension is rarely foregrounded in the extensive literature on globalization. The reason why this should come as a surprise is simply that globalization is tantamount to a particular form of acceleration, which reduces the importance of distance, frequently obliterating it altogether. In the era of wireless communications, there is no longer a connection between duration and distance. In 1903, Theodore Roosevelt sent a round-the-world telegram to himself, and it reached him in nine minutes (Anderson 2006: 3). Today, such an exercise would not have made sense, but a century ago, it indicated that the world had become a smaller place; the space–time continuum had been compressed enormously compared with the situation only half a century earlier, when there was no way in which Roosevelt could have sent a telegram even to London.

Technological changes are necessary conditions for time-space compression. The jet plane and the satellite dish automatically enable people to communicate fast in both senses of the word, but their mere invention says nothing about their social importance: Who has access to these technologies, how are they being used, and how do they contribute to transforming economies and everyday lives worldwide. When we study technological changes, therefore, they must always be placed in their social context. One of the most interesting findings in the interdisciplinary research on information and communication technologies is that they have hugely different social implications and cultural connotations in different societies.

Harvey defines time-space compression like this:

[P]rocesses that so revolutionize the objective qualities of space and time that we are forced to alter, sometimes in quite radical ways, how we represent the world to ourselves. I use the word "compression" because a strong case can be made that the history of capitalism has been characterized by speed-up in the pace of life, while so overcoming spatial barriers that the world sometimes seems to collapse inwards upon us. (1989: 240)

This "speed-up" is then illustrated graphically (Harvey 1989: 241) by looking at four maps of the world indicating the fastest available transport technology at the time:

1   1500–1840 (best average speed of horse drawn coaches and sailing ships was 10 mph).

2   1850–1930 (steam locomotives averaged 65 mph, and steam ships averaged 36 mph).

3   1950s (propeller aircraft, 300–400 mph).

4   1960s (jet passenger aircraft, 500–700 mph).

A similar table showing the acceleration in the communication of messages would be no less striking, but less tidy. For hundreds, indeed thousands of years, the fastest widespread means of communication was the written document, transported by a horse (trained pigeons were unusual). Intercontinental communication could take place no faster than a sail ship. With the coming of the train and steamship in the early decades of the nineteenth century, the speed of communication increased as much as the speed of ground communication; however, long before the steamboats had fully replaced sail ships, a truly transformative innovation saw the light of day—namely, the telegraph, which was first demonstrated in 1838. For the first time in history, a message could be transported without being embedded in a physical object. The first transatlantic cable between New York and London was opened in 1866; the first cable from London to Bombay was opened in 1870. Huge rolls of copper wire enmeshed in waterproof gutta-percha rubber from Malaya were laid out across the ocean floor. No wonder science fiction became a popular literary form only a few years later. Although the telegraph was used chiefly for short messages, transmitted in Morse code (now obsolete, but learned routinely by Boy Scouts as late as the 1980s), it revolutionized the way people experienced time and space.

The significance of the telegraph was recognized by contemporary commentators, and the London *Times* wrote, in 1844, about the telegraph: "Since the discovery of Columbus, nothing has been done in any degree comparable to the vast enlargement which has thus been given to the sphere of human activity" (quoted in Chanda 2007: 62).

Suddenly, a remote city could be experienced as very near if it was connected by cable; similarly, towns or villages in the neighborhood appeared to be remote if they were unconnected by telegraph. The train and the telephone (invented in 1877) similarly contributed to changing the time-space continuum. As from the late nineteenth century, one could no longer draw on an intuitive connection between distance and delay. Some towns and cities were connected fast through ground transportation, instantaneously through the telegraph and telephone. This led, among other things, to the standardization of time zones. Before the train and the telegraph, there was no reason why New York and Cincinnati should keep synchronized time, as travel and communication between the two cities took days anyway.

Accelerated Change

As one of the most original theorists of speed and power, Paul Virilio (2000), has often said: we now live in an era with no delays. Virilio has the Internet family of technologies in mind, and in this respect, he is not overstating the point. (It should be quite clear that he is not thinking of commuter trains into London, of rush hour traffic in the greater Los Angeles area, nor of citizens waiting to speak to a civil servant on the phone.) Global telecommunications and other communication based on satellites are placeless and immediate. All the nodes connected through the Internet are, in a certain sense, everywhere and nowhere. In practice, there is no difference between sending and receiving e-mail from Melbourne or from the office next door or from watching a direct transmission from a soccer game in Belgium, New Year celebrations in Kiribati, or an interview transmitted from one's local television studio. Time, regarded as a means to create distance and proximity, is gone.

This familiar fact has many unintended consequences, some of which are explored by Virilio, who talks of his own field of study as *dromology*, the study of speed and acceleration. One of his special fields of interest is the military. At the outset of the twentieth century, it would have taken weeks or months to invade a country like Poland: The speed of war was identical with the average speed of the cavalry. Although horses are fast animals, they need food and rest, and they are further delayed by hills, swamps, and rivers—not to mention intransigent villagers who are liable to destroy bridges and set traps. At the beginning of the twentieth century, the tank and the double-decker airplane were introduced, and suddenly, the speed of war was increased several times. Then came the Spitfires and medium-range missiles, and today, a warlike state can in principle inflict unspeakable damage on another country in a matter of minutes.

Technologies spread faster and faster. It took forty years for the radio to gain an audience of fifty million; in the case of personal computers, the figure was fifteen, and only four years after its introduction in 1992, fifty million people were using the World Wide Web. By 2007, the figure was about a billion, but only six years later, in 2013, the number of Internet users had skyrocketed to 2.4 billion—probably to a great extent through the spread of Internet services for mobile phones. This means that at the time of writing, more than a third of the world's population has access to the Internet. Still, access to the Internet is very unevenly distributed. In the North Atlantic region—North America and Western Europe—the vast majority now has simple if not continuous access, while the penetration in Africa is only 15 percent. (As late as 2005, just 1 percent of Africans, bar South Africa, had Internet access.)

The new technologies can spread incredibly fast to new areas. In the late 1990s, text messages were unknown in China. In 2006, between twelve and fourteen billion text messages were sent every month in the same country. If this sounds like a lot, we should add that by 2012, the monthly number of text messages sent in China had gone up to eighty-six billion.

The Information Society

Acceleration hinges on technology, and the acceleration of global communication depends on information and communication technology. In fact, these technologies—from the cell phone to the computer terminal—are now so pervasive and so ubiquitous that many have taken to describing our era as an information society, or a global information society.

Such terms are not unproblematic, and at the very least, they need defining. Quite obviously, every human society is an information society in the sense that information is important for the distribution of social rank, for survival, and so on. What distinguishes the contemporary era from previous ones is chiefly that information is rapidly becoming a central value generator for business and the most valuable raw material in the world economy (cf. Castells 1996). This is not just the case in the financial economy, or in that part of the economy that deals in information (such as software companies) but also in the industrial part of the economy.

In other words, the information society is not a postindustrial society. Even in the most technologically advanced countries, such as Germany and the United States, a large proportion of their economic output consists in industrial goods. What distinguishes the information society from industrial society is that in the former, electronic information technology pervades the productive process and is an important, integral part of it.

The transition from an agrarian to an industrial society did not entail the end of agriculture but its transformation. Agriculture was industrialized through new machinery and, to some extent, new forms of production and distribution. Similarly, the information society does not entail the end of agriculture nor industry, but their informatization. Sennett (1997) writes about a bakery in New England where the employees are no longer capable of baking bread, since the productive process is now managed via computer screens.

To take another, perhaps even more telling example: Before the so-called Y2K scare in late 1999, when it was widely feared that a huge number of mainframe computer systems would break down on January 1, 2000, because of simplified programming in the past, among the most anxious of all professional groups in the North were gardeners. The temperature in many greenhouses is regulated by thermostats run by computers. If the computers suddenly collapsed on New Year's Eve, enormous amounts of flowers would freeze across the cold part of the world. This is a way of describing the information society: it is a place where even the greenhouses have to be compatible with the latest operating system.

Needless to say, the informatization of the economy, and of society as such, takes place unevenly and chiefly in the rich countries and wealthy enclaves elsewhere.

Friedman's "Flatteners"

In a widely read book about globalization with the tantalizing title *The World is Flat*, Thomas Friedman (2005) refers to one of his earlier books, published back in 1999, by saying that the globalization processes that interest him were just beginning back then. Speaking of contemporary globalization as "Globalization 3.0," Friedman argues forcefully that only in the first years of the twenty-first century, momentous changes have led to a much more integrated, "flatter" world than the world of even the last decade of the twentieth century. One may shrug at this generalization—Friedman's most convincing defense of the view is the commonplace that China's economic impact on the world has grown tremendously and very fast—but his view illustrates a widespread feeling, not altogether unjustified, that changes are happening quickly.

Friedman mentions ten flatteners, which have each contributed to leveling the playing field. All of them are to do with information and communication technology and with acceleration, ranging from the explosion in twenty-four-hour parcel delivery (FedEx has the fifth-largest fleet of aircraft in the world) and broadband connections to computerized logistics on a huge scale. Software developers in India, he notices, no longer have to move to the United States to have a career, since their geographic location is henceforth unimportant. He also describes the Wal-Mart supply chain in some detail, showing how it profits from deterritorialized markets and remarking that if Wal-Mart had been a country, it would have been China's eighth-largest trading partner! Friedman tells many other stories in his readable book, of innovators dreaming up new products, cutting prices, or speeding up production or distribution, all of them involving computers in one way or another. Partly, Friedman's evolutionist scheme (he really believes that the world is moving in one direction) is like an undialectical form of Marxism—a Marxism without contradiction—and partly, it is an extension of the theory of industrial society developed by sociologists and economists in the twentieth century. What is new, in his view, is global simultaneity under informational capitalism.

In the domains of information technology, consumption, and retail trade, the world is doubtless becoming "flatter," to use Friedman's term, although it should be kept in mind that perhaps half the world's population does not take part in this. If we look at acceleration from a spatial point of view, it becomes evident that certain places change much faster than others. The central nodes of any disembedded activity are characterized by a much higher speed than the rest of the system, and outside the nodes—in unconnected areas—the speed may approach zero. There are about 70 television sets for every 1,000 persons in sub-Saharan Africa (2013), while the figure for the United States is 1,140, and a large (if shrinking) part of the Indian population has never made a telephone call. In spite of a certain degree of deterritorialization, therefore, the central principle of world-systems theory in dividing the globe into center, periphery, and semiperiphery is still relevant in many respects.

Under a regime of accelerated change, obsolescence becomes an everyday thing. The anthropologist Andreas Huyssen (2003) relates a story of an attempt to buy a computer in New York, when he encountered unexpected difficulties: "Whatever was on display was relentlessly described by the sales personnel as already obsolete, that is, museal, by comparison with the imminently expected and so much more powerful next product line (70)." Approaching parody, this anecdote nonetheless illustrates the incredible speed of change in certain domains, not least to do with consumption, communication, and production. Commenting on accelerated consumption, Zygmunt Bauman writes:

> There is a natural resonance between the spectacular career of the "now", brought about by time-compressing technology, and the logic of consumer-oriented economy. As far as the latter goes, the consumer's satisfaction ought to be *instant*, and this in a double sense. Obviously, consumed goods should satisfy immediately, requiring no learning of skills and no lengthy groundwork; but the satisfaction should also end—"in no time," that is in the moment the time needed for their consumption is up. (1999: 81)

We live in an era when the cigarette has replaced the pipe, cornflakes have long ago replaced porridge (both cigarettes and cornflakes are now being replaced by nothing, which can be consumed even faster—increasingly, American children don't eat breakfast), e-mail is replacing paper-based correspondence, and the two-minute newsreel is one of the hottest products in the media field. The newspaper articles become shorter, the transitions in films more frequent, and the time each of us spends responding to an electronic letter is reduced proportionally by the number of e-mails we receive. The restless and shifting style of communication that was introduced with MTV has become an accurate image of the spirit of the age. Speed is an addictive drug: Horrified, we watch ourselves groping for the fast-forward button in the cinema, the public loses interest in slow-moving sports; in my part of the world, ice skating and cross-country skiing have serious problems of recruitment and audience appeal, as people switch to more explosive sports, such as ice hockey and downhill skiing; we fill the slow gaps by talking on mobile phones when walking down a street or waiting for a traffic light to change; we damn the municipal transport authority when the bus is five minutes late, and consumers are still, after all these years, impatiently waiting for computers and Internet connections that are sufficiently fast.

With these examples in mind, we should not forget that accelerating technologies are extremely unevenly distributed, although it needs to be pointed out that in this respect, differences are shrinking. In the time of the landline telephone, it may still have been true that Manhattan had more telephone lines than sub-Saharan Africa and Italy as many as Latin America. In the era of wireless mobile communications, however, this kind of arithmetic no longer works. It is true that in the very poorest African countries, such as Niger or Chad, fewer than fifty in a thousand have a telephone; but in most countries in the Global South, at least a quarter of the population have one and, even more importantly, most people know someone whose phone they can ask to borrow.

Acceleration in the Media

Since its inception, journalism has always been a profession characterized by speed. The notion of today's paper is both a symbol and a sign of modernity. It is worth nothing if it is not current. Typically, the newspapers had their major breakthrough in the late eighteenth century, at the same time that clocks began to be used to monitor work, which was also the same period that the French and American revolutions introduced their individualistic freedom ideals, the steam engine began to utilize fossil fuels to release hitherto unknown amounts of energy for human use, and the industrial revolution began to transform labor. There was now a critical mass of people, especially in the major cities, who felt an acute need to keep up to date with contemporary events. Then, as now, a newspaper was ephemeral. Its life span lasted exactly one day.

Other media are faster. Radio and television can update their content any time, and this is also the case with the media, which may eventually replace the newspapers—namely, some kind of electronic publications based on text. (In this field, technological change happens so fast that there is little point in attempting to make accurate predictions, and it has been predicted regularly since the early 1980s that the e-paper or e-book would soon fully replace the printed versions.)

It makes no sense to talk about the life span of an Internet newspaper: any item survives only as long as it is being accessed by a minimal number of readers, or until the staff has managed to update or replace it. There is a whirling dance going on between user clicks and editorial updates, and the more attuned the editorial updaters are to the users' preferences, the more advertising they get. An average reader of the leading purely electronic newspaper in Norway—the only newspaper, incidentally, that does not have a paper version—spends forty-five seconds browsing the paper. News addicts go there several times a day, especially during dramatic events (civil wars, hostage crises, soccer finals). This kind of media instills a new rhythm and a new restlessness, and—not least importantly—new routines in the consumption of news.

Bourdieu's Pessimism

In a profoundly pessimistic and critical essay about the misery of television, Pierre Bourdieu (1996, my translation) develops a familiar, but far from unimportant, argument. He argues that the fragmented temporality of television, with its swift transitions and fast-paced journalism, creates an intellectual public culture, which favors a particular kind of participant. Bourdieu speaks of these participants as "fast-thinkers." Whereas the Belgian cartoon hero Lucky Luke is famous for drawing his gun faster than his own shadow, fast-thinkers are described sarcastically as "thinkers who think faster than an accelerating bullet." They are the people who are able, in a couple of minutes of direct transmission, to explain what is wrong with the economic policies of the European Union, why one ought to read Kant's *Critique of Pure Reason* this summer, or explain the origins of early twentieth-century racist pseudoscience. It is, nonetheless, a fact that some of the sharpest minds need time to reflect and more time (much more, in some cases) to make an accurate, sufficiently nuanced statement on a particular issue. This kind of thinker becomes invisible and virtually deprived of influence, according to Bourdieu, in this rushed era. (In a banal sense, Bourdieu is obviously wrong. Few contemporary thinkers were, until his death in 2002, more influential than Bourdieu himself, and clearly he did not regard himself as a fast thinker.)

Bourdieu's argument is congruent with the observation that media appeal has become the most important capital of politicians—not, in other words, their political message or cohesive vision. This is not an entirely new phenomenon; in the United States, the first clear indication of this development came with John F. Kennedy's victory over Richard M. Nixon in 1960. Anyway, a result, in Bourdieu's view, is that it is the people who speak like machine guns, in boldface and capital letters, who are given airplay and influence—not the slow and systematic ones.

What is wrong with this? Why should people who have the gift of being able to think fast and accurately be stigmatized in this way? In a word, what is wrong about thinking fast? Nothing in particular, apart from the fact that some thoughts only function in a slow mode, and that some lines of reasoning can only be developed in a continuous fashion, without the interruptions of an impatient journalist who wants to move on (where?) in the program. Bourdieu mentions an example with which many academics will be able to identify. In 1989, he published *La noblesse de l'Etat* (*The State Nobility*), a study of symbolic power and elite formation in the French education system. Bourdieu had been actively interested in the field for more than twenty years, and the book had been long in the making. A journalist proposed a debate between Bourdieu and the president of the alumni organization of *les grandes écoles*; the latter would speak "for" and Bourdieu would speak "against." "And," he sums up sourly: "he [the journalist] hadn't a clue as to why I refused" (Bourdieu 1996: 23).

In general, news is becoming shorter and shorter. A tired joke about the competition for attention among tabloids consists in the remark that when war eventually breaks out for real, the papers will only have space for the "W" on the front page. The joke illustrates the principle of diminishing returns (or falling marginal value). In basic economics courses, teachers tend to use food and drink as examples to explain this principle, which is invaluable in an accelerating capitalist culture: If you are thirsty, the first soda has very high value for you. The second one is also quite valuable, and you may even—if your thirst is very considerable—be willing to pay for the third one. But then, the many soda cans left in the shop suddenly have no value at all to you; you are unwilling to pay a penny for any of them. Tender steaks, further, are highly valuable if you are only allowed to savor them once a month; when steak becomes daily fare, its value decreases dramatically. The marginal value of a commodity is defined as the value of the last unit one is willing to spend money or time and attention on. Although this principle cannot by far be applied to everything we do (a lot of activities, such as saxophone playing, become more rewarding the more one carries on), it can offer important insights into the situation described by Bourdieu and other cultural critics—how news, and more generally information, is being produced and consumed.

Acceleration, seen from a general perspective, can be fruitfully understood as a function of capitalism. Growth is necessary for capitalist operations to survive in competition with others who also grow, and it can be achieved either through conquering new markets or through intensification of consumption in existing ones. Reducing product life span and increasing the turnover rate is one way of ensuring growth; filling vacant niches with new forms of consumption is another. Both have an accelerating effect on consumption and, perhaps, life in general.

Simultaneity

As the anthropologist Johannes Fabian (1983) famously pointed out, there has always been a marked tendency in the West to think of peoples elsewhere as somehow belonging to another time. That which is distant in space is thought of as being distant in time as well. Even if the notion that primitive peoples represented us at an earlier stage in social evolution was abandoned by professional anthropologists in the early twentieth century as a figure of thought, this idea remained deeply embedded, even in anthropology itself, argued Fabian in the early 1980s. This kind of argument, although it makes its appearance occasionally in the media, would have been difficult to sustain in the academic community today.

There is a Gary Larson cartoon that depicts an unspecified tribal group shouting at the imminent arrival of a group of people in khakis: "Anthropologists! Anthropologists!" while they quickly put their TV sets and PlayStations away in order not to disappoint the researchers. Today, even in the places thought of as most remote from Western civilization, e-mail facilities are rarely far away, and locals use cell phones if they can afford to, which they increasingly can. This does not mean that they are fully integrated into the "flattened," globalized world described by the likes of Thomas Friedman—in many cases, they have no regular work, they have never been to a large city, they may be illiterate (especially the women), and they continue to make most of their purchases in the local market—but that they are connected with the world of instantaneous global communication and of monetary exchange. With both information technologies, like television, and communication technologies, like e-mail and telephony, becoming deterritorialized, there is a real sense in which humans everywhere have become contemporaries for the first time in history. Historical events, such as the fall of Communism in Eastern Europe, could be followed day by day by people everywhere (I was myself in Trinidad in the autumn of 1989, and had it been two or three years later, I could have discussed the events in Hungary and Romania instantaneously with my northern European friends over e-mail). The dramatic events unfolding during the Arab Spring of 2011, leading to the toppling of regimes in Tunisia, Libya, and Egypt (and a horrible civil war in Syria), were covered as they took place, and not just by foreign and domestic journalists, but by anyone with access to a smartphone. Some of the most memorable video clips from these dramas—technically inferior but emotionally poignant and acute—were placed on YouTube by ordinary citizens.

Still, it is important to keep in mind that not everything is in sync with everything else. First, as James Mittelman (2001: 7) points out, "the [global] system affects its components in very different ways. Globalization is a partial, not a totalizing phenomenon. Countries and regions are tethered to some aspects of globalization, but sizeable pockets remain removed from it." Hardly anywhere is this more true than in that aspect of globalization of which I speak as acceleration. Although there has been an IT boom in India since the turn of the millennium, that vast country emerging as a major power in the production of information technology, poverty remains very widespread in India today.

Second, we all live in a number of different temporal regimes, the accelerated simultaneity of global information society being only one, and our participation in it varies from zero to considerable. Moreover, even the super-efficient, successful Indian computer engineer may occasionally visit a Hindu temple where time moves as slowly as it did a thousand years ago or more. Although the general tendency is that everything fast spreads at the expense of everything that is slow (cf. Eriksen 2001c), slowness continues to exist, both because of the exclusion of millions from the fast world of global capitalism and ICTs (information and communication technologies), and because significant sociocultural domains are scarcely influenced by it. Yet, for all the talk of acceleration and speed as markers of globalization, there have been few sustained studies of the variations in speed lived by people who are part of this.

Popular Music and Temporal Structures

In a bold and daring book about the qualities of progressive rock, the North American philosophy professor Bill Martin has tried, in his broad defense plea for classic rock groups he admires (including Yes, Rush, and King Crimson), to explain what is wrong with the computer- and studio-based dance music developed since the late 1980s, including house, techno, drum'n'bass, and other genres that have little in common, apart from the fact that they can be described as varieties of nonlinear, repetitive, rhythmical dance music. This is music, which in his view, lacks progression and direction, which—unlike, say, Beethoven, Miles Davis, and Led Zeppelin—is not heading anywhere. Enjoyment of such music is generally undertaken through entering a room full of sound where a great number of aural things are happening and staying there until it no longer feels cool. Martin's preferred music is linear and has an inner development, although it may often be partly improvised. About the new rhythmic music, he has this to say:

> As with postmodern architecture, the idea in this stacking is that, in principle, any sound can go with any other sound. Just as, however, even the most eclectic pastiche of a building must all the same have some sort of foundation that anchors it to the ground, vertically stacked music often depends on an insisting beat. There are layers of trance stacked on top of dance, often without much in the way of stylistic integration. (Martin 1998: 290).

Martin doubts that this music will be capable of creating anything really new. He says, "The vertical-stacking approach implicitly (or even explicitly) accepts the idea that music (or art more generally) is now simply a matter of trying out the combinations, filling out the grid" (1998: 291). There are layers upon layers on top of each other, every vacant spot is filled, and there is little by way of internal integration. Stacking replaces internal development.

The listener's situation is radically different between rock/jazz and the new rhythmic music. The latter goes on and on; the former has a beginning, a long middle (internal development), and an end or climax. Interestingly, Indonesian gamelan music has been a significant source of inspiration to many of those who work with repetitive music, among them the minimalist composer Steve Reich. This is music developed in a traditional, ritualistic culture with no linear concept of development. The link with gamelan music is far from uninteresting, considering the view to the effect that an essentially nonlinear way of being in time is being strengthened in contemporary culture.

Interestingly, Manuel Castells (1996: 306) writes about new age music as the classical music of our era and describes it as an expression for "the double reference to moment and eternity; me and the universe, the self and the net." Desert winds and ocean waves create the backdrop for many of the repetitive patterns that make up new age music. It is a droning, timeless, and lingering kind of music—an antidote to the quotidian rat race, but also perfectly symmetrical to it, since it brackets the passage of time.

Put differently: When growing amounts of information are distributed at growing speed, it becomes increasingly difficult to create narratives, orders, and developmental sequences. The fragments threaten to become hegemonic. This has consequences for the ways in which we relate to knowledge, work, and lifestyle in a wide sense. Cause and effect, internal organic growth, maturity, and experience; such categories are under heavy pressure in this situation. The examples from music are just illustrations. The phenomenon as such is more widespread, and journalism, education, work, politics, and domestic life, just to mention a few areas, are affected by vertical stacking, a result of acceleration.

Some Further Implications of Acceleration

The sociologist John Urry (2000) has written usefully about the contrast between "glacial" and "instantaneous" time as two opposing temporal regimes, in a similar vein to what I have elsewhere (Eriksen 2001c) called cumulative, linear time versus the time of the moment: Glacial time is historical and developmental, while instantaneous time is just now, with few connections with a past or a future. In a list of characteristics of instantaneous time, Urry mentions the technological changes dealt with above, a "heightened temporariness of products, jobs, careers, natures, values and personal relationships," "the growth of 24 hour trading," and "extraordinary increases in the availability of products from different societies so that many styles and fashions can be consumed without having to wait to travel there" (2000: 129). All places now appear to be contemporary—but, as I have stressed before, we should pay more attention to the places that are not and are, for obvious reasons, rarely dealt with in studies of globalization.

Pessimistic analysts like Paul Virilio, who laments "the pollution of distances and delays which make up the world of concrete experience" (2000: 116), seem to overemphasize everything that is fleeting and transitory and are fascinated with the extreme, at the expense of neglecting the mundane and everyday, where there may be more continuity. Yet, in spite of such objections, it is clear that global capitalism, as a system of production, of distribution, and of consumption, favors speed over slowness because it is more profitable. As David Harvey sums up:

> Given the pressures to accelerate turnover time (and to overcome spatial barriers), the commodification of images of the most ephemeral sort would seem to be a godsend from the standpoint of capital accumulation, particularly when other paths to relieve over-accumulation seems blocked. Ephemerality and instantaneous communicability over space then become virtues to be explored and appropriated by capitalists for their own purposes. (1989: 288)

In this context, it is tempting to propose a whole series of contrasts that may illustrate the transition from industrial to informational society, from nation-building to globalization. We may, for example, depict the changes like this:

Table 2.1 sums up some of the critical concerns voiced by many writers about acceleration and globalization. To what extent these contrasts accurately depict the contrast between two temporalities, one tied to the nation-state and industrialism and one tied to global networks, neoliberal capitalism, and informationalism is naturally subject to controversy, and this is not the place to give a final verdict. What should be noted, however, is that all these assumed transitions point in the same direction, although the examples are taken from vastly different domains; the trend can be described as a movement from continuity and coherence (the book and the lifelong marriage as telling examples) to flickering fragmentation.

Table 2.1. Some possible dimensions of the transition from industrial to informational society (adapted from Eriksen 2001c).

Industrial society	Informational society
CD/vinyl record	MP3, streaming
Book	Web, handheld gadget
Single-channel TV	Multichannel TV, streaming
Letter	E-mail, Facebook, Twitter, etc.
Landline telephone	Mobile telephone
. . . and while we are at it, why not also:	
Lifelong monogamy	Serial monogamy
The era of the gold watch	The era of flexible work
Aging, maturing	Eternal (or faded) youth
Depth	Breadth
Linear, cumulative time	Fragmented contemporariness
Scarcity of information	Scarcity of freedom from information

The Unevenness of Speed

In the 1980s and 1990s, I carried out anthropological research in Mauritius, an island about which it was often said that "it changed fast." Always part of a global system—it had been a sugar producing colony since it was first settled in the early eighteenth century—it successfully went through an economic diversification process from the early 1980s onwards. Tourism and textile industry were the new main earners of foreign currency. From the early 1990s, Mauritius was quickly incorporated into the new informational regime. The speed of everyday life picked up. New highways ensured that commuters into the capital lost less time travelling to work than before. Mobile telephony, ubiquitous by the mid-1990s, ensured fast and instantaneous communication. The airport was expanded, fast-food outlets made their appearance, and both productivity and consumption levels soared.

In 2011, I visited Mauritius after having been absent for some years. As always, I noticed changes: new shopping malls, new brands, new buildings, and—most spectacularly—an entire new town had been built during my absence, dubbed Cybercity and located near the university. It consisted of a relatively modest (but imposing by

Mauritian standards) cluster of high-rise buildings, a slick new business hotel, offices, and restaurants. The patrons of the hotel bar were mostly youngish Mauritians of all ethnic communities, tapping away on their smartphones and sipping cocktails. The scene gave the impression of fast change in a society, which had, until recently, been seriously ethnically segregated, rurally dominated, and totally dependent on sugar exports.

Later, I visited some of my old haunts—namely, a small town and a fishing village on the coast. It was easy to see that change had not taken place there in a way remotely comparable to the building of the Cybercity. The physical environment was somewhat more dilapidated than before, otherwise similar. There were few visible indicators of change, although people did have flat-screen TVs and mobile phones here as well, and the cafes in town were by now nonsmoking. The contrast was nevertheless striking and a reminder that it is irresponsible to talk merely about social and cultural change in a given place without specifying where that change takes place.

From the 1940s into the 1970s, Zambia (North Rhodesia until 1964) went through a series of changes widely regarded with optimism and assumed to consist in a linear process of development, with copper mining as the central export-oriented industry. The country, and in particular the Copperbelt, subsequently went into sharp economic decline and was delinked from global networks into which it had formerly been integrated. As early as 1941, the anthropologist Godfrey Wilson wrote about the newly urbanized miners that they were moving from tribal to world society, a "huge world-wide community" (1941, quoted in Ferguson 1999: 234). Carrying out a re-study of the same areas many decades later, James Ferguson (1999) found a population that was nostalgic for a kind of modernity that they used to possess, but had lost. In some respects, Ferguson points out, the people of the region were just as up to date as anybody else, regarding style, music, and other urban sensibilities. But concerning their integration in the world economic system, and not least the belief in progress and development, they had been disconnected. Life had gone through a process of deceleration.

When you think you have discovered something, you should always look for its opposite. An important paradox of enlightenment is that when something is lit up, something else is left in the dark. And when something accelerates, something else decelerates, either in absolute or at the very least in relative terms. Keeping up with changes can be difficult enough; coping with enforced delinking, as the example from the Copperbelt suggests, can be deeply demoralizing and humiliating in a world where change in the guise of development and global integration is still seen as meaningful, valuable, and realistic.

* * *

Every generation has a tendency to regard its own era as being unique, and with good reason: All epochs are in their way unique. At the same time, it can also be claimed that much of that which is perceived as novel, has in fact existed for quite a while— say, since Plato, or since the Agricultural Revolution, since Marco Polo, Columbus, Gutenberg, the Prophet Mohammad, or the Reformation (pick your choice). Regarding speed and acceleration, one may object to those who stress the unique effects of jet planes, mobile telephones, and the Internet, that the most important changes in the history of modern world society took place when the telegraph was invented, or the steamship, or for that matter, the fast Roman two-wheel chariot. In other words, seen from this perspective, there is little or nothing new under the sun.

This kind of argument has its limitations. Although the telegraph was an invention with enormous consequences, the Internet signifies more than a mere footnote to Marconi. Global telecommunications based on real time creates a framework for human existence that differs radically from all earlier technologies because of the huge, and growing, number of nodes connected to each other in real time. Yet, it is perfectly reasonable to regard the electronic revolution as a direct extension of earlier innovations and accelerations. The great informational divides in Western cultural history—writing, money, printing, the clock—contributed to liberating, as it were, communication from its immediate context; writing made knowledge timeless and cumulative, the clock made time mechanical and universal, and money made values comparable. Whether you are in Canberra or in Kanpur, a dollar, an hour, and a news headline mean pretty much the same. The circumstances continue to vary, but the common denominators link places together.

Standardization and time saving are true-born children of the Industrial Revolution, and it was during the disruptions caused by industrialization that the foundations for the tyranny of the moment were laid. Only in industrial society could the clock be used to promote synchronized efficiency in a large and complex industrial work setting. It was also in this era that time and money were tightly coupled; punctuality had been a virtue at least since the time of Calvin, but the notion that time saved is money made became a guiding principle in production only when industry replaced traditional crafts on a large scale. The industrial revolution, which began towards the end of the eighteenth century, would need the entire nineteenth century to be completed in the West, culminating in the introduction of assembly lines and time recorders. The twentieth century ended with the globalization of simultaneity, and this particular plot thickens as we move deeper into the twenty-first century.

- Time-space compression refers to the squeezing together of time and space due to economic and technological changes, and it appears as acceleration.
- Technologies that accelerate communication—from jet planes to cell phones—have spread fast in the last decades, but unevenly, leading to the exclusion of vast numbers of humans, largely in the Third World.
- Both the logic of capitalist growth and expansion, and the availability of technologies of instantaneous communication, lead to acceleration in communication, production, and consumption.
- A consequence of accelerated communication is the enhanced knowledge, even if skewed, of remote places and the global system in most parts of the world.

Questions

- Describe some consequences—personal, political, cultural, economic—of the telegraph for transnational communication in the nineteenth century.
- Mention a few areas where acceleration has been perceptible from your parents' generation to yours, and discuss how this process relates to globalization.
- In what ways can acceleration of communication make people more vulnerable?
- Why are people who are excluded from accelerating processes likely to be politically powerless?
- The author seems to argue that the acceleration of communication, and the compression of messages into tiny packets of information, is related to globalization. How? And do you agree?

Further Reading

Castells, Manuel (2009) *Communication Power*. New York: Oxford University Press. Drawing on his theory of the global network society, Castells argues that ownership, control, or influence over communication networks are the main source of power in the present world.

Hassan, Robert, and Ronald E. Purser, eds. (2007) *24/7: Time and Temporality in the Network Society*. Stanford, California: Stanford Business Books. This is one of the few existing books that systematically explores the effects of the new communication technologies on work, business organization, and life in general in the West.

3

Standardization

The creation of comparability is a central feature of globalization (as well as modernity). This is evident in as different areas as communication, identities, trade, and politics. The establishment of global standards in measurements (notably the metric system), political organization (the state system and parties), time (twenty-four universal time zones), and language (English as a global means of communication)—to mention some important dimensions—has accompanied and facilitated the growth in transnational connectedness and has in some cases been necessary for these ties to be possible at all. However, standardization also takes place in less noticeable ways—for example, in the development of a global grammar of identity politics, software, and the size of shipping containers.

Imagine a nonstandard world. You would live in a town or village with your relatives, with few prospects of moving anywhere else. Everything you knew was handed down by your older relatives; all skills were taught face to face. The language you spoke was mutually intelligible with that of neighboring areas, but not quite identical, and comprehension faded with distance. Trade with outsiders took place through barter, but within your local area, certain goods could be exchanged for shell money. Your religion was associated with ancestors and the nature surrounding your home area. There was no script, no money, no calendars, and no standards of measurement operating beyond the immediate neighborhood.

In the premodern world, most products and services were nonstandard. They did not conform to a commonly established norm or set of parameters. They could not be mass produced, and if they travelled, they were recognized as exotic and precious. Language, too, was mostly local, spoken only in a restricted area and with marked dialect differences between localities. With the coming of literacy and later printing, the development of the modern state and its institutions (Anderson 1991 [1983]; Gellner 1983), standardization of phenomena such as language, measurements, and law took place at the national level. The development of the banking system contributed to the standardization of money and eventually other financial instruments.

In an important sense, globalization continues the work of nation building by creating shared standards, comparability, and bridging principles of translation between formerly discrete and largely incommensurable worlds (Barloewen 2003; Eriksen 2003; Meyer et al. 1992). Anything from consumer tastes to measurements and values are now being standardized at a global level. This does not mean that everybody is equally affected (it would be foolish to assume this), nor that standardization is all-encompassing. There is considerable resistance against standardization in almost all its forms from people and organizations who insist on remaining unique and locally embedded. According to an influential school in economic anthropology, going back to the critique of disembedded market economies in the 1930s and 1940s and associated with names such as Marcel Mauss and Karl Polanyi, it is in the very nature of human communities to resist commodification and disembedding of the economy from life in general (Hann and Hart 2012). In spite of imperfections and resistance, it is indisputable that the range of common denominators is widening in its scope and deepening in its impact as a result of the accelerated disembedding processes discussed in the previous chapters and that such emerging commonalities influence lives worldwide, for better and worse.

Some Standards of a Global Modernity

Standardization implies comparability. Shared measurements ensure that a buyer in a distant land gets the amount he or she has paid for; shared temporality makes synchronization and timetables possible; a shared (or convertible) currency makes economic transactions across space easy; a shared language makes communication across borders possible. Some of the social and cultural features of modernity are preconditions for globalization—if rural Turks had not known about wage work, they would not have migrated to Germany, and if middle-class Brazilians had been illiterate, they could not have learned English at school—and I will therefore quickly outline some of the most important forms of standardization entailed by modernity and required by globalization.

First, a *monetary economy* has become the norm, if not a universal practice, in most parts of the world. Such an economy is encouraged by states, which receive important revenue through direct and indirect taxation. Even land and labor, which tended not to be commodities in traditional societies, can now be sold and bought almost everywhere. Notwithstanding the neoliberal deregulation of recent decades, states remain the most powerful absentee landlords, and the omnipresence of money integrates an unlimited number of people anonymously into a vast system of exchange. The temporal structure on which this depends is linear and irreversible.

Second, *formal education* is nearly universally recognized as an important means for the achievement of rank, wealth, and related benefits. This entails, among other things, literacy, the standardization of languages, and the suppression of minority languages. Two hundred of the original two hundred fifty Australian languages have been eradicated, and most of the remaining ones are on the verge of extinction, which is a testimony to the loss of cultural diversity resulting from unequal encounters between modern states and indigenous peoples. Systems of higher education have increasingly been standardized across the world, and since the turn of the millennium, global ranking of universities—measuring their achievements in research and teaching outcomes—has become routine.

Third, political units of significant importance to the majority of mankind are *political parties*, organized at a nation-state level with local branches. Position in political parties is ostensibly achieved, not ascribed.

Fourth, official ideologies in virtually every country in the world are *nationalist* in character (although nationalism comes in many flavors), and individual rights and duties are to a great extent vested in citizenship. For those who are deprived of citizenship—internally displaced people, certain ethnic minorities, undocumented migrants—it thus becomes very difficult to assert their rights. The nation-states require their citizens to adhere to an abstract ideology of metaphoric kinship and to make personal sacrifices for the betterment of the abstract community of the country. In return, the nation-state presumably offers protection, collective identity, and career opportunities.

This list could have been made much longer, but I shall stop here. The main point is that the fact of the modern nation-state seems to create a uniform and universal framework for social organization on a very large scale. Of course, hardly two persons are affected by these and other dimensions of modernity in the same way, but virtually everybody has to cope with aspects of the nation-state and capitalism. Hardly anybody is totally unaffected in the contemporary world.

Some Contemporary Forms of Standardization

While traditional crafts were transferred directly from master to apprentice, production in a factory is so standardized that it ideally only requires a few, general skills. One of the aims of standardization of skills is to make workers interchangeable. As the early sociologists, from Marx to Durkheim, were concerned with, production in a factory entails splitting up the process so that each worker only produces a tiny bit of the whole. Criticism to the effect that this led to alienation was taken up not just by Marx but by a lot of concerned observers in the nineteenth century—in other words, a generation or two before Henry Ford invented the modern assembly line in the years before the First World War. Things would, in other words, only get worse. Or—perhaps—better: Like books following the printing press, manufactured goods became cheaper and more easily available as a result of mass-production and standardization.

Industrial production synchronizes work and standardizes its products. An item, such as a smartphone, is identical with all other items of the same make and model, and if it is unique, that is because of some defect (or because it is a pirated copy). In the society of craftsmanship, on the contrary, each object was individually made and unique. Mass-produced objects are interchangeable, like the skills of an engineer; the persons possessing them are interchangeable, and the skills can be applied to new contexts with (at least theoretically) minimal problems of translation involved in adapting them.

A world of standardization is a world of many common denominators and bridgeheads for communication.

Writing, money, wage work, the political party, and the state form are some of the key dimensions of standardization making global integration possible. The clock, the main source of mechanical time, is also important. The technology of the clock led to both the standardization of time units and the synchronization of large populations. The larger the number of people there were who needed to coordinate their movements with minute precision, the larger the number of regions there were that had been comprised by the new standards. When the last stretch of the Great Western Railway was opened in June 1841, the clocks in Bristol were ten minutes behind clocks in London. There had been no need for an exact synchronization of the inhabitants of the two cities yet. This need for synchronization came partly with the railway and partly with the telegraph during the following decades. The railway reduced the twenty-hour journey from London to Bristol to four hours, but the telegraph soon reduced the time required to send urgent dispatches almost to zero.

The present global system of twenty-four time zones was established in 1884. A maze of local time zones had made conversion difficult earlier. Passengers had been forced to set their timepieces in every city, and the need for a common standard had been voiced for years when an international panel finally reached an agreement at a meeting in Washington, D.C.

Like disembedding and acceleration, standardization takes place unevenly. Speaking about the "nodes" of global communication, such as airports, conference venues, and business hotels, the anthropologist Ulf Hannerz (1990) has proposed the term "global switchboards." Those who meet there, originating from different societies, speak a shared language (often English) and also have other things in common; they conform to a number of shared cultural standards. However, other members of their respective societies have less in common with each other, and are to that effect less standardized on a global scale.

Standardization is attempted in many areas, and the goal is always to create comparability in order to enhance communication, trade, and various forms of exchange. Units of measurement have to be standardized for goods from different origins to be compatible, but standards also concern the quality of steel, the size of crates, the shape of cucumbers, and many other features of trading goods.

In the realm of interpersonal interaction, the plastic card and the bar code are two everyday examples of global standards that make it easier to cross boundaries. An early-twenty-first-century, much-publicized attempt at standardization from a different field, moreover, is associated with the so-called Bologna agreement in Europe.

In 1999, ministers of education from twenty-nine European countries met to discuss the future of higher education in the continent. This was the starting point of a highly consequential and controversial restructuring of higher education in Europe, aiming to standardize courses and degrees continent-wide, to enhance comparability, student mobility, and to ensure consistent quality. As a result of the Bologna reforms, many countries have had to change their degree system dramatically, to conform to the requirements laid down for MA and BA degrees internationally. The advantages are obvious in that they create a level playing field, making it easy for students to take courses (giving them standardized credit points) at various universities in different countries, and the standardized system of evaluation (using the Anglo-American A–F scale) supposedly makes degrees from different universities comparable.

However, there are problems with such attempts at standardization. A grade on a BA course is not a meter; it has no objective standard of which to relate. As a result, the grades are used differently in different countries (the grade A, I happen to know, is quite rare in the social sciences in Norway). There are also serious misgivings about the assumed loss of local specificity and old academic traditions in several countries. The German Magister degree entailed years of independent study; it has now been replaced by a two-year taught MA degree. As is often the case, locals protest against standardization imposed from above or outside, but in this case, largely to no avail.

Obsolescence

A consequence of standardization is that many practices, knowledges, skills, and crafts disappear. The nonstandard is either marginalized or rendered obsolescent, like beer bottles too tall to fit the standardized supermarket fridge shelves. Historically and today, this happens in many domains. A famous anthropological travelogue, Claude Lévi-Strauss's *Tristes Tropiques* (1989 [1955]), is largely built around the idea that entire life-worlds are being rendered obsolete by modernization. The onslaught of modernity, in Lévi-Strauss's view, entailed the loss of unique ways of life, worldviews, and real-life showcases of human variation as it were. A generation before Lévi-Strauss, another great anthropologist, Bronislaw Malinowski, complained, a tad more cynically, that anthropology, or ethnology as he still called it is:

in the sadly ludicrous, not to say tragic, position, that at the very moment when it begins to put its workshop in order, to forge its proper tools, to start ready for work on its appointed task, the material of its study melts away with hopeless rapidity. Just now, when the methods and aims of scientific field ethnology have taken shape, when men fully trained for the work have begun to travel into savage countries and study their inhabitants—these die away under our very eyes. (1984 [1922]: xv)

Nostalgic laments about the disappearance of unique cultural forms are a common feature of perceived globalization—indeed, a popular British series about other cultures produced towards the end of the twentieth century was called *Disappearing World*. This concern is not new; it is a part of modernity's critical self-reflection and can be traced at least back to the Romantic movement in Germany around the year 1800. However, the speed with which cultural worlds (and other things) are rendered obsolete is greatly enhanced in our intensively globalized era. The quaint and local is replaced with that which is comparable along a set of common denominators in order to enhance intelligibility, trade, exchange, and—many would emphasize—exploitation. General-purpose money of the Western type, thus, renders shell money and copper sticks obsolete; the great religions of conversion (Islam and Christianity) have conquered most of the societies that used to have local religions; formal education replaces learning by watching, and hundreds of languages are predicted to vanish within a few decades. In the contemporary North Atlantic world, typical examples of obsolescence would refer to commodities such as locally manufactured soft drinks (in the early 2000s, it was reported that Coke was for the first time the largest selling soft drink in Scotland, dethroning the national beverage Irn-Bru, which may eventually become obsolete) and computer operating systems (there were lots of incompatible systems in the 1980s; now there are essentially three—Windows, MacOS, and Linux).

EFL as the Medium of Globalbabble

Although the global percentage of native English-speakers is declining, the number of people using English as their main foreign language is growing. According to the British Council (2009), about 25 percent of the world's population speaks English "to some level of competence," and they add, in a perhaps not overly disinterested vein, that "demand from the other three-quarters is increasing. Everybody wants to speak it."

You may be reading this in a language different from the one you use as an everyday medium for carrying on with your life. As for myself, I'm writing in a language that is not the medium of my everyday trivia, and there are a lot of things I cannot say in a satisfactory way through the idiom of English. Exactly how these limitations affect our communication is difficult to assess, but in general, English as a foreign language (EFL) has certain characteristics not shared with English as a native language. In fact, there are courses available for translating between plain English and EFL. One such online course, or really a teaser for a course (McAlpine 2006), offers a great deal of advice—not, this time, for the foreigner wanting to express himself better in a foreign language but for native speakers wanting to be understood by foreigners. As everybody knows, English as a foreign language is not the same language as English spoken by natives. More than one first-time foreign visitor to London, with top marks in English from his or her school, has been shocked upon discovering that it is plainly impossible to understand what the cockney cabman is saying.

The examples discussed in the online course are instructive in suggesting some changes to be expected when an increasing amount of communication takes place between people who are not using their first language:

- One is advised to use short sentences.
- One is advised to avoid false subjects, such as "It" in sentences like "It is extraordinary how warm the weather is." It is better to say "The weather is extraordinarily warm."
- Miniwords, or fillers, such as "get, go, lot, by, for, it, he, the, a, of," are discouraged as they can lead to confusion.
- Complex questions are discouraged, such as "You don't have the courage to acknowledge that your allegations have no factual basis whatsoever, do you?" Rather, say, "Do you admit that you have made false allegations?" (I like this example. It prepares the native speaker for encounters he may expect with foreigners.)
- Similarly, double negatives are discouraged: "The results were not displeasing" should be avoided. Instead, say, "The results were pleasing."
- One is moreover advised not to use idioms such as "the tip of the iceberg," "just around the corner," and so on.
- Plainly, all kinds of ambiguity are discouraged to avoid misunderstandings. Negative words are also discouraged, as in "The shipment will not arrive until late January"—it is better to say "The shipment will arrive in late January."

In other words, authors of courses like this one encourage native speakers to avoid colloquialisms and idioms, understatement, and metaphor. The result can be described as a disembedded language, an efficient, simplified, practical means of communication where there would otherwise have been none.

Bilingualism and Standardization

A closer look at language obsolescence may be instructive in showing the forces of standardization and globalization at work. In a prestandardized world, it was difficult to draw the boundary around one language. It was largely with printing and mass education that languages were standardized in the sense that a speaker from Bayern (Bavaria) could easily communicate with, and relate to the same literary standard of German (*Hochdeutsch*), as a speaker from Schleswig. In other words, it is impossible to fix the number of languages spoken in the year 1400. Only in Italy, a linguist might have found forty distinct languages or more.

Only a tiny minority of the world's several thousand languages underwent this process of standardization, which was often associated with the growth of a nation-state (Anderson 1991 [1983]). These languages often ousted or marginalized unwritten languages or even written languages with no political support. Nation building, in this way, functioned as a great leveler.

In the early twenty-first century, the work of the nation-state continues, this time at a higher pace and a larger scale. The total number of languages spoken was estimated to be six thousand at the turn of the millennium (Crystal 2000). Interestingly, only 4 percent of these languages account for 96 percent of the speakers. A quarter of them have fewer than one thousand speakers. In a typical sequence, a language becomes obsolete when the speakers first become bilingual (adding a dominant, often national language to their repertoire), followed by a decline in the use of their original language, largely for pragmatic reasons—the radio, the newspapers, and the people in town all use the dominant language. It is widely believed that English is the main global leveler here, imposing its standards on people everywhere else; so far, this is an overstatement. The vast majority of the people who are learning English use it as a foreign language or lingua franca. Bahasa Indonesia, the national language of Indonesia (which is almost identical to Malay), has probably eradicated more local languages than English, to take one example. However, the growth of bilingualism in English has been phenomenal over the last few decades, and this is a process of globalization proper (neither imperialism nor nation building) since most of the countries that adopt English as a second language today have no shared colonial history with Great Britain. Moreover, English as a second language is making inroads not chiefly among the small peoples speaking languages with no literature and no public sphere but among speakers of national languages like Dutch and Polish, and even in countries such as Vietnam and Rwanda, where the second language used to be French. Many specialists envision a future where English will gradually replace national languages in certain domains—in academic publishing, this has already largely happened—while the national languages, often in a hybridized form with many loanwords from English, continue to be used, at least for some time, in other fields. To mention but one example, there is great pressure on European universities now, especially in smaller countries like Portugal and Finland, to offer courses in English in order to facilitate student mobility. Thus, we have entered a period of linguistic standardization, which is not a result of nationalism or imperialism but of transnational networking.

The Globalization of Nothing

In a thought-provoking book about standardization called *The Globalization of Nothing*, the sociologist George Ritzer (2004) contrasts what he sees as two pervasive tendencies in the contemporary world: the *grobalization* of nothing and the *glocalization* of something. He defines glocalization as that which is "locally conceived and controlled and rich in distinctive substance" (2004: 8), while grobalization is defined as "generally centrally conceived, controlled, and comparatively devoid of distinctive substantive content" (2004: 3). In other words, standardized, mass-produced goods catering to an assumed common denominator of disembedded market tastes are the outcome of grobalization, while anything that couldn't have been produced anywhere but in a particular location is defined as glocalization.

Indirectly framing the debate about standardization, Ritzer says that there "is a gulf between those who emphasize the increasing grobal influence of capitalistic, Americanized, and McDonaldized interests and those who see the world growing increasingly pluralistic and indeterminate" (2004: 80).

Concentrating largely on consumption, Ritzer distinguishes between the grobalization and glocalization of places, things, persons, and services. The more personalized, place-bound, and unique something is, the more glocalized. For example, while a craft barn represents the glocalization of something, Disney World stands for the grobalization of nothing. A bar frequented because of its skillful bartender or because it is where one's friends hang out is something, whereas hotel bars with new customers every evening and a standardized, transnational selection of cocktails is a nothing. The big and standardized stands for nothing, while the small and locally fashioned stands for something in Ritzer's account.

Ritzer agrees that things are really more complicated. He admits that "grobalization can, at times, involve something (for example, art exhibits that move among art galleries throughout the world, Italian exports of food like Parmigiano-Reggiano and Culatella ham)" (2004: 99), and conversely, that the glocal can also produce nothing, such as tourist trinkets. He even concedes that there are "people today, perhaps a majority, who prefer nothing to something and who have good reason for that preference" (2004: 16), thinking about those—hundreds of millions—who scarcely have the opportunity to participate in the consumption of nothing. People in poorer countries produce much of the richer world's nothingness, but can scarcely afford any of it for themselves.

Inspired not only by Marc Augé's concept of non-places but also by Max Weber's early twentieth-century theory of disenchantment and rationalization, Ritzer establishes a series of simple contrasts where everything mass produced, ready-made, and instant appears dehumanized and where everything one of a kind (be it a product or an employee) is "enchanted" and authentic.

Many writers on globalization would be inclined to see Ritzer's analysis as simplistic. As pointed out by Jean-Loup Amselle (2001: 22), even in McDonald's restaurants, "as one may discover by visiting its outlets throughout the world, [they] do not sell the same products everywhere." In India, where the first McDonald's outlet was opened in New Delhi in 1996, 75 percent of the menu has been Indianized. Notably, the majority of the population does not eat beef, and so the Big Mac was transformed into a Maharaja Mac made with mutton, and vegetarian burgers were added to the menu. Moreover, apparently identical products and services are perceived in distinctly local ways. Coca-Cola, an everyday product in most of the Western world, is associated with weddings and other rituals—for example, among Luo of Western Kenya. The Macintosh computer, according to Amselle (2001), became a symbol of identity among French intellectuals resisting the global dominance of Microsoft (although the Mac is, of course, just as American as Microsoft). In other words, rather than being overrun by the grobalization of nothing, locals invest the nothing with something in discriminating, critical ways. And yet, Ritzer has a point when he argues that the transnational standardization of commodities and services is one important dimension of globalization, even if the meaning of the products and services thus disseminated vary locally.

McWorld and Its Discontents

One influential writer on globalization who is likely to be sympathetic to Ritzer's perspective is the international relationist Benjamin Barber, whose book *Jihad vs. McWorld* (1995) has exerted major influence inside and outside the academy—it is even rumored that it was read by Bill Clinton during his presidency. Thinking along similar lines to Ritzer, Barber is more interested in the political implications of globalization than its commercial ones.

Like Ritzer, Barber describes the emergence of a bipolar world pitting global capitalism and consumerism against local resistance and alternatives. The word jihad in the title has led many to assume that Ritzer's book is somehow about the West and Islam, but he uses it as a generic term for all kinds of countermovements resisting the homogenizing effects of global flows.

McWorld, in Barber's usage, "is a product of popular culture driven by expansionist commerce" (1995: back cover). It is a close relative to the old Marxist term "monopoly capitalism," which is wedded to consumerism. Barber describes the spread of standardized popular culture, such as MTV, at some length, showing that nearly all countries outside Africa had access to MTV as early as 1995. Today, the example seems dated since YouTube has taken over much of the music video market. In a general way, nevertheless, the example is relevant not only as a description of transnationally standardized consumption but also as an indicator of economic power. Comparing today's media magnates to earlier industrial tycoons, he reminds the reader that "theirs [the media moguls] is power not over oil, steel, and railroads—mere muscles of our modern industrial bodies—but over pictures, information and ideas—the very sinews of our postmodern world" (Barber 1995: 298; see also Castells 2009). Although Barber shows how the oil oligarchy seems to stimulate local countermovements in many countries, especially among local people who are not beneficiaries of the giant corporations, he also seems to argue that standardized global media and information products lend themselves more easily to local political protest—they seem to be colonizing people's minds—than to industrial products.

What is at stake for Barber, whose book is not just diagnostic but genuinely worried in its tone, is civil society and with it democracy. In a world where citizens can choose to either become integrated into a blandly homogeneous global market or to join an antimodern resistance movement, he argues, there is little room for the citizen as a member of a public sphere deliberating over politics, making compromises and ensuring a fair distribution of goods and benefits. Like many others, Barber is not opposed to the market as such, but says that the virtues of the global marketplace "scarcely warrant permitting the market to become sovereign over politics, culture, and civil society" (1995: 298). Barber's jihad metaphor resembles Ritzer's notion of the glocalization of something, but it differs through its chiefly political content and for being overtly antiglobalist. Like all simplifications, Barber's dichotomous world can be criticized, but as a very general description of a global dynamics with manifold local expressions, it stands up to scrutiny quite well. As a matter of fact, many if not most writers on the politics of globalization employ some kind of dichotomous divide between, on the one hand, universalist globalizing processes and, on the other, local alternatives or resistance—"cosmopolitans and locals" (Hannerz 1990), "the Net and the Self" (Castells 1996), "system world and life-world" (Beck 1999), "fundamentalism and ambivalence" (Bauman 1999). These are attempts to give some substance to a general dualism between the universal and the particular, which constitutes a central tension in all globalizing processes.

MS Word

There is a healthy and vigorous body of literature dealing with standardization—some of it laudatory, some of it critical, some of it just curious—but surprisingly little is written about the medium of standardization through which more than 90 percent of that literature is produced—namely, Microsoft Word. This is even more surprising given that many critics of global homogenization through expanding markets are especially concerned about information technology and the media.

Microsoft Word, which began its career in 1981 as one of many word processors on the market, eventually became market dominant (from around 1990) and has virtually destroyed all competition in the world of Windows, where alternative word processors are difficult to come by and have to be Word-compatible in order to have a commercial potential. Most Macintosh users, too, use Word.

Compared to the alternatives, there is nothing remarkable about Word as a word processor, except for its size (being part of a huge Office package, it takes up an extraordinary amount of space on the hard drive). Its near-monopoly must be understood as a direct result of the dominant position of the associated operating system, Windows. The strength of Microsoft was never its ability to innovate, but it has skillfully developed ideas and concepts borrowed elsewhere to fit its own mold and has marketed its alternative more efficiently than anybody else would be capable of doing—Excel resembles Lotus, Word in its early incarnations resembled several Macintosh word processors (MacWrite, WriteNow, etc.), Internet Explorer resembles other web browsers, and the very Windows interface was in its day so similar to the Finder (the Macintosh's graphic interface) that Apple sued for plagiarism.

Word is regularly launched in new versions, always larger and lumpier than its predecessors, often requiring the user to buy new hardware. Even if a user resists and wants to stick to her 1995 version of Word, she will eventually have to upgrade in order to be able to exchange documents with others.

How could it be that Word and Windows steadily increased their market shares from the early 1990s onwards, in spite of the existence of cheaper and possibly better alternatives? One answer, which gives an interesting spin on the discussion about standardization, is "path dependence" (David 1992, 2007): The more people who use a particular technological solution, the more difficult it becomes for an alternative to make headway, even if it is a better product. Nothing succeeds like success, and the dissemination of an emergent standard creates snowball effects, through deals with government agencies, major corporations, and other big consumers.

The theory of path dependence has been criticized (see, e.g., Liebowitz and Margolis 2013) for lacking empirical evidence and for not taking into account the possibility that consumers can change their minds. However, it should be said in defense of the theory that certain decisions are irreversible, and in a given network of communication and exchange, shared standards often enforce, and reinforce, themselves. When a standard rail gauge (width of railway tracks) has been decided, there is no turning back afterwards. Nonetheless, the standards are not ubiquitous, and the standard gauge is used only by 60 percent of the world's railways. Travelers by train from France to Spain, for example, have to change trains on the border because the tracks have different gauge. Several of the European countries that chose nonstandard gauge did so for military reasons, to prevent alien powers from invading by train. This kind of argument is interesting in the context of the contemporary debate over how to prevent terrorists from entering one's country: the contrast shows how much more deterritorialized our present world is than that of the mid-nineteenth century.

Muslim countries and China have challenged the Christian calendar, generally with mixed success, while nobody, to my knowledge, has tried to posit alternatives to the colonially imposed global system of time zones. Microsoft's attempts to close the open standards on the Internet in the early 2000s (by creating their own version of the HTML programming language) would, if it had been successful, create the same kind of path dependence as the clock and calendar standards: you could have stuck to the old, open-source code, but in the end you would have few left to talk to.

This brings us to one of the clear advantages of standardization, seen from a user's perspective. Shared standards for time, measurements, and word processing make it easy to communicate across borders. It is easier to manage an organization where all employees use a single software package than one where people have chosen their software eclectically. Compatibility, support, and networking are factors here.

Using MS Word can be a frustrating experience for writers who are accustomed to other word processors. It is difficult to turn its helper, spell-checker, and automatic formatting off once and for all, and its menus are often counterintuitive. Fortunately, conversion filters are available for all nonstandard word processors (that is to say, all except Word itself—the majority, as is well known, never has to learn the languages of minorities).

All word processors influence the way we write and think by laying down incentives and constraints. For this reason, the historical transition from WordPerfect to Word as the globally dominant word processor is less trivial, from a cultural perspective, than the shifting market shares between, say, Coke and Pepsi. The significance of Word's global dominance can be compared with the transition from parchment to paper, from the quill to the fountain pen: It influences language, the style of working, and the style of thought. For this reason, an interest in software standards is not just motivated by an interest in standardization and globalization, but it also has wider intellectual and political implications.

The Metric System

Britons, Americans, and a few others have rebelled against it for decades, but the metric system is the closest bid we are likely to get for a universal, coherent global standard for all important measurements. Bushels, pounds, yards, and ounces, and a myriad of locally defined measurement units across the globe, have been giving way to the metric system for two centuries, and the process seems to be nearly complete by the early twenty-first century.

Now officially named the International System of Units (SI), the metric system began in France in 1790 when a government commission defined the meter as one ten millionth of a quarter of the earth's meridian passing through Paris.

At the first international General Conference on Weights and Measures in 1889, a prototype meter bar was established, made of 90 percent platinum and 10 percent iridium, measured at the melting point of ice. The meter is the standard from which all other units in the metric system derive. A liter (originally pint) is defined as the volume of a cube having a side equal to a tenth of a meter (a decimeter). The unit for mass, the grave (now kilogram), is defined as the mass of one liter of distilled water at the temperature of melting ice.

The decimal system on which the metric system is based is another globally accepted standard, a cultural one and not a god-given one, as is the Celsius system for measuring temperatures. Their almost universal acceptance (again, many Anglo-Saxons still swear by the Fahrenheit scale) is an instance of globalization; it has not come about by itself.

Even the A formats for paper (common almost everywhere except in some English-speaking countries) are based on the metric system. All formats are defined such that the height divided by the width of the paper is the square root of two. The rare format A0 has an area of one square meter. Format A1 is A0 cut into two equal pieces, and so on. This entails that the common A4 format is one-sixteenth the size of A0—that is, one-sixteenth square meter.

The meter as such is a fairly random unit, but all the other measurements of mass, density, and so on follow logically from it, and it is also used in compounds with other systems of measurements, creating standards such as kilometers per hour.

The Shipping Container and Standardization

Although globalization is often associated with the Internet and satellite television, travel, the global spread of computers, standardized consumer habits, and so on, it may well be argued that the invention of the standardized shipping container in the 1950s was an equally important precondition for contemporary globalization as the launching of the first communication satellites by the Soviets in 1957 and the Americans in 1960.

Before the introduction of a standardized container that could be loaded directly from a truck onto a cargo ship, cargo was characteristically nonstandard. A typical cargo ship as late as in the 1950s could contain barrels, drums, crates, reels, bundles, boxes, cases, bags, and cartons, mostly loaded manually by stevedores. Larger containers did exist, but there was no standard size or shape. Freight costs were high and hampered trade. In the mid-1950s, the trucker Malcom McLean, long frustrated by the inefficient and half-hearted relationship between transportation on land and by sea, devised the prototype of container shipping, when he had an oil tanker refitted to accommodate fifty-eight standard size containers, lifted by cranes directly from trailers onto the ship, and sailing with them from Newark to Houston (Levinson 2006). This new, efficient way of moving goods initially met with resistance from established transport companies and trade unions, but it was so much cheaper and more efficient than the competition that it slowly transformed the entire logistical chain from production to consumer.

Railway cars, trailers, and ships were increasingly made, or adjusted, to fit with the new metal containers. Seaports were built or rebuilt to accommodate container ships as well as the trucks and trains carrying the containers. Those that were slow to adjust, such as Liverpool, went into recession.

Container shipping combined with container transport over land—fast, cheap, and reliable—did not only lead to the downfall of the dockers' guild and the almost total reconstruction of commercial port areas, but it is also a key to China's rise to prominence as an industrial exporter, having brought freight rates down so much that even a producer of cheap goods far from its markets could remain highly competitive. The shipping container also led to the decline of the warehouse, replacing it by sophisticated logistics where products reached their destination directly and just in time, instead of wasting away in dusty warehouses waiting to be picked up. Indeed, the term *logistics* as a nonmilitary concept owes its existence largely to the shipping container (Levinson 2006).

The box, the modern shipping container, embodies several aspects of global standardization: The container itself, the cranes, port facilities, railway cars, trailers, and containerships had to be standardized so that a container filled in California and shipped from Oakland could easily and inexpensively be off-loaded in Sydney and driven directly to its final destination. The rapidly growing amounts of goods contained by these metal boxes have contributed in no small degree to standardizing consumer tastes worldwide. Finally, the logistics involved in producing, moving, and selling the contents of the containers are comparable everywhere in the world. The shipping container is a homogenizing machine.

Resistance to Standardization

Standardization, a key feature of modernity as such, is greatly facilitated on a transnational scale thanks to acceleration in communication, the predominance of a globalized capitalism, and the instruments of disembedding. It should nevertheless be kept in mind that the scope of global modernity, even if it is truly global, is not universal. In a strong critique of overenthusiastic "globalizers," Jean-François Bayart (2003) thus points out that "the extension of capitalism to a world scale cannot be taken for granted" (308). He speaks of the "ambiguous relationship to capitalism" in Latin America, sub-Saharan Africa's "refusal to integrate into the capitalist economy," and the "failure of 'political Islam' in defining a specific and viable economic orientation" (309), concluding that globalization, certainly if we speak of it in terms of global capitalism, is patchy and far from all-encompassing. Indeed, a vast number of people in the world are integrated in the capitalist world without contributing to its reproduction at the institutional and systemic level. They operate in the informal sector, as producers, buyers, sellers, and consumers, in the grey zones of the economy that never make it to the national statistics or the tax office (Mathews et al. 2012). These depend on local knowledge and personal networks. Transactions take place independently of the medium of writing, and taxes are evaded rather than paid.

Standardization only works for some human activities and products. *Scalability* is a necessary condition for standards—that the same things can be replicated in more or less identical form everywhere (Tsing 2012). The nonscalable, or that which cannot be standardized, have qualities that anchor them to particular contexts and settings. Tsing mentions particular forms of complexity (such as an ecosystem) and emotions (such as love) as nonscalable phenomena, but as a rule, we may say that every human life-world has nonscalable features. Even strongly standardized organizational forms, such as the plantation (Tsing's example), or forms of consumption (from fast food to clothes) take on a local significance because they are incorporated into particular, nonscalable life-worlds.

In addition, the extent of standardization is limited simply because not all areas are equally affected by the forces of incorporation and global networks. Many small languages may survive the twenty-first century—not because their speakers stubbornly stick to the idiom of their forebears, or because they are able to obtain support from transnational agencies favoring linguistic pluralism, but because they are left alone, overlooked and neglected by globalizing forces. Research in this area must ultimately take on the question of whether this is a good or a bad thing. Isolated pockets of tribal people, say, in the New Guinea highlands, may avoid the oppression of the state, the disintegration of certain customs, the loss of language, and oral traditions, but they will similarly not have the benefits of modern health care, a variety of job opportunities, a wider range of experiences, and a more comprehensive freedom to shape their lives than before. In a comparison of the situation of the Baruya (a New Guinean people) in the 1960s and in the 2000s, the anthropologist Maurice Godelier (2009) laments that they no longer constitute an autonomous society. They have been incorporated into the Papua New Guinea state as citizens, classified by statisticians as forming a segment of a larger ethnic group, proletarianized, and dragged into formal education and wage work. Whether this is good or bad depends on one's position; Godelier's point is that they have lost self-determination as a people.

There are few autonomous groups left, although there remain pockets and even larger territories where the inhabitants have successfully managed to keep the state at bay (Scott 2010). The people Bayart has in mind are not, as a rule, isolated tribal people or otherwise stateless groups but rather poor people in slums and impoverished peasants, formally educated people living in countries that accord them few citizen rights, and marginal groups everywhere. However, he does not give a conclusive answer to the question of whether one is necessarily worse off for being marginal to world capitalism or if it would have been better for the people in question not to be part of a monetized economy at all.

There can be no unequivocal answer to this incredibly complex question, but in a very different part of the world (namely the affluent North Atlantic), reflexive—that is to say, self-conscious—resistance to globalization has become widespread in certain milieus. It can be grouped in two main varieties. First, the alterglobalizers, formerly known as the antiglobalization movement, a loose coalition of farmers, students, and political idealists from across the world (but dominated by the North Atlantic), have made strong protests and organized huge demonstrations against the instruments of global capitalism, including the World Trade Organization (WTO), the International Monetary Fund (IMF), and the U.S. Treasury, arguing—among other things—that it is unfavorable to the needs of poor countries, that neoliberalism is an exploitative and cruel form of economy, which creates uncertainty, inequality, and leads to mass unemployment, and that current practices lead to an unhealthy and demeaning standardization of production everywhere. It is to be noted here, and it has no bearing on the arguments put forward by the movement, that the antiglobalizers are themselves globalized and not really opposed to globalization as such: they share a transnational mindset inspired by ideological developments in the North Atlantic, they communicate electronically, and they travel to demonstrations by jet. It is, in other words, globalization narrowly defined as global capitalism they rebel against (see also Chapter 9).

Exclusion is a major theme in research on globalization, and it affects many more than the people participating in antiglobalization movements. For many of the millions of poor in the Third World, who have only experienced the negative effects of globalization (such as loss of land, pauperization, loss of tradition, and autonomy), being standardized to the extent of getting an education and a job at the local McDonald's would, in many cases, be preferred to being neglected. Capitalism creates both wealth and poverty simultaneously in the lack of a state, or a transnational political body, serving the needs not only of the market but of society. This gap—between a globally standardized and synchronized economic system on the one hand and weak transnational political instruments on the other—can probably be described as the main contradiction, or source of conflict, in a globalized era. Some want the train of globalization to stop so that they can get off; others want it to stop so that they can get on, while yet others want it to change track. But all groups depend on a political power willing to and capable of creating conditions for a society that contains something more than standardized market forces.

- Standardization refers to the imposition of shared standards, which render events and objects comparable and conversion or translation possible.
- Standardization entails the establishment of common denominators, but it also marginalizes and sometimes destroys that which is locally unique.
- In some cases, as with language, global or international standards coexist through a stable division of labor, side by side with the local.
- Many of the tensions and conflicts resulting from globalization are based on a contrast between universalizing standardization and local alternatives or resistance.

Questions

- What does standardization have to do with globalization?
- How does standardization in production affect transnational investments?
- Discuss some consequences of synchronization for globalization or transnational processes in general—financial, political, interpersonal.
- In which areas is standardization actively resisted? Give examples from your own society and a country on a different continent.
- What does Ritzer mean by grobalization and glocalization? Is the dichotomy useful or not?
- Do you see a structural similarity between identity politics (ethnic, religious, or nationalist) and resistance to standardized consumer goods (McDonald's, Microsoft, etc.)?

Further Reading

Levinson, Marc (2006) *The Box: How the Shipping Container Made the World Smaller and the World Economy Bigger*. Princeton, NJ: Princeton University Press. A fascinating and compelling story about the history of the shipping container and its fundamental significance for globalization, influencing not only distribution and consumption but also production and economic development.

Ritzer, George (2004) *The Globalization of Nothing*. London: Sage. Using simple but original dichotomies, the author argues—with examples chiefly from consumption and marketing—that globalization follows two main itineraries: homogenization and monopoly capitalism, and locally anchored adaptations to the global field.

4

Connections

A sensible rule of thumb for connectedness might be that the actions of powerholders in one region of a network rapidly (say within a year) and visibly (say in changes actually reported by nearby observers) affect the welfare of at least a significant minority (say a tenth) of the population in another region of the network. Such a criterion indubitably makes our own world a single system; even in the absence of worldwide flows of capital, communications, and manufactured goods, shipments of grain and arms from region to region would suffice to establish the minimum connections.

—CHARLES TILLY, *BIG STRUCTURES, LARGE PROCESSES, HUGE COMPARISONS*, 62

Some of the most widespread metaphors for globalization are based on ideas about networks and connectedness. And rightly so: Never before in human history have so many people been so closely connected as today. And the networks are continuously becoming denser and more diverse. In the early 1990s, the jet plane and the television satellite would be used as examples of increased interconnectedness. Ten years later, e-mail, mobile telephony, and the World Wide Web would figure prominently. Another ten years on, Facebook, migrant remittances, and trade with China—both formal and informal—exemplify the kinds of connections that make almost every locality translocal, almost every local phenomenon glocal. This chapter covers a broad range of networks, from formal organizations (FIFA, the WTO, etc.) to informal petty trade networks, from telecommunications to the use of English and Microsoft software as a means of transnational communication.

The culinary capital of India may be London, that of China San Francisco. In order to finish an anthropological study of a town in the Dominican Republic, you have to spend at least a few months in New York City, since that is where a good portion of the population spends much of its time. The little trolls, "Scream" t-shirts, and exorbitantly priced knitted sweaters sold to wealthy tourists visiting Oslo are made in Taiwan, Pakistan, and Sri Lanka, respectively. The largest city in the English-speaking Caribbean is London. And if the classical patriarchal kinship system of the Taiwanese had been unable to withstand the pressure of individualism from modernization, several shop owners in Silicon Valley might still have been in business: The patriclan is an efficient economic unit where interest-free loans and free services are available, and when shops in California (and elsewhere) have to close down because their customers have lost their jobs, this is partly a result of competition from East Asia. There were several interlinked causes for the global economic crisis starting in 2007, but it began in earnest when millions of American homes were revealed to be both overvalued and financed by subprime mortgage loans leading to massive defaults on the part of the borrowers. As a result, the housing bubble burst. Beginning as a modest, seemingly manageable problem, the economic crisis grew in a totally uncontrolled and unforeseen way, leading to financial bankruptcies, mass unemployment in a number of countries, and the placing of the entire country of Iceland under administration (Pálsson 2013).

Such is the extent of global interconnectedness, and I still haven't even mentioned satellite television, the Internet, cheap flights, and cell phones. Some theorists compare the complex webs of connectedness in the current era to chaos and complexity in physics (e.g., Thrift 1999; Urry 2003), mining complexity theory for models that can be used to understand social change.

The most famous metaphor from chaos theory is that of the butterfly effect: A butterfly flapping its little wings on the Brazilian coast whips up some air and changes the direction of a tiny wind. This wind connects to other streams of air, changing parameters in the atmosphere ever so slightly for each step, and one of the cumulative effects is, say, a blizzard in Maine. The reasoning behind the butterfly effect is old as the hills, as witnessed by this familiar English rhyme:

> For want of a nail, the shoe was lost;
> For want of the shoe, the horse was lost;
> For want of the horse, the rider was lost;
> For want of the rider, the battle was lost;
> For want of the battle, the kingdom was lost;
> And all from the want of a horseshoe nail.

The general point here is that small changes can have momentous effects, or rather, that tiny variations in the initial parameters of a process may, through complex feedback processes, lead to major differences in the outcome. Butterfly effects, as such, are relatively uncommon in globalization processes, but the point is rather that in a steadily more interconnected world, the distance between cause and effect is often enormous. Space is relativized; urban Trinidadians may feel that Barbados and even Miami are closer than Mayaro in rural Trinidad, and although you exercise little power over your neighbor, you may work in a company with the power to hire and fire people in a Malaysian town. In this kind of world, the power of the nation-state is increasingly being questioned. The deregulation of markets has weakened the state in many rich countries, while structural adjustment programs imposed by the International Monetary Fund (IMF) on many countries in the Global South in the 1980s and 1990s entailed a slimming of the public sector and the privatization—in many cases de facto disappearance—of services that had formerly been public.

While few contend that the state is withering away, its power to govern is being challenged from several directions, mostly transnational—large corporations, transnational rights movements or religious ones, informal networks ranging from petty trade to migration chains and migrant remittances, and ultimately, the world market. Global climate change and other environmental issues demonstrate that single states are unable, on their own, to regulate the conditions for their own survival. Media flows, flows of people, goods, and commitments, virtual communities on the Internet, and transnational interest groups undermine the power of the nation-state to some extent. The question, and here scholars disagree, is to what extent.

Criticism of Methodological Nationalism

Few would disagree that the boundaries between societies and cultures, which were never absolute, are becoming increasingly contested. The sociologist Charles Tilly's pioneering book *Big Structures, Large Processes, Huge Comparisons* (1984: 12) argued that social science and sociology in particular ought to develop a truly global outlook, leaving the "pernicious postulates" of classic sociology behind, which presupposed that the world as a whole could be divided into distinct (mainly national) societies, that social change is a coherent general phenomenon, that large-scale change takes all societies through a more or less standard set of stages, and that times of rapid change necessarily entail a range of disorderly behaviors, such as crime, suicide, and rebellion. In contemporary language, one might say that Tilly calls for a transnational, nonteleological social science able to hold its own when confronted with paradoxical complexities.

First, it is clearly not the case that the world is moving in one direction, nor that modernity entails the death of everything nonmodern. Kinship continues to play an important role even in the most modern and individualist societies in the world; religion continues to be important, both as personal religiosity and as organized religion, and interpersonal trust and informal networks continue to function as a crucial glue, even in thoroughly bureaucratized societies. Even science, that hallmark of modern rationality, has emerged, and continues to develop, as a socially and culturally embedded form of knowledge, as Bruno Latour (1993) showed in a book aptly entitled *We Have Never Been Modern*.

Second, in Tilly's view, "methodological nationalism," to use Ulrich Beck's more recent term (2005; see also Wimmer and Glick Schiller 2002), seriously limits the comparative scope and contextual understanding of sociology. It is plainly impossible to understand a single nation-state, even a huge one, if the analysis is not based on an understanding of transnational processes. Transnationalism must be a premise, not an afterthought.

Third, global interconnectedness is not new and has a centuries-old legacy in trade, migration (enforced and voluntary), and colonialism. Yet, the extent to which transnational connections have become a defining feature of the world is unsurpassed in history and has intensified enormously only in the decades following the publication of Tilly's book.

Many sociologists and other social and cultural theorists have, in the decades following Tilly's book, taken his admonitions seriously—in addition to social scientists, such as Immanuel Wallerstein (1974–79) and Eric Wolf (1982), who were already working within a global framework. One of the most comprehensive recent attempts to define and delineate a sociology of globalization is arguably Manuel Castells's three-volume *The Information Society* (1996–98; updated editions were published in 2000–2004). The central idea in Castells's 1,500-page treatise is that of interconnectedness, and he approaches the issue from numerous viewpoints in a bid to show that the emergent world of transnational informational capitalism is qualitatively different from the one that preceded it.

The Network Society

The central concept in Castells's first volume (1996) is the network, which in his view "constitute[s] the new social morphology of our societies" (469). What he argues is that the main mode of social organization in politics, the economy, and civil society is shifting from the relatively stable hierarchy to a more fluid network form. The networks are interpersonal, transnational, and transitory. Although a fixed hierarchy is absent, networks do not accord equal power to all. While the most powerful person in a hierarchy could be located at the top of a pyramid, the most powerful person in a network is the spider, the one to whom everybody has to relate, who knows everybody, and who can coordinate activities. In other words, the greatest personal capital in a network society belongs to the best connected person.

According to Castells, "our societies are increasingly structured around a bipolar opposition between the Net and the Self" (1996: 3). In this, he means that the main conflicts take place between autonomy and dependence, the life-world and the system-world (Niklas Luhmann's terms [1995]) or, put more prosaically, between "abstract, universal instrumentalism, and historically rooted, particularistic identities" (Castells 1996: 3). Networks are not necessarily transnational, but this is increasingly the case, finds Castells, who sees the deregulation of world markets, the growth of information technology, and the end of the Cold War as parallel processes creating conditions for an accelerated and intensified globalization.

Put differently, the concept of the Net combines two related processes—namely, economic globalization and the spread of information technology, which makes distance irrelevant. Whereas classic industrial society was organized through the space of places, information society takes place through the space of flows, where the degree of connectedness, not physical proximity, is the decisive factor.

Networks are built around nodes—that is, points where lines intersect, or, less technically, a site where relevant activities connected with other activities (or nodes) elsewhere take place. A node can be and often is a person with relevant connections to others. Networks are, importantly, "open structures, able to expand without limits, integrating new nodes as long as they are able to communicate within the network" (Castells 1996: 469).

Let us take a brief look at some of the transnational networks that contribute to making the world a smaller place.

Communication Networks

Communication networks are obviously of prime importance. Nobody denies this, not even the global skeptics. The Internet, which was invented under the name Arpanet in 1969, had few and specialized users for two decades. Between 1995 and 2013, the number of people who had access to the Internet soared from 26 million to 2.4 billion (Internet World Stats 2013). The number of websites worldwide has grown from zero in 1992 (the year the World Wide Web was introduced) to 100 million in 2000 and 767 million active websites in 2013 (Netcraft 2013).

Mobile telephones were rare as late as 1990, which was before most countries had a telecommunication infrastructure ensuring coverage. Many mobile phones at that time were just car phones jacked into the lighter socket of the car and connected through a huge transmitter/receiver in the trunk. By 2013, the global number of mobile telephones is approaching the six billion mark, up from ten million in 1991. In China alone, four hundred million people had a mobile phone in 2006, but by 2013, the number had increased to one billion. More than six hundred million sub-Saharan Africans had mobile phones by 2013, up from zero in 1994.

Although networking through computers and mobile phones is in principle spaceless and deterritorialized, most of it is local. The most popular websites are usually, if not always, domestic ones, and the vast majority of SMS (Short Message Service) messages sent have a local addressee. Still, both technologies bear the mark of the deterritorialized network. During my first fieldwork trip in Mauritius in 1986, making a phone call home was exhausting, expensive, and unsatisfying. By the late 1990s, I could comfortably speak to anyone from a terrace overlooking the Indian Ocean, far from the nearest town. Both e-mail and mobile phone calls militate against firm hierarchies: they are flat, immediate media of communication with no intermediate secretary or other filter between the sender and the receiver. Formal modes of address are unusual in both media—polite forms of address are in fact disappearing in several languages, possibly partly as a result of the new media—and communication through e-mail or cell phone is expected to be swift and efficient.

Still not satisfied that the global network society is a fact? Well, take the communications satellite. These satellites are used for a number of purposes, from weather forecasting to telephony, surveillance, television transmissions, and, more recently, GPS navigation—you can now buy a small, touch-sensitive screen, place it on your dashboard, plot in your itinerary, and the voice of your preference will tell you exactly where to turn right and where to turn back. Recent improvements to map services even entail that they are updated continuously on road works and traffic.

The communications satellite was first described by the science fiction writer Arthur C. Clarke in a short article published in 1945. Indeed, he described it so well that it couldn't be patented later. Although both the Soviets and the Americans sent satellites into space in 1957 and 1960, respectively, it would take nearly twenty years from Clarke's description for the first successful audiovisual experiments to be conducted with communication satellites—parts of the 1964 Tokyo Olympics were televised via satellite—and in 1965 there was one such satellite. By 2013, there were more than two hundred, in addition to all the other, specialized satellites used for scientific research and other purposes. In the mid-1960s, a few million watched television programs broadcast via satellite; today, several billion do. In principle, anyone can watch any program, although in practice, most people watch local programs anyway.

Well over half the global population is to some extent affected by the telecommunications revolution, but to many it makes little subjective difference in their everyday lives. Contrary to many people's expectations, the Internet and mobile telephony are mostly used locally or domestically. Sometimes it seems that it was easier for a northern European to get a pen-friend in Brazil back in the 1970s than it is to join a virtual chat room today. Nonetheless, the placeless character of these new technologies affect all the people who use them, even if unconsciously. A standard opener for a contemporary telephone conversation is, "Where are you now?" This would not have been the case in the era of landlines, which predominated in most of the world until the mid-1990s.

Transnational media, drawing on the same satellite technology as the new communication technologies, lead to similar forms of deterritorialization, but it would be difficult to argue that the transnationalization of media lead to global homogenization. Rather, as many writers in the field have shown (see, e.g., Hannerz

1996; Hemer and Tufte 2005), what is being globalized are chiefly the media forms, not the content. National public spheres are to some extent being deterritorialized, when you can access your daily newspaper on the Web from anywhere in the world or watch your favorite domestic sitcom every Wednesday on your travels abroad, but such examples testify to the enduring strength, not the dissolution, of national public spheres. Content on the Internet is often believed to be largely in English; in fact, only about half of it is. There are thousands upon thousands of Czech, Japanese, Spanish, and Danish websites in existence. They share the technological form of the Web and its deterritorialized character, but not necessarily anything more.

A Networked Global Economy?

Castells (1996), among others, writes about "the network enterprise" as a new kind of company. It is loosely organized, there is little job security, it has assets in several places, and it stands in a complex relationship to other businesses. Many have described recent changes in capitalism as a transition from mass production to flexible production (and accumulation), or from Fordism to post-Fordism. This means a shift from large, stable enterprises, often involving assembly lines and mechanized production of large quantities of standardized goods. With the growth of a diverse world market and rapid technological changes, this system became too rigid and was to a great extent replaced with a more flexible system of production, which was more responsive to market trends and more adaptable. Another trend described by Castells (1996) is the "crisis of the large organization"; much of the contemporary job creation and innovation comes from middle-sized and small enterprises functioning in a larger network of complementary and competing businesses.

On the other side, some huge corporations have grown and benefited from increased globalization, adapting to the new situation. By 2004, Unilever had more than five hundred subsidiaries located in one hundred countries, and the mass media conglomerate Bertelsmann had more than six hundred affiliates in fifty countries (Scholte 2005: 178). Production sites are more easily moved overseas than before, and markets are more easily accessible than they used to be. Certain services can easily be outsourced overseas—American call centers in India being the most commonly cited example (but if you call Norwegian Airlines' service number, the person taking your call may well be an Estonian working from Tallinn and addressing you in flawless Norwegian). Statistics confirm the feeling shared by many to the effect that transnational corporations are becoming ever more powerful. Some of them have a turnover that exceeds the GDP (Gross Domestic Product) of many countries, and the annual total sales by all companies that form part of transnational corporations increased from $2.7 trillion in 1982 to $17.6 trillion in 2003 (Scholte 2005: 179). Many of these companies are believed to be locally owned and run, and many are joint ventures with local capital; the point is that these figures suggest a tighter integration and closer networking in the global economy than earlier.

Tellingly, the very technologies that make networking possible have moved to the core of the global economy. Some of the fastest growing companies in the world deliver hardware, software, or services associated with computing. Nokia, which basically produced rubber boots and a few TV sets in the 1980s, sold more than 450 million mobile phones a year at the height of its market dominance in 2008 (on the eve of the introduction of the touch phone). IT companies, some telecommunications service providers (like Vodafone), and content producers (like Time Warner, Bertelsmann, and Sony) are now among the most profitable corporations in the world.

The now virtually universal existence of capitalism as a system of production, distribution, and consumption on the planet—the monetary economy, supply-and-demand mechanism, and wage work are almost everywhere present—is underpinned by the breadth of economic involvement by major enterprises. The network structure of the global economy—with subsidiaries, joint ventures, a global scattering of assets—have led critics like Antonio Negri and Michael Hardt to describe the new world in bleak terms. Hardt and Negri, in their much discussed book *Empire* (2000), depict the world as being ruled by a web of overlapping networks of transnational corporations and organizations—an empire with no geographical center nor a government or an executive committee. Their vision is like a dark version of Castells's account of the network society.

Not everyone agrees that the world economy has entered a distinctly global phase. Paul Hirst and Grahame Thompson (1999) are among the most vocal critics of the globalizers' views. They argue that (a) in some respects, the contemporary international economy is less integrated and open than that of the period from 1870 to the First World War, (b) that most ostensibly transnational companies are in fact based and firmly rooted in national economies, (c) that most investments take place domestically or among the rich countries, and (d) that the major economic powers (Europe, North America, Japan) are able to regulate and control important aspects of the world economy if they coordinate their policies.

Hardt and Negri appear to exaggerate the reach of the global network society (and so, probably, does Castells). Governments still regulate domestic trade and use incentives at home, often with tangible results. Environmental problems, usually blamed on globalization, are often the result of government policies, such as the Brazilian government subsidies to logging companies (Gilpin 2002). There is nothing even resembling a global labor market, given the severe restrictions on immigration in rich countries. As a citizen, you are endowed with particular rights and obligations towards a territorial state, and some states continue to maintain ambitious welfare programs for all their citizens. As the ex-World Bank executive Joseph Stiglitz quips in a bitter critique of the free-trade hypocrisy he has seen in international organizations, Americans are all for free trade but against imports (2002). In other words, there are few reasons to believe that the global network society is omnipresent and omnipotent. Yet, a look at the figures is sufficient to convince me, at least, that there are strong tendencies towards wider and denser transnational networks, which lead to new forms of capital accumulation and increased concentration of economic power. Interestingly, the patterns of capital accumulation largely follow the center-periphery-semiperiphery triad developed by Wallerstein, although the rise of East Asia as contender for a place in the center is a new development. Countries like Brazil, South Africa, and Russia remain semiperipheral, and Western Europe and North America (plus Japan and Australia) remain part of the center.

Networks do not preclude centralization. Writing about transnational business, Saskia Sassen points towards the emergence of an "inter-urban geography that joins major international financial and business centers: New York, London, Tokyo, Paris, Frankfurt, Zurich, Amsterdam, Los Angeles, Sydney, Hong Kong," more recently incorporating cities like São Paolo, Buenos Aires, Bombay, Bangkok, and so on (2003: 271). The point is that as these intercity networks have become denser because of the growth in transnational financial transactions, the economic, political, and cultural distance between the cities and other parts of their countries has increased. Networks appear to be open-ended, but their boundaries can be as rigid as those of the closed structure.

Globalization from Below

A networked global economy does lead to the concentration of power in certain hubs, and under a global neoliberal economic regime, inequality has increased within most countries. At the same time, fiscal loopholes enable powerful transnational corporations, such as Starbucks and Kentucky Fried Chicken, to evade taxation in most of the countries in which they operate.

At the same time, other stories about interconnectedness and globalization, which create a very different picture, are no less true or relevant. In fact, it may well be argued that a main feature of economic globalization consists in the increased mobility of persons and goods, as well as the forging of interpersonal connections. The traffic in money, goods, and persons increased enormously in the last decades of the twentieth century and continues to do so in the twenty-first. This will be dealt with comprehensively in the next chapter; for now, we will just make some observations on the economic dimension of connectedness from below.

A fair number of the people involved in transnational trade are petty traders. Some buy secondhand clothes from Western charities and sell them in markets, some travel to Dubai or China in order to return with cheap, marketable goods, some ply the streets or beaches of tourist spots with their fake Rolex watches or Ray-Ban sunglasses, and others smuggle the goods across international borders, at the peril of being caught and jailed. Increasingly, the source of much of the goods sold in the informal sector is China, and a considerable amount is pirated goods, from cigarettes and perfume to cameras and jeans. The vast majority of people in the Global South can never afford to buy an Armani suit or a Dior dress, but quite a few can afford a fake copy. While the corporate world of the North Atlantic sees piracy as a threat to business and a violation of moral principles—in short, a serious crime—those who form part of it, either as producers, vendors, or consumers, see piracy as their only opportunity to take part in the consumer culture they are exposed to daily through the media.

Only since the turn of the millennium, the importance of China for globalization has increased many times. Chinese companies are involved in land acquisition, mining operations, shipping, and real estate investments all over the world now, but one of the most significant and fascinating aspects of the growth of Chinese global dominance is that of small trade. As Olivier Pliez (2012) explains in an essay about "the new Silk Road" from China to North Africa, the city of Yiwu (virtually unknown in the West) is the site of fifty-eight thousand shops "specializing in the sale of 'small commodities', i.e. small household goods, jewelry, razors, toys, and religious artifacts" (27). Clothing is nevertheless the main export from this region. Blank CDs are another sought-after commodity; it is estimated that two in three CDs sold in Mexico are pirated (Aguiar 2012: 41).

Goods intended for the informal sector usually have to be collected in person in order to evade customs but also because of a general lack of trust in a transnational business world without written contracts. Investments can be risky but also lucrative. Gordon Mathews (2012) estimates that about 20 percent of the cell phones sold in Africa were bought by itinerant African traders in the ramshackle wholesale center Chungking Mansions in Hong Kong, but Yang Yang (2012) states that more than half the African traders who come to Guangzhou go bankrupt and never return. These multiple ties, connecting people through what is known in Mexico as *la fayuca hormiga* (the ant trade)—that is, the semilegal or downright illegal traffic in goods, often pirated, across national boundaries in order to provide a taste of affluence and consumerism to people who would otherwise have been deprived of it. This kind of globalization from below, unlike remittances from migrants, represents a shadow economy existing side by side with the formal economy of major brands and Western dominance and is an excellent example of south–south relationships forming as a result of intensified globalization.

Cuban Exceptionalism

A central location in an early—some would say the first—phase of globalization in the sixteenth and seventeenth centuries, following Columbus and the emergent conceptualization of the New World, Cuba subsequently became, like the rest of the Caribbean, something of a backwater economically and politically. By the mid-twentieth century, Cuba was a typical Latin American country: politically authoritarian, economically dependent, ridden by deep class differences correlated with race, still based on a plantation system based on relatively simple technology, and dominated by U.S. interests, from investors to mafiosi. Following the 1959 revolution, Cuba severed its ties with the capitalist world, forging a strong ideological, military, and economic alliance with the Soviet Union and its Eastern European allies. With the collapse of the Communist bloc around 1990, many predicted that Cuba would follow suit within a few years. This was not to happen. At the time of writing, Cuba remains a centralized one-party society with a planned economy, limited civil rights, and a very piecemeal and partial integration into the global networks of the early twenty-first century.

Cuban exceptionalism—some would say autonomy—is suggestive of the extent to which much of the rest of the world is enmeshed in a plethora of transnational networks:

- Controlled flow of information. Censorship effectively limits the access to information, including critical information about the state, for the vast majority of Cubans. Internet access is extremely limited, and satellite channels on television are only available in tourist areas.
- Lack of market mechanism in the peso economy. Most Cubans receive their salaries in *moneda nacional*, a nonconvertible currency, which enables them to buy goods and services at subsidized prices. A meal in the university canteen at Cienfuegos, for example, costs the equivalent of 5¢, a local bus ticket 2¢. Prices are fixed by the state rather than through a supply/demand mechanism.
- Limited integration into the world market. Much of Cuba's foreign trade is still (in spite of the disappearance of the eastern European market) regulated through bilateral trade agreements with friendly states like Venezuela. The availability of imported goods in the peso sector is limited.
- Limited flow of persons. Cubans are not free to leave their country, and obtaining a passport is in most cases impossible.
- Absence of transnational corporations. There is no McDonald's in Cuba, and you'd be hard pressed to find a spare part for your Macintosh laptop in Havana.

There are several cracks and fissures in this system. Two parallel economies operate alongside the planned, subsidy-based peso economy. First, foreigners use the *peso convertible*, a hard currency with which one may obtain many imported and luxury goods theoretically unavailable to Cubans. Many tourist hotels are joint ventures between the Cuban state and foreign, often Spanish, companies, and dollar shops sell international brands. (But, tellingly, video films aimed at the tourist market were still, in 2013, mostly in the obsolete VHS format.) Second, a thriving informal economy, operating among Cubans and between Cubans and foreigners, entails that many Cubans sell goods and services to tourists (sometimes goods stolen from the state, such as cigars), often in or beyond a legal grey zone (this activity is known as *jineterismo* [hustling]), giving them access to pesos convertible. In spite of this, Cuba remains largely aloof from many of the forms of globalization characterizing most of the world: disparities in wealth are modest compared to other Caribbean and Latin American countries—most private cars are old and either American (pre-1959) or Soviet (pre-1991)—print media are few and censored, television is state-controlled, internet is rare, foreign travel is illegal unless one marries abroad, and so on. Although Cuba is committed to international cooperation through NGOs (nongovernmental organizations) and the UN system, it has resisted global capitalism and the global information economy surprisingly efficiently, not least when we take its geographical location into account.

Global Governance?

What about politics? Many writers on globalization have pointed out that the degree of transnational economic connectedness far exceeds the degree of transnational political regulation. As David Held and Anthony McGrew (2000: 26–27) put it, "the globalization of economic activity exceeds the regulatory reach of national governments while, at the same time, existing multilateral institutions of global economic governance have limited authority because states, jealously guarding their national sovereignty, refuse to cede them substantial power."

It should, nevertheless, be borne in mind, as Held and McGrew also point out (2000: 11–12; see also Held et al. 1999: 54), that the number of international organizations has grown enormously in the last hundred years. The number of international NGOs was 37 in 1909 and had grown to more than 40,000 in 2013. The degree of diplomatic connectedness between states, defined as the number of connections through at least one resident emissary, grew from 2,140 in 1950 to 5,388 in 1970 and 7,762 in 1991.

International cooperation has, in other words, grown tremendously over the last decades. Much of it falls short of deserving the label global, being international: Development cooperation and diplomatic ties, which account for much of the growth, tend to be bilateral and governed by nation-states. Truly transnational organizations are more interesting, and they proliferate in areas such as environmentalism and human rights issues. Such nonstate, often network-based organizations, may exert considerable political influence. Nevertheless, when one speaks of *global governance*, one usually has something more in mind, something that is binding on states and commits their power to a transnational good. International treaties over workers' rights or greenhouse gases are attempts at global governance, of an admittedly limited scope. International peacekeeping forces also express, from a different area, an ability among a number of countries to give up, temporarily, some of their sovereignty and use their diplomatic and military power to help resolve conflicts in which their country has no direct interest.

As a counterpoint to Negri and Hardt's grim outlook, George Monbiot (2003) has suggested the establishment of a world government, building on and extending both the power and the democratic legitimacy of the United Nations' General Assembly. Seen by many as utopian, this kind of proposal illustrates the widespread feeling that everything seems to be globalized except democracy. Summing up some of the main obstacles to global governance, Fred Halliday concludes the following:

> the success of peace-keeping . . . continues to run up against the reluctance of sovereign states to commit their forces to combat, and of states criticized by the international community to yield to UN pressure; growing awareness of the ecological crisis . . . goes together with contention and evasion, in north and south; the rising recognition of the importance of women's position in society has produced outright rejection of change in some states, in the name of sovereignty and national

tradition . . .; a greater stress on the rights of individuals produces denunciation of international, and specifically 'western', interference from others. (2000: 498)

An additional argument against the idea of global governance is the idea that its instruments "are not and are not likely to be democratic" (Dahl 2000: 538) because they may lead to majorities consistently overruling minorities. Against this pessimism, David Held et al. (2005) has forcefully put the case for a cosmopolitan social democracy aiming to extend rights and obligations globally, to keep transnational in check, and to prevent meaningless wars. The discussion about the prospects and limits for global governance is bound to continue for some years, indeed as long as the gap between economic and communicational integration and political nationalism remains.

An alternative perspective sees the increased contact across borders as a source of conflict due to competition over scarce resources, deep cultural differences, and the loss of ideological differences due to the end of the Cold War. The most influential representative of this school of thought is Samuel Huntington (1996), a political scientist famous for his notion of "the clash of civilizations." In Huntington's view, the most important conflicts in the world of the near future are likely to follow "civilizational faultlines"—that is, they will be fought across the border areas between civilizations. In Huntington's view, a civilization is a cluster of closely related cultures, which forms natural alliances. There is a Western civilization, a Latin American one, an Islamic one, a Hindu one, and so on. However, so far, few conflicts in the world have followed the lines predicted by Huntington (Fox 1999), and his concept of the civilization has been criticized for being simplistic and based on an obsolete idea of the world as consisting of clearly bounded, territorial cultures.

Notwithstanding the arguments surrounding the propositions for a global government, it should be kept in mind that global governance is not the same as a global, or world, government (Scholte 2011: 10). Governance is carried out by the United Nations, the World Trade Organization, the Organization of the Islamic Conference, and the Internet Corporation for Assigned Names and Numbers (Scholte 2011: 1). Although the power of these and other organizations is limited—they do not pass laws and cannot always impose sanctions—it should not be underestimated. If the ant trade of the Ciudad Juarez–El Paso area represents globalization from below, the powerful networks developed by the Bretton Woods institutions and the United Nations conglomerate of transnational organizations similarly stand for globalization from above, but both kinds of interconnectedness contribute to the shrinking of the planet and the tighter integration of its inhabitants.

Translation

The global dominance of English is reflected in many ways, not least through the linguistic insularity, indeed parochialism, of the English-speaking parts of the world. On a wonderful website called Index Translationum (UNESCO 2013), the UNESCO (United Nations Educational Scientific and Cultural Organization) has collected a variety of statistical material on translations published since 1979. It reveals that 1,257,542 books were translated from English from 1979 to 2012—the figures for French, the runner-up language, are 222,587, while the figure for Finnish is 8,486.

Regarding target languages, the German-speaking world appears to be the keenest on being enriched by impulses from abroad: 301,700 books were translated into German (204,426 books were translated from German), while 154,925 books were translated into English, which was surpassed by a comfortable margin by both French (239,885) and Spanish (228,885). The impressive number of 48,311 books were translated into Finnish.

In other words, while the Finns translated six times as many books into Finnish as the number of Finnish books translated abroad, and the Germans translated a third more into German than that which went in the opposite direction, about eight times as many books were translated from English as into English. While just 15 percent of the books translated from German had English as their destination language, about two-thirds of the books translated into German were from English.

It is almost difficult to believe it, but if the UNESCO statistics are correct, more books were translated in Denmark (five million inhabitants) than in the United States (over three hundred million inhabitants), and more books were translated in Hungary than in the United Kingdom.

According to statistics on Internet use, 51.3 percent of communication on the Internet is in English (while a mere 5 percent of the world's population speaks it as their first language), and 56 percent of all web pages are in English. Regarding academic publishing, I have been unable to find reliable figures, but everyone seems to agree that the proportion of English has increased steadily since the Second World War. In some fields, more than 90 percent of publications are in English; in many universities, a publication has to be in English if it is to count as an international publication in the annual report.

Remittances and Cheap Calls

Contemporary migration is another excellent example of interconnectedness. It is clearly better described as the ongoing negotiation of transnational ties than as a one-way movement creating permanent diasporic populations in host countries—to be integrated and, perhaps, eventually assimilated after one, two, or three generations. Migration will be discussed in some detail in the next chapter; for now, one dimension of migration will suffice to demonstrate some of the many emergent forms of interconnectedness crisscrossing the world—namely, remittances.

Remittances are transfers of money from migrants to relatives or other close associates in the home country. In the United States, a main immigrant country, the value of remittances sent from the country is estimated to have grown from $3.3 billion in 1981 to $20.5 billion in 2003 and a whopping $48 billion in 2009—a dramatic increase in less than thirty years (Congress of the United States 2005, 2011).

Globally, the total amount of formal remittances increased from slightly over $1.5 billion in 1970 to $84 billion in 1999, increasing almost by 1,000 percent in slightly over ten years, to reach $534 billion in 2012 (World Bank estimate), which by far exceeds the amount spent on development aid. Moreover, the actual figure may be quite a bit higher, as remittances are often transferred via informal channels. However, the informal remittances transferred outside the banking system, although impossible to measure accurately, are estimated to be twice or three times the formal ones (Van Doorn 2002). The value of remittances easily exceeds that of global foreign aid.

There is, in a word, a massive transfer of wealth going on from the rich countries to the poor ones, which takes place at an individual, small-scale level and is therefore relatively unknown outside policy and research circles—and which shows the extent of moral interconnectedness between migrants and the people they have left. A precondition for remittances to function efficiently is trust and moral obligation, which continue to be operative years and decades after the migrant's departure. With informal transfers, this is even more the case than with formal money transfers: Very often, middlemen are involved, and the money is carried as legal tender. The courier has to be trustworthy.

As shown by Nigel Harris (2002) and others (e.g., Carling 2008; Levitt 2001), remittances are spent in a variety of ways, with considerable variation between countries. However, almost everywhere, a proportion is invested in land or small enterprises. It has been speculated that every dollar sent back to the Philippines leads to a further three dollars in local growth, either through investment or through boosting local demand. An estimated nine million Filipinos work abroad, many of them women, and their remittances make up 10 percent of the national GDP (Standing 2011: 109).

A fascinating aspect of remittances is their low-key, small-scale character, creating strong ties of commitment, obligation, and economic transactions between millions of individuals located sometimes at opposite ends of the globe, without many taking notice. But take a stroll in the Pakistani town of Kharian, and you will notice a not insignificant Norwegianization of the town. People carry plastic bags from Oslo shops, many speak Norwegian, and at least one barber has a faded, framed photo of the late King Olav V on display in his shop. Most of Norway's Pakistani hail from the Kharian area, and many travel back and forth as often as time and money allow.

A parallel development to the spectacular growth in remittances, which further contributes to a deterritorialization of trust and moral obligation, is the rapid spread of cell phones since around 1990 and the reduced cost of using them. Steven Vertovec (2004) remarks on the significance of the phone card (precluding a regular subscription) for the transnational connectedness of ordinary immigrants in Europe and North America. In many poor to middle-income countries, cell phone ownership and use seems to be spreading faster than any other new technology. Heather Horst (2006) reports that in Jamaica 86 percent of the population over fifteen had a mobile phone in the early twenty-first century and that by 2003, three-quarters of all phone traffic was cellular. By 2013, the figure was approaching 100 percent. Before the mid-1990s, Horst reports, telephone communication between Jamaica and the outside world was cumbersome, erratic, and expensive. Most Jamaicans relied on phone booths, which were often out of order, and calls tended to be brief and slightly breathless since there were often others waiting to use the phone. As Horst says—her work is in Jamaica, but it is relevant for many places—the cell phone enables people to stay regularly in touch with loved ones overseas and to negotiate personal relationships as well as financial transactions, to give urgent information (such as a death or illness), and so on. Cheaper and more mobile than computer-mediated e-mail, new generations of cell phones are increasingly versatile; they can be used to send instant images of the newborn baby to the parents at home, mood updates, and gossip on an everyday basis.

Remittances and phone calls are two ways of staying in touch, and they sometimes go together. Horst (2006) writes of an elderly lady in Jamaica who needed a bit of money, who phoned her family overseas, and received the amount in one hour. These are some of the networks rarely given much attention in the literatures on either migration or globalization, but which in important ways create and maintain strong webs of transnational commitments worldwide. Most significantly, such networks are interpersonal and based on personal commitment—unlike rather a lot of the other transnational or global networks often considered in research on globalization, but like several of the phenomena considered in this chapter. With the next example, it becomes evident that globalization from above and from below can often be two sides of the same coin.

Soccer and Globalization

As pointed out by Richard Giulianotti and Roland Robertson (2004), few of the many scholars who write about globalization have studied sport. The recent history of soccer, in particular, can serve both as an illustration and as an indication of the extent of transnational interconnectedness.

Soccer, a sport played to varying degrees in most parts of the world, has British origins but is, unlike cricket, not strongly associated with colonialism. Its rules are easy to learn, it requires no expensive equipment, and it can be played in alleys, on lawns, in schoolyards, and on open fields. Goalposts can be made from anything—schoolbags and sweaters were standard in my childhood—and the size of the team is not important. No special skills are required to play soccer.

As a spectator sport, soccer also has enormous appeal with its combination of complexity and simplicity, elegance and brute force, its many variations and possibilities for individual players to shine.

This does not in itself explain the global popularity of soccer nor its failure, so far, to penetrate some of the largest and most populous countries in the world (it is not so widespread in India, China, or the United States). However, in all European and Latin American countries, in most of Africa, and in large parts of Asia, including most of the Middle East, soccer is the single most popular sport for spectators and practitioners alike. At a transnational level, the game, its tournaments, the ranking of national teams, and so on are governed by FIFA (Fédération Internationale de Football Association—a mighty body of global governance, by the way). More than 300,000 clubs with altogether 240 million players are registered with FIFA.

Following Roland Robertson (1992), one may say that globalization involves a heightened awareness of the world as an interconnected place and that processes of globalization tend to be met with glocalization (Robertson's term)—that is, local adaptations of global trends. Both aspects of globalization are clearly present in the soccer world: international games, at the club or national team level, are prestigious, and fans are increasingly familiar with the soccer scene in countries other than their own. Yet, teams continue to be locally based and are associated with a home ground and a team mythology. Many teams are invested with political and cultural capital extraneous to the game: The Glasgow Rangers is a Protestant team, while Celtic is Catholic (and the tension between these Scottish teams is played out between Catholics and Protestants in Belfast as well). Liverpool is associated with the working class, Everton with the middle class. Matches between Barcelona and Real Madrid are symbolic battles over Spanish politics—namely, the tension between Catalonia and the central power in Madrid, with echoes that go back to the Civil War and the Fascist period, with Franco's power base mainly in Madrid and some of the most fervent left-wing resistance based in Catalonia.

Increasingly, soccer has become transnational in two main ways. First, the number of foreign players on major teams has increased steadily. In its starting lineup for the 2013–14 season, the London team Arsenal would usually have between one and three English players (twenty years earlier, they had just one foreigner), and the Antwerp team Beveren reached the Belgian cup final in 2004 with a team composed almost entirely of players from the Ivory Coast!

Even the changing face of nations in an era of transnational migration is illustrated in soccer. The French national team that won the 1998 World Cup was led by Zinedine Zidane, a player of Algerian origin, and the team was denounced by the right-wing nationalist leader Jean-Marie le Pen as "not a real French team." Another example is the Nigerian striker Emmanuel Olisadebe, who performed so well in the Polish league in 2000 that he was fast-tracked for citizenship to strengthen the Polish national team, where he played during the 2002 World Cup. Although Olisadebe remains a Polish citizen, he would play for a number of clubs in several countries until his retirement in 2012.

Fan bases are increasingly becoming transnational as well. Several English soccer clubs have far more registered fans in Norway than even the most popular domestic clubs. Expensive merchandise, ranging from shirts to bed linen and curtains, is sold worldwide. Some of the richest clubs, like Real Madrid, Barcelona, Bayern München, and Manchester United, can indeed be seen as transnational corporations selling goods to fans all over the world. There is a strong glocal element here, in that supporter culture carries different cultural connotations in different localities. Tottenham Hotspur is not associated with the Jewish community of North London outside the UK, nor do most Man U supporters in Japan relate to the club's history, but they are more interested in its current stars.

Being a soccer supporter has become more complicated and reflects the interconnectedness and emerging complexity of the contemporary world. Before the 2006 World Cup, I discovered that my son (who was then nine) disapproved of the Swedish striker Zlatan Ibrahimovic. I asked if it had anything to do with the Swedes as such (there has been friendly rivalry between Sweden and Norway for many years, not least in sport) or with Zlatan's controversial personality. I ruled out the possibility that the animosity had anything to do with Zlatan's Yugoslav origins, as my son was too young to have developed xenophobic prejudices. Eventually, it turned out that the problem was that Zlatan played for Juventus, a team my son disliked. As a faithful Arsenal fan, he supported France in the 2006 World Cup, since Arsenal's star player Thierry Henry had a pivotal place in the French squad.

A factor that should not be underestimated in an analysis of the evolution of soccer as a global language is the procurement of global TV rights and the growing internationalization of the fan base. The roughly half a million people who physically turn up at stadiums in England and Wales every weekend to watch the Premier League are increasingly becoming stage props, creating ambience and atmosphere for the real supporters, who watch the games on a pay channel somewhere in the world, thereby generating important revenue for the clubs and—not least—for the owner of the exclusive TV rights, the Australian media magnate Rupert Murdoch, who has controlled Premier League rights since its inception in 1992. Matches, which used to be played exclusively on Saturday afternoons, have now been spread out over several days in order to generate maximum revenue from the TV rights. On a varying scale (but no other league matches the English one in this respect), similar arrangements have been made in other countries. Even in peripheral Norway, not exactly a superpower in the world of soccer, match schedules in the domestic elite division have been adjusted to suit the demands of the owners of television rights.

The organization of soccer today involves many cross-cutting ties of loyalty, deterritorialized fandom, and global governance (with considerable democratic deficit), but its global dimension is limited, as pointed out by McGovern (2002). The flow of players between countries is far from completely global and deterritorialized; most of it takes place between metropolitan countries and ex-colonies or within a region sharing many cultural characteristics, such as northern Europe. Clubs remain attached to a semisacred place (the home ground) and tend to be domestically owned (with some much-publicized exceptions).

Soccer also exemplifies economic globalization. As much as 60 percent of all leather soccer balls are hand-stitched in the city of Sialkot, northeastern Pakistan. The workers earn, on an average, the equivalent to $1,000 a year, twice the average wage in the country. Some of the soccer balls can cost up to $150 apiece in Europe. Ironically, cricket-addicted Pakistan is one of the countries where soccer is not a major sport.

Anarchist Connectivity in Early Globalization

Benedict Anderson, best known for his influential book on the growth of nationalism, *Imagined Communities* (1991 [1983]), has more recently published a book about "anarchism and the post-colonial imagination," which he describes as an essay on "early globalization" (2006: back cover).

Set in the Philippines of the late nineteenth century, Anderson's book describes the growth and indeed the invention of the Filipino nation, focusing on the role of a handful of intellectuals—the novelist José Rizal, the folklorist and journalist Isabelo de los Reyes, the political leader Mariano Ponce, and a few others.

This was the era of the steamship and the intercontinental telegraph, a period that must have appeared dizzyingly novel, with fast communications and a shrunken planet. Anderson describes how the Filipino intellectuals were crucially influenced by events elsewhere in the world and how their personal networks covered most of the planet. Taking courage from the insurgencies of Cuba (another Spanish colony), Filipinos rebelled unsuccessfully against Spanish rule; they learned from anarchists in France, syndicalists in Spain, humanist scholars in Germany, nationalists in China, and modernizers in Japan. They were cosmopolitan in their outlook and transnational in their networks.

An obvious question, which can be raised in connection with Anderson's book, is what has changed? In what important ways is our period of globalization and transnationalism distinctive and different from the late nineteenth century, which was also a period of powerful nationalist ideology, capitalist expansion, and technological innovations?

One striking difference is to do with language. The Filipino intellectuals described by Anderson (2006: 5) corresponded in many languages, since—as the author puts it—there was no "ugly, commercially debased 'international language'" available at the time. Another difference is to do with speed—travel from the Far East to Europe still took weeks. A third difference is that capitalism, while already hegemonic, was far less widespread then than it is now. Yet, at the same time, many of the social and cultural dimensions we associate with globalization today were already in place, in embryonic form, then, and this is Anderson's point. French ideas could be borrowed and transplanted instantly to East Asia, local ways of life could be compared to life elsewhere through a growing scholarly literature, and a global consciousness about political change and human rights was spreading in Europe and the colonies. There was disembedding, movement, interconnectedness, acceleration, and mixing—not to the same degree as now, but Anderson's book is still a reminder that contemporary globalization has been under way for quite some time, and that it may well be seen as an integral aspect of modernity as such.

Delinking, Chosen, and Enforced

As many writers on globalization have noted, one particularly visible feature of it is the emergence of strong localist and traditionalist identities. The tension between a borderless global network society on the one hand and fervent isolationism on the other is like flypaper for journalists and scholars, and book titles like *The World is Flat* (Friedman 2005) and *Jihad vs. McWorld* (Barber 1995) may well prove to be irresistible when the browsing customer in an airport bookshop stumbles across them. There is a simple but productive dialectic to be identified here: The transnational network economy and its cultural correlates create opportunities for some and powerlessness for others. French filmmakers are unhappy with Hollywood's global dominance (which is, incidentally, somewhat less total than often assumed), pious Muslims are unhappy with permissive images from cable TV and from the London and Paris streets they walked as students, Scandinavians worry about the future of their welfare state in a situation of global economic competition and increased migration, and indigenous leaders worldwide are concerned with how to retain a way of life and a culture that at least embodies a few central features of their tradition while simultaneously benefiting from modernity. Global capitalism, or neoliberalism, it is often said, produces both losers and winners, both poverty and wealth, and it tends to increase inequalities. It could be added that even in the cases where capitalism does provide increased (measurable) wealth, it can also produce poverty at the cultural or spiritual level. "We have everything now, but that is all we have," laments the popular folk singer Ole Paus, who lives in a leafy Oslo suburb where everybody is wired in every conceivable way but few know their neighbors and even fewer have the time to read Dostoyevsky, being too busy with their Facebook status updates, tweets, and media consumption. Countermovements against the limitless standardization and homogenization seemingly resulting from globalization can thus be founded in a variety of motivations, but all of them are to do with *autonomy* at the personal or community level. I shall have much more to say about this in later chapters, but at this point, we should note that globalization, even when met with little or no resistance, can usually be described as glocalization: the preexisting local is fused with global influence; the particular merges with the universal to create something true to the universal grammar of global modernity but at the same time is locally embedded. Even the transnational trademark of Manchester United is irreducibly connected to the physical city of Manchester and the lore surrounding Old Trafford Stadium, and it is totally unlikely that the trademark would have survived a move to, say, New York City or Brussels.

Possibly because most of the literature concentrates on the people who are actively part of the process, who make their imprint and contribute to shaping the economy, politics, and culture of the planet, a huge part of the world's population is plainly left out of most globalization studies. I have slum dwellers in mind, those fast growing populations largely comprising of people who have moved from rural areas because life was no longer sustainable there.

To what extent urban slum growth is a direct result of globalization is debatable. Depletion of agricultural land combined with population growth is one way of describing it. On the other hand, the neoliberal deregulation of national economies (which often have followed the advice of the IMF and reduced the public sector dramatically) has made millions superfluous in the labor force. Mechanization and informatization reduces the need for manpower in the economy, and few states in the Third World have policies effectively preventing slum growth. At the same time, perhaps paradoxically, some slums grow precisely because of the need for labor, not least in industrializing China, where workers' salaries may be extremely low, making life in informal housing the only viable option. Mike Davis (2006) presents some thought-provoking figures.

A World of Slums

Around 2007, for the first time in human history, there were more urban than rural people in the world, and most of the urban growth had taken place in poor countries. Cities in the rich countries grow somewhat, but in a slow and fairly controlled way. The growth in poor cities lacks historical precedent. Between 1800 and 1910, the population of London grew by a factor of seven. This sounds dramatic, but in a much shorter period—from 1950 to 2000—the population in cities like Dhaka, Kinshasa, and Lagos has increased forty times!

Buenos Aires and Rio de Janeiro were large cities already in the mid-twentieth century, with 4.6 and 3 million inhabitants, respectively. In 2006, both had around 12 million inhabitants. Cairo has grown, in the same period, from 2.4 to 15 million, Delhi from 1.4 to more than 18 million, Seoul from 1 to 22 million. African cities like Nouakchott and Mogadishu, which were just oases or trading posts a few decades ago, are now home to millions. The Congolese city Mbuji-Mayi has grown from next to nothing to 2 million since the mid-1990s. Urban slums emerge, especially in China and parts of Africa, in areas where there were initially no urban settlement at all—gigantic slums without a city proper. In Kenya, 85 percent of the population growth now takes place in the seething slums of Nairobi and Mombasa.

Certain areas are about to grow into enormous, continuous settlements of cardboard and corrugated iron, with millions upon millions of inhabitants—seen by the authorities as human driftwood—but with little by way of plumbing, electricity, or police protection. Davis (2006) mentions the five-hundred-kilometer stretch from Rio to São Paolo (pop. thirty-seven million), the central Mexican highlands around Mexico City (estimated to contain half of Mexico's population by 2050), parts of China, and the coastal strip from Benin City via Lagos to Accra, which is predicted, in a few years' time, to contain the largest concentration of poverty in the world.

People move to town for a variety of reasons. Traditionally, a main cause, or cluster of causes, has been a combination of relative overpopulation in rural areas and possibilities for work. The bright lights perspective also had its supporters—people left boredom, or so they believed, for excitement. Such explanations may still hold true in parts of China and India, but not in Africa or Latin America, where urban economies have, in fact, been in decline during the last decades, at the same time as the urban population has doubled several times. An explanation would have to take into account factors such as war and depleted resources as a result of population growth or ruthless modernization (the construction of motorways and resorts for the rich, etc.), along with a dream of prosperity and work, which becomes increasingly unrealistic as the years go by.

The main headache for government and comfortably-off people concerns how to control and contain the slum population in order to prevent them from spreading, with their rags and stink, into prosperous quarters and commercial centers. In many colonial cities, high-ranking military officers, apparatchiks, politicians, and businessmen have joined expatriates from rich countries in taking over the lush residential areas left by the colonials. Increasingly, such suburbs of affluence and freshness are becoming gated communities where nobody is allowed to enter without permission. In parts of Cape Town, electrical fences have now replaced human guards. New forms of apartheid-like exclusion develop as a result of rich people's wish to be left alone with their wealth. They have effectively divorced themselves from greater society in their cosmopolitan, transnational homes.

How do slum dwellers survive at all, given that only a minuscule minority have formal work? The answer is the "informal sector" (a term coined by Hart 1973)—that is, unregistered economic activity. Some make a living by selling each other services, from haircuts and sex to transport and protection; some run little workshops producing tourist trinkets—or they sell cheap goods made in China; some grow cannabis or distill alcohol; and some make a living from the rubbish of the rich, be it old furniture or edible things. Many, not least of all children, are informally employed by large enterprises. They survive, but just barely.

The distance between life in the slums and the rich suburbs grows. The rich have their health centers and shopping malls, their fast-food restaurants and private schools (in Ritzer's terms, they have an abundance of nothing, but try to say that to a slum dweller), and in the weekends, they can whisk out to their country houses or resorts on new highways, which are built on land that would formerly have been used for other purposes. They are the beneficiaries of a globalization and a standardization of lifestyles, which liberates them from the poor in their own countries, connected as they are to the rich world through numerous bridgeheads and networks. In substantial parts of the Global South, certainly in large parts of Africa, it now appears that nation building and development for the whole people was something one tried to achieve in the twentieth century, a project now abandoned.

Connectedness and Disjunctures

Both at the individual level and at the macro level of states, the *degree of interconnectedness* usually measures the degree of success. This is what counts in the network society. Few individuals who are never sought after either online or by telephone, who rarely leave home, and who don't know anyone beyond a radius of five minutes' walking distance, are successful and thriving in this society. About states, it can be said with even greater confidence that no isolated state is successful in providing material security for its inhabitants or offering them civil rights and personal freedom. The degree of connectedness, and the reach of the connections, indicates the degree of participation in all kinds of contexts. Voluntary delinking at the individual level is a luxury indicating affluence; at the level of the state, it is always selective, never comprehensive.

Interconnectedness is, thus, both a central feature of globalization and a way of measuring success in a globalized society. It is beyond doubt that the scope and compass of connections, which are often deterritorialized and transnational, are characteristic of the present era; another question, more difficult to answer, is whether connectedness has been similarly valued in earlier periods? The answer seems to be that at the individual level, wide-ranging personal networks and mutual ties of obligation would mainly be an asset—not least for people engaged in trade and politics. At the societal level, trade and openness to the world would also be profitable in most cases, but not always. In a seminal paper on some of the dimensions of globalization, the anthropologist Arjun Appadurai (1990) argues that the globalization processes are "disjunctive" in that they move along different axes and with different ends. He distinguishes between ethnoscapes, mediascapes, technoscapes, finanscapes, and ideoscapes as five relatively separate fields affected by, and affecting, globalization. Appadurai argues that global flows take place through these five distinctive dimensions, which collide and enter into conflict with one another. The degree of transnational interconnectedness varies along such dimensions (a country may be financially transnational, but ethnically parochial, for example), so that interconnectedness is rarely an either-or issue but a question that needs a more considered answer: What kind of interconnectedness is under investigation, what is the underlying motivation, and what are the social consequences? Individuals, groups, and states have restrictions imposed on their connections with the outside world, deliberately or not. These restrictions are often associated with the movement of goods and people, to which we now turn.

- Through trade, communication, and movement, most of the world is increasingly interconnected, with political, economic, and cultural consequences.
- Economic interconnectedness develops not only through huge transnational corporations but also in small and medium-scale enterprises spreading their assets, investments, and collaboration internationally.
- Technological interconnectedness through ICT (information and communications technology), for example, does not necessarily mean enhanced interaction; for example, local languages often predominate.
- Mass migration has led to new patterns of transnational interconnectedness, linking people interpersonally, often through kinship, across continents.
- The growth of the NGO system indicates an increased interdependence and integration of a different kind from the economic and technological connectedness.

Questions

- What is methodological nationalism? What are the alternatives?
- What are the main objections, among the critics of globalization theory, against the view that the world is becoming ever more interconnected and integrated? Do you have any to add yourself?
- Does the transnationalization of economic power through large corporations lead to a change in the global power relations? Are there any indications that such a change may come about soon? And which areas are lagging behind?
- Present the main arguments in favor of and against global governance. What is your view?
- In what ways do transnational media enhance a subjective sense of globalization? Give examples from sports, news, and entertainment, and, if possible, counterexamples.
- Contrast chosen and enforced delinking from global interconnectedness. Do they have anything in common?

Further Reading

Appadurai, Arjun (1996) *Modernity at Large*. Minneapolis: University of Minnesota Press. An influential anthropologist looks at globalization, identifying themes and methods appropriate for anthropology and arguing throughout that globalization creates tension and unevenness, far from being a source of homogenization.

Mathews, Gordon, Gustavo Lins Ribeiro, and Carlos Alba Vega, eds. (2012) *Globalization from Below: The World's Other Economy*. London: Routledge. Focusing almost exclusively on the flow of goods from China through informal channels to sites ranging from Mexico to Egypt and India, this book reveals much of what goes on behind the curtains of formal globalization.

Scholte, Jan Aart, ed. (2011) *Building Global Democracy? Civil Society and Accountable Global Governance*. Cambridge: Cambridge University Press. An excellent collection of essays examining the importance and influence of formal transnational bodies of governance, ranging from the WTO to the G8 meetings and the Organization of the Islamic Conference.

5

Mobility

Nowadays we are all on the move.

—ZYGMUNT BAUMAN, *GLOBALIZATION—THE HUMAN CONSEQUENCES*, 77

Globalization does not just entail the accelerated transportation of goods, ideas, and technologies. People, too, are capable of moving faster and more comfortably than before. (Until the nineteenth century, all overland travel was de facto outdoors.) The different forms of mobility and transnational movement demonstrate differences in power structures between regions and countries better than most other aspects of globalization. The tourist, the foreign student, or the conference participant moves with much greater ease and with a different purpose to the refugee from a war-torn country, the young man desperate for work, the domestic servant, or the sex worker. The creation of internal markets facilitating mobility within regions such as the European Union enhances the mobility of those inside but may exclude those outside in efficient and telling ways. Just as mobility can be chosen or enforced, so can immobility.

In the town of Garachico, Tenerife, a monument to the emigrant has been erected. Facing the Atlantic Ocean, it depicts a man with a suitcase looking out to sea, knowing that he will leave his home in search of a better life in a foreign land. However, there is something conspicuously missing in the sculpture. Where the man's heart should have been, there is instead a hole.

Tenerife, and the Canary Islands more generally, have been transit ports for centuries. Columbus and other early explorers in the Americas would stop there en route to replenish supplies. During the period of the Franco dictatorship (1936–75), many Spaniards fleeing the regime to settle in Latin America left via the Canary Islands, and the monument in Garachico was, perhaps, erected to commemorate the many thousands who fled from Fascism.

In the 2000s, the Canary Islands have been the site of three different forms of mobility and migration. First, thousands of northern Europeans are moving, seasonally or permanently, to the balmy climate and high quality of life in the Canaries. They buy terraced flats and make the islands their new home, often living off state pensions or savings. Second, the people involved in building these terraced flats and providing other kinds of services, from cleaning to waiting tables, are often foreigners, from origins ranging from Venezuela and Ecuador to Poland and Romania. Their project consists in improving their lives and perhaps giving their children improved prospects. (The economic crisis in Spain has led many of them to return more recently, sometimes joined by Spanish emigrants!)

The third kind of migration originates in Africa. Boats, often rusty and dilapidated, regularly depart from Dakar or Nouachott, literally filled to the brim with prospective refugees, who have sold everything they have, and often borrowed money in addition, in order to get into the European Union. While the northern Europeans have left their home in order to do as little as possible, and the migrant workers have arrived to improve their lot, the African refugees have left their previous lives behind in order to be able to support their families at home. The vast majority are returned unceremoniously. The passage, by the way, costs around €1,000 ($1,300), roughly the same price as a northern European tourist would pay for a two-week holiday at one of Tenerife's best hotels, flight included.

The juxtaposition of these three categories of migrants tells us something about the extent of mobility in the contemporary world, but perhaps more importantly, about the kind of world in which we live and its unequal distribution of opportunities. And yet all kinds of stories exist about migration, not least from the Global South. Tracing the itineraries of the people who used to live in his Kumasi (Ghana) neighborhood when he was a child, the philosopher Kwame Anthony Appiah observes:

> Eddie, from across the street, who never finished school, called to wish me a Happy New Year from Japan; Frankie, my cousin from next door to Eddie, lives in England; Mrs Effah still lives next door, but visits her children in the United States; even my mother and sister have moved across the city. (2003: 195)

As pointed out by Jan Aart Scholte (2005: 65), "methodological territorialism has had a pervasive and deep hold on the conventions of social research; thus globalization (when understood as the spread of supranationality) implies a major reorientation of approach."

Scholte, a political scientist, argues that researchers have tended to take territorial units for granted in their studies, seeing the world "through the lens of territorial geography" (2005: 56), assuming that societies take a territorial form. Although Scholte and others (e.g., Marcus 1998; Urry 2000) try to develop methodologies for the study of nonterritorial, or deterritorialized, phenomena—diasporic groups, tourism, the Internet, financial capital—they do not proclaim the end of territoriality. Scholte stresses that "the end of territorial*ism* does not mean the 'end of territorial*ity*'" (2005: 76; italics in the original). However, in an interconnected world, few territories can be merely territories, and few if any territories can be bounded territories. They become territories interlinked with and responding to processes taking place far beyond their limits, and therefore *reterritorialization*, the attempt to fix and stabilize a place, a country, or a region, is itself a product of its own dialectical negation—that, deterritorialization.

Although it sounds hyperbolic to say that we are all on the move, it is true in several senses that mobility is characteristic of contemporary globalization. Tourists, business and conference travelers, refugees and labor migrants, students and seasonal workers—there are more of them than ever before. There is a sense in which boundaries that may have been considered firm and reliable in the mid-twentieth century are dissolving. Anthropologists are no less uneasy than geographers when confronted with the seemingly unbounded (or at least unevenly bounded) cultures of today, and many follow the lead of Arjun Appadurai (1996), Ulf Hannerz (1992), Jonathan Friedman (1994), Michael Kearney (1995), and others in refashioning their concept of culture to fit a more complex, interrelated, and paradoxical reality. Sociologists conceptualize a "sociology of mobility" (Urry 2000), and political scientists are busy discussing human rights and transnational politics. Whether posterity will judge these tendencies in social theory as fads or ripples or whether they constitute something like a paradigm shift in the social sciences is too early to tell. Less risky is the assertion that *mobility* has to be a key concept of globalization.

From Diasporas to Super-Diversity

Unlike the situation in a city like London as late as around 1990, when most immigrants came from ex-colonies, the city's immigrants now truly come from everywhere. Described as "the world in one city" (Vertovec 2007), London may be exceptionally diverse regarding the breadth and numbers of its residents of foreign origin, but the tendency described by Steven Vertovec with reference to London can also be seen elsewhere in the world. While over 300 languages are now spoken in London, which is an impressive number by any standard, as a matter of fact, 124 languages are spoken only in the southern Oslo suburb of Holmlia!

Foreigners resident in a country are classified according to their circumstances: they are either refugees or economic immigrants, students or tourists, diplomats or spouses of citizens. In recent years, such classificatory schemes have increasingly been seen as unsatisfactory. Contemporary flows of people into the great (and not so great) cities of the world include people who cannot easily be classified as either this or that: students who have stayed on, getting a boyfriend or girlfriend and a McJob, tourists who forgot to return, Polish seasonal workers, legal or not, visitors who are neither quite jobseekers nor exactly not jobseekers. There is an increased degree of imagination in the current movement of people, from Nigerian soccer players and prostitutes to fake chemical engineers, young brides and grooms brought by established immigrants from the home country, huge trade delegations, and northern

Europeans who settle seasonally in the Mediterranean. It is sometimes said by Lithuanians that cities like Vilnius and Kaunas are virtually emptied of people between twenty and thirty-five in the summer months as they are all in the West, working or looking for work. In Poland, there has for years been a shortage of construction workers, since many of them work semipermanently in Germany, Sweden, and other high-salary countries—in most cases without being immigrants in those countries.

Vertovec notes that whereas most of the immigration into the UK before the 1990s was of Commonwealth origin (similarly, most immigration into France came from its ex-colonies), immigrants now come from everywhere—rich, middle-income, and poor countries. In London, there were in 2005 fifty nonindigenous nationalities numbering more than ten thousand. The diversity is staggering and impossible to describe in simplifying terms. Within each group, there is great variation in people's immigration status (some are refugees, some spouses, some students, some undocumented, and so on), their educational level, and their way of integrating into British society. The era of the settled, stable, spatially concentrated diasporic population—Bangladeshi in Tower Hamlets, Jamaicans in Brixton—is gone. In its stead, there is now a dynamic, forever changing ethnic mosaic in a city like London, where some are there to stay, others to commute, yet others to leave for greener pastures, or just home, wherever that is. The new situation, familiar in many other cities as well, puts pressure on local government to provide services adapted to a super-diverse and shifting situation with extremely heterogeneous neighborhoods and hugely varied needs. There is a fleeting and undefined quality to transnational migration these days, which is captured well in Vertovec's term "super-diversity." As he concludes: "more people are now moving from more places, through more places, to more places" (2010: 86).

Transnational Migration

Migration is one of the central facts of transnational processes (see Schiller et al. 1992 for a pioneering contribution). Those who trace globalization back to the beginning of the modern era (around 1500—e.g., Wallerstein 2004; Wolf 1982) emphasize European colonization of the New World and the Transatlantic slave trade as constitutive events. Those who go even further back (e.g., Chase-Dunn and Hall 1997; Chanda 2007; Friedman 1994) stress not just large-scale trade and cultural standardization as features of the Roman Empire but also the movement of people from Italy to the Iberian Peninsula, Gaul, Britannia, and elsewhere. This is also the case with respect to premodern empires outside Europe, such as the Aztecs in Mesoamerica and the Han in China.

Large-scale immigration has been the norm in the Americas and Australia for centuries, and in countries where the vast majority of the population are descendants of immigrants, public opinion and policy regarding immigration is bound to differ somewhat from the European countries, where modern mass immigration is a recent phenomenon, which continues to stir up controversy. Nevertheless, immigration into Europe continues in spite of economic uncertainties (the Euro crisis and related challenges) and political measures in some countries to reduce immigration. Some countries are entirely reliable on labor migrants. In 2010, 90 percent of the labor force in the United Arab Emirates was foreign, more than 80 percent in Kuwait and Qatar (Standing 2011). In the United States, the migrant share of the workforce went down from 21 percent in 1910 to 5 percent in 1970, but it rose again to 16 percent in 2010 (Standing 2011: 90).

Contemporary globalization is characterized by several streams of people: a small trickle of North Atlantic expatriates living temporarily or semipermanently in the South as diplomats, businessmen, or aid workers, and more substantial streams of people from southern countries to other southern countries (South Africa is a magnet in southern-central Africa, many refugees live in camps in the neighboring country, Morocco is a transit country for hundreds of thousands of sub-Saharan Africans hoping to get into Europe, and so on) and from south to north. In the New World countries of the United States, Canada, and Australia, immigration has been seen as a normal process since their inception as settler societies. In European countries, the situation is different, and as should be well known, debates over migration policy and the integration of immigrants into the majority societies are omnipresent and cover everything from immigrants' voting patterns to gender roles, the significance of religion (usually Islam), and discrimination in the labor market.

It should be pointed out, though, that although migration has changed the face of Western cities in recent decades, the proportion of migrants (people living outside their country of birth) is lower today than it was in the early twentieth century. Although more people, in absolute numbers, live outside their country of birth today than earlier in the history of the state (Papastergiadis 2000), only 3 percent of the world's population are immigrants today, while the proportion in 1913 was around 10 percent (Cohen 2006; International Organization for Migration 2013). Yet, the numbers of people on the move have been growing fast since the turn of the millennium. Only in the United States, about a million legal migrants enter the country every year, and to this, another half a million irregular migrants may perhaps be added.

Migration can be an unsettling, confusing, and frustrating experience, especially if it is prompted by push factors rather than pull factors. Immigrants are often ostracized by the majority and denied full civil rights by governments. Many, perhaps most, belong to the precariat—that is, a precarious part of the labor force with little job security. Many respond through devising both local and transnational strategies strengthening the coherence of their local community and networks, often based on ethnicity or religion, as well as their ties to the countries of origin. Remittances and telecommunications as ways of maintaining moral and economic ties have been discussed earlier; it should be noted that migrant minorities pursue many other strategies as well. Many migrants in Europe reconnect with the homeland through marriage, usually by arranging to move the spouse to the European country. Some send their children to school in the home country for shorter or longer periods. Yet others are involved in long-distance political activities.

Transnational Connections

Transnational connections among migrants are often economically important. A study of Senegalese Wolof in Emilia Romagna (northern Italy) by Bruno Riccio (1999) demonstrates several important features of transnational entrepreneurship. Wolof are traditionally associated with trade in West Africa, and they have successfully adapted their skills to function transnationally, spanning Senegalese and European markets in their business flows. Riccio argues that in a manner similar to the Hausa of Ibadan, Wolof in Italy are morally and socially bound by their allegiance to Muslim brotherhoods in Senegal (the Mouride), but he also points out that without a strong organization of Wolof wholesalers based in Italy offering not only goods but also training of itinerant salesmen, the individual Wolof peddler would have been chanceless.

The Wolof trade system studied by Riccio functions in both directions. Traders live in Italy part of the year and in Senegal part of the year, and the goods offered for sale in the Senegalese markets range from hi-fi equipment and other electronic goods to the trader's own secondhand clothes. Although Riccio takes pains to describe the variations in the circumstances of migration, an unambiguous pattern emerges from his material, which shows that Wolof migrants to Italy are positioned in Italian society in a unique way, due to particular features of their cultural background and their local organization in Senegal. Somewhat like Gujerati traders in postwar London (Tambs-Lyche 1980), they draw on preexisting social and cultural resources in developing their economic niche under new circumstances.

As shown in the previous chapter's discussion about globalization from below, transnational microeconomies have become very widespread during the last decades, and migration must increasingly be envisioned as a transnational venture rather than as a one way process resulting in segregation, assimilation, or integration in the receiving society. The economics of transnationalism can be observed in Congolese *sapeurs* (Friedman 1990) flaunting their wealth in Brazzaville following a frugal period of hard work in Paris, in the informal *hawala* banking system whereby Somali refugees send remittances to relatives, in the flow of goods into and out of immigrant-owned shops in any European city (increasingly of Chinese origin), and most certainly in thousands of local communities, from Kerala to Jamaica, which benefit from the work of locals working overseas. Seen from a global structural perspective, this kind of transnational economics can easily be seen as a vertical ethnic division of labor whereby the exploitative systems of colonialism are continued; seen from the perspective of the local community, it may equally well be seen as a much-needed source of wealth, and seen from the perspective of the individual, it entails a new set of risks and opportunities.

Many migrant populations are forced to establish webs of security and trust independently of the state in which they live, creating stable minorities with distinct identities. Thus, globalization and migration presents challenges to the state from within (see Barkan et al. 2008 for the United States; Carmel et al. 2012 for Europe). As cultural similarity as a normative basis for society becomes unrealistic, social cohesion at the level of the territorial state becomes less likely, and the normative and cultural basis of the state needs to be redefined.

The heightened mobility enhanced by globalization at the technological, social, cultural, and sometimes political level is counteracted by a renewed emphasis on borders (Green and Malm 2013). A salient aspect of migration, thus, is border control. The national borders of rich countries are increasingly becoming militarized, physical walls and fences are being raised like the one along the U.S.–Mexican border, and the density of patrol boats and armed forces along coastal borders is growing (Aas 2007). Simultaneously, prison populations in the same countries are swelling with immigrants and other foreigners. Beginning to resemble gated communities in more than one respect, the rich countries try to stem and direct incoming transnational flows, sifting "tourists" from "vagabonds," to use Zygmunt Bauman's (1999) terms.

Outsourcing the Nation-state?

Nation-states are often seen as the victims of globalization, but they may sometimes profit from it by deterritorializing some of their activities. Let me give a couple of examples from the country where I live.

Bits of Norway are being exported to places where it is more pleasant or interesting to be. Students, pensioners, and various service providers migrate seasonally, some permanently, to more temperate places. The numbers of retired Norwegians who spend part of the year in southern Europe (with a particularly high density in the Costa Blanca segment of the Spanish coast) is rising. They do not necessarily have any interest in Spain as such and make sure to get their *Aftenposten* every morning, participate in Norwegian clubs and organizations, get Norwegian nurses and dentists to look after their medical needs, and have even succeeded in opening Norwegian schools in their preferred areas. Norwegian students, for their part, increasingly do part of their studies in other countries, Australia having been the country of preference for a number of years—not because of the quality of their universities; Australian universities are, on the whole, neither better nor worse than their Norwegian counterparts—but for other, easily understood reasons to do with climate, excitement, cultural similarities, and expectations of a higher quality of life. Some even bring their teachers and reading lists with them; on a few occasions, I have taught groups of young Norwegians abroad— Latin American history and globalization in Cuba, cultural pluralism and ethnicity in India. These groups typically leave Norway in January and return in late May for their exams.

A different, but similar phenomenon is the transmigration engaged in by many immigrants and their descendants to Norway. Spending part of the year in their country of origin if they have the chance, many immigrants have developed attachments and obligations towards two places in disparate countries, and it may well be argued that certain parts of Pakistani Punjab (notably the Kharian area) have been just as Norwegianized as the Norwegian-dominated villages in southern Spain.

A second, economically more important kind of outsourcing consists in making others do the work. A rich country like Norway relies increasingly on foreigners doing the work. Just after the turn of the millennium, shops around the country suddenly began to fill up with all kinds of goods; everything was really cheap and it was all made in China. Simultaneously, growing numbers of temporary workers from Poland and the Baltic states make major contributions to the economy—in Western Europe, so many Poles work in construction that there is a shortage of construction workers in Poland, where one now has to subcontract Ukrainian entrepreneurs to get buildings finished. (One wonders what they will eventually do in Ukraine; the answer is probably Chinese firms).

These are some of the things a nation-state can use globalization for, without losing its integrity as a nation-state. The question is how long these kinds of processes can go on before new, more complex allegiances are being forged.

The Growth of Tourism

The inhabitants of Norway in 1850 never went on holiday. Some of the very rich went on once-in-a-lifetime tours of Europe, some from the privileged classes studied in Copenhagen or Berlin, and thousands of sailors travelled abroad because it was their job. Half a century later, this began to change. The imported idea of the seaside resort materialized, and mountain trips dear to the emerging middle-class nationalism began to resemble tourism in the modern sense, featuring the exotic (local peasants) and the magnificent (the mountains). Half a century later again, the package trip to the Mediterranean was introduced, but most Norwegians still spent their holidays (which they were now entitled to) at home or in another Scandinavian country.

Similar developments took place earlier in a few other countries, notably Britain, where forty-eight London coaches a day served the seaside in Brighton as early as the summer months of the 1830s, and the package trip was invented by Thomas Cook already in 1844. Nevertheless, the emergence of mass tourism has taken place and has unfolded fairly synchronically in the rich countries since the mid-twentieth century. Whereas my parents spent their summer holidays in the family cottage or perhaps in neighboring Sweden or Denmark when they were young, I went to southern Europe with my friends on an Interrail ticket, and the next generation would similarly travel to South America or Thailand. This illustrates the evolution of tourism, from local to regional to global, as it has unfolded in most parts of the rich world.

The word tourist was still a recent invention in the mid-nineteenth century. Due to economic growth and technological changes (including, notably, cheap flights), the tourist industry has grown steadily in the last fifty years, making it the possibly largest economic sector in the world. By the mid-1990s, 7 percent of the global workforce—around 230 million people—were employed in tourism (Löfgren 1999: 6). By 2012, tourist organizations counted 1.035 billion international tourist arrivals worldwide, which indicates a perceptible growth only since 2010, when the comparable figure was 940 million. The Mediterranean area, the most popular foreign destination for northern Europeans, received about six million tourists annually in 1955. In 2011, the number was 300 million (Lanquar 2011), and continued growth is expected (unless something unexpected happens, such as paleness becoming fashionable again or rapid climate change making the heat unbearable in summer). Many tourists in the Mediterranean area, Orvar Löfgren comments (1999: 187), "have to get used to vacationing in an eternal construction site."

Similar statistics could be made for Florida, a malaria-ridden, poor, and thinly populated state until after the Second World War. Today, the state receives up to eighty million tourist arrivals a year, and a poll conducted in 2011 indicated that 42 percent of the residents of the northeastern states planned to visit Florida during the spring break.

How American is Globalization?

Every country in the world (with the likely exception of the United States) has its own domestic debate about Americanization, and almost everywhere, the middle classes and establishment media worry about it. They write and say that Hollywood and American cable companies dominate on TV and in the cinema, that the fast-food giants invade and transform the national food culture, that American telecom and computer corporations dictate the new media, that bad American pop music is ubiquitous, and that transnational companies based in the United States dominate the world economy.

To what extent are these assumptions correct? Take television first. It is true that American soaps and sitcoms are broadcast in many countries, and CNN is available in an incredible number of hotel rooms. But the most popular TV programs are nearly always locally produced. Besides, Mexican and Brazilian soap operas (*telenovelas*) are more popular than the American ones in many countries, especially in the Third World.

A similar statement could be made with respect to fast food. Yes, McDonald's restaurants are astonishingly widespread, but they rarely have a market-dominant position. In a city like Avignon, there is one McDonald's and about two hundred other restaurants and bars. In Japan, several chains, including Yoshinoya, which serves traditional Japanese food, have more restaurants than McDonald's. McDonald's isn't even the largest fast-food corporation in the world. That position is held by the British corporation Compass, which owns Burger King, Sbarro, and other chains. Even 7-Eleven, that archetype of Americanization, is owned by a Japanese company.

What about American corporations? Don't they, at least, dominate the world? In fact, no. They dominate in the United States, but not many other places. Volkswagen sells more cars in China than all the American car makers combined. Toyota is the number three car maker in the United States, making one suspect that the Nipponization of the United States is more tangible than the Americanization of Japan!

On the other hand, a quarter of the world's one hundred largest nonfinancial enterprises are American. Yet, most of them have their main assets in the United States itself. Whereas the British telecom company Vodafone has 80 percent of its assets overseas, the figure for McDonald's is only 40 percent.

In some areas, American companies dominate the world economy. This is the case with oil companies like Exxon, airplane factories like Boeing, and computing companies like Microsoft, Dell, and Apple. In the media and entertainment world, American giants like Time Warner and Disney retain a strong position, although Sony may be the world's largest media company and the Dutch company Polygram the largest music company.

Globalization is, in other words, not Americanization, even if we restrict our scope to consumer habits and economic flows. In some areas, the United States is, in fact, less globalized than many other countries. Far fewer Americans than South Koreans have Internet at home, and regarding mobile telephony, the United States has been lagging behind for years. Americans travel far less abroad than Europeans—most don't even have a passport—and the international standard meter of 1889, described in an earlier chapter, is stored safely in Sèvres and is unlikely to cross the Atlantic any time soon (Marling 2006).

Perspectives on Tourism

Global tourism can be interpreted along several lines. One is homogenization, industrialization, and mass production along the lines described by George Ritzer in *The McDonaldization of Society* (1993). Leafing through the free catalogues distributed by the large tour operators, it is difficult to notice where the Spanish section ends and the Brazilian section begins. There is a global grammar of package tourism, which entails that tourist destinations have to conform to a minimal set of requirements. If the destination is of the sun and sand type, nightclubs, snorkeling trips, air conditioning, swimming pools, playgrounds, and charming, open-air markets are de rigueur. Food is either international or modified local. Tennis courts and mini golf are ubiquitous. If the destination is a city, standardized sights (the Rijksmuseum, the Sacre Cœur, the Tower of London) are featured along with advice on shopping opportunities. Hotels are classified according to an international ranking system.

Another perspective on global tourism would emphasize its glocal dimension, blending local culture, food, and music with the common denominators required by the global grammar of tourism. Toilets and bathrooms, the tourist staff's language skills, and food preparation, to mention a few dimensions, cannot be tampered with too much within this grammar, which ensures that any tourist destination should in principle be accessible to middle-class travelers from anywhere. However, local flavor is sometimes considerable and is indeed often a main attraction. Along the lush and picturesque Gudbrandsdal valley of central-southern Norway, numerous converted farms and newly built guesthouses in an old-fashioned style are calibrated to attract tourists (many of them Norwegian-Americans) in search of the authentic. Staff are paid to wear traditionalist clothes, to serve dishes rarely seen on Norwegian dinner tables, and to perform fiddle music. In general, the cultural dimension of tourism has become more and more pronounced as the number of tourists grows and their interests diversify. The folklore show has become a staple in many exotic tourist locations, and in some areas (e.g., South Africa and Indonesia), cultural tourism to real villages or real townships has become an important source of income to people living there. In many parts of the world, ethnic groups have to some extent redefined themselves from being political interest groups to offering authentic culture for tourists (Comaroff and Comaroff 2009) through a process that could be called the commercialization (or even touristification) of identity.

Tourist destinations are at least two places at one and the same time: A holiday destination and a local community. People from Benidorm live in a Spanish town, while tourists are on holiday in southern Europe, a place with totally different connotations. Residents of Dubrovnik, Croatia, complain about the feeling of living in a museum. In many popular tourist destinations, not least in the Mediterranean, locals are shocked and outraged at what they see as a hedonistic culture of permissiveness, especially among the young vacationers, coming from northern Europe. A colleague in Cyprus was visibly relieved, but also expressed concern, when I told him that the young Scandinavians who engage routinely in casual sex and take recreational drugs in the clubs dotting the island's southern coast would never dare to behave in the same way at home.

As always, there are exceptions to this rule. Cancun, on the Caribbean Maya coast of Mexico, was nonexistent as late as the mid-1970s. At the latest count in 2013, it had about 630,000 inhabitants, virtually all of whom are employed directly or indirectly in the tourism industry. It is a place with no history and no established collective identity, constructed because of the need among U.S. tour operators to find a new appropriate destination—Florida was filling up—four hours or less by plane from the main U.S. cities. (Slightly south of Cancun, a town apparently designed for European tourists was developed—namely, Playa del Carmen, with smaller hotels, less traffic, and pedestrian streets with quaint shops and sidewalk cafés.)

The tourist, as described by Urry (1990) and Löfgren (1999), is a skilled vacationer who knows the cultural codes and rules regulating the role of the tourist. However, tourism has diversified, and today it would probably be correct to speak of a plurality of tourisms. Antitourism of the generic backpacker kind, for example, has been institutionalized and standardized for decades, so that popular alternative travel guidebooks, like the Lonely Planet and Rough Guide series, can be bought in every airport or bookshop, giving sound advice as to which local bus to take to see temples off the beaten track and which guesthouses to avoid because staff tends to steal from the guests. In recent years, the website TripAdvisor, featuring authentic reviews of hotels, sights, and sites by real tourists, has become established as a supplement, or perhaps competitor, to the printed or app-based guides.

The Tourist and the Refugee

Tourism entails leisure and easy, laid-back consumption. Adrian Franklin (2004) has suggested that city centers are, in the early twenty-first century, being redesigned in order to enable people to be "tourists at home," with a proliferation of sleek buildings, coffee-bars, riverside or seaside promenades lined with restaurants, and so on. Scott Lash and John Urry (1993: 258) also suggested, writing in a period (the early 1990s) when many inner cities that had fallen into decay—owing largely to the unintentional effects of the car—were being refurbished and turned into commercially viable places, that whereas some tourists make an effort to mingle with the locals, many local residents behave like tourists in using tourist facilities in their own countries. In deeply class-divided societies, tourist areas may need to be physically closed off from the rest of society for the sake of security and in order to avoid friction. The beaches in Jamaica's Montego Bay are patrolled by armed guards, as is the Cape Town waterfront.

Bauman phrases an important difference like this: "One difference between those 'high up' and those 'low down' is that the first may leave the second behind—but not vice versa" (1999: 86). Although most people in the world continue to lead the majority of their lives near the place where they grew up, some are free to travel on vacation (or business), while others are forced to leave their homes as refugees or economic migrants. According to figures from the IOM (International Organization for Migration), there were 214 million international migrants in 2012. To this may be added tens of millions of internal migrants, not least in populous countries like China and India. According to the UNHCR (United Nations High Commission for Refugees), the number of forcibly displaced persons worldwide reached 42 million in 2011. Most of them live in a neighboring country, and the largest recipient country in 2011 was Pakistan, hosting 1.7 million refugees, nearly all from Afghanistan. Number two was, perhaps surprisingly, Iran, which hosted 886,000 refugees, again nearly exclusively from neighboring Afghanistan.

The contrast between the tourist and the refugee is stark. The tourist can travel anywhere or almost anywhere with a minimum of friction; the refugee is interrogated at every international border and is likely to be turned away. The tourist moves in a third culture where everybody has a smattering of English and can easily buy everything he needs. The refugee is usually penniless and dependent on charity and often encounters serious problems of understanding with the locals due to lack of a shared language. The tourist, of course, is free to leave any moment, while the refugee is ordered back and forth. Tellingly, the tourist, always short of time at home, makes a virtue of reducing his or her speed and limiting the daily activities while on vacation; the refugee's life, however, is full of slow, empty time where nothing happens. Both exemplify the predominance of movement in the contemporary world, and between them, the refugee and the tourist give an accurate depiction of the uneven distribution of resources in the globalized world.

Long-distance Nationalism

The "multiple identities that arise from globalization, especially as more and more people live in more than one country" (Castles and Davidson 2000: 87) often result in hyphenated identities, which have been especially pronounced in the New World. On a visit to Canada many years ago, I noticed that my Canadian friends spoke of each other as "Ukrainian," "Portuguese," and so on. This was not meant to question their national loyalty, but indicated something about origins and networks. Their Canadianness was taken for granted; the predicate before the implicit hyphen suggested, if anything, that having a mixed identity was legitimate.

For decades, it was believed in North America that immigrant minorities would generally become assimilated, that their markers of difference would gradually fade away. At least this was assumed to be the case of immigrants with European origins; with people of nonstandard appearance (blacks, Latin Americans, Asians), it was another story. Nonetheless, since the 1960s, social scientists and others have discovered that ethnic and national identities did not vanish—indeed, that they were in some cases strengthened. Even third- and fourth-generation Irish or Danes considered themselves somehow as Irish and Danes, often even without having visited the country of their ancestors. Although they became culturally assimilated, the identity remained attached to origins.

Benedict Anderson (1992) coined the term "long-distance nationalism" to describe some political implications of continued allegiance to a country, or region, where one either no longer lives or indeed has never lived. Some of the older minorities in the United States, such as Irish and Jews, have members who have for many years been actively involved in politics in Ireland and Israel, often supporting nationalist movements and trying to influence American policy through lobbying and strategic voting. However, the practices of long-distance nationalism have become much more widespread in recent years, due to (1) the great increase in the numbers of immigrants and (2) the increased facility in swift communication.

To take a few examples: The Hindu nationalists of the BJP in India (*Bharatya Janata Party*, or the Indian People's Party) have depended crucially on financial and moral support from NRIs (Non-Resident Indians), many in North America. During the breakup and subsequent wars of Yugoslavia, Yugoslavs in countries like Sweden and Australia began to emphasize their *ethnic* identities as Bosnians, Serbs, and Croats and made active contributions to the war. Many Tamils in Western Europe remain involved in the Tamil independence struggle in Sri Lanka—indeed, for many, their potential contributions to the Tamil Eelam's secession attempt has been their main cause for being abroad (Fuglerud 1999).

Anderson's only extended example illustrates the case well. He speaks about a Sikh living in Toronto, who actively supports the Khalistani movement in Indian Punjab, a violent movement, which has often targeted civilians in terrorist attacks. This man does not participate in Canadian political life but "lives, through E-mail, by long-distance nationalism" (Anderson 1992: 11; see also Cohen 1997: 110–15). Asked by a fellow Sikh why he does not move back, he explains that it is too dangerous and that he prefers his children to grow up in peaceful Toronto.

In Anderson's words:

> his political participation is directed towards an imagined *heimat* in which he does not intend to live, where he pays no taxes, where he cannot be arrested, where he will not be brought before the courts—and where he does not vote; in effect, a politics without responsibility or accountability. (1992: 11)

Yet, at the same time, this kind of politics is, it may seem, an inevitable outcome of intensified transnational connections. Sometimes, as the examples above suggest, the diasporic populations, nostalgic for the imagined authenticity of their childhood (or that of their grandparents), support cultural purity movements opposed to faceless modernization, political compromises, and cultural hybridization. As a result, they often support—from the safety of exile—militant nationalist groups. On the other hand, there are also examples of long-distance nationalist movements with other political agendas—for example, Arab, Iranian, and South Asian feminist groups working from exile in Western Europe to improve the conditions for women in the home country.

Gendered Migration

Migration is rarely entirely gender neutral. Already the enforced migration of slavery was heavily slanted in this respect, the vast majority of the slaves being men. Later movements of people in search of work or protection are also gendered in significant ways. It is commonly assumed that labor migrants moving into Western Europe or Latin American migrants heading into the United States and Canada have tended to be dominated by men. Certain forms of labor are almost exclusively male, such as construction work, mining, and some kinds of factory work.

Yet, at the same time, some of the growth trends in international migration are largely feminine. Domestic services, nursing, and housework are widely considered women's work. In the wealthy Gulf states, from Kuwait to the United Arab Emirates, large numbers of Asian women work as domestic servants, cleaners, and in the health service. The Filipina maid has become widespread in Western Europe as well, while many Latin American women find similar kinds of work in the United States. Some hope to find a husband in the new country, while others have families to support at home. In the United Kingdom, most immigrants from countries like Slovakia, Thailand, Madagascar, and the Czech Republic are women, mostly working in the domestic or health services, while the majority of asylum-seekers from countries like Nepal, Algeria, and Afghanistan are men (Vertovec 2007).

There is a considerable informal sector here as well. Since nearly all sex workers are female, the international sex trade is heavily feminized, and most sex workers in the rich countries are foreign—Nigerian, eastern European, Thai, and Latin American. However, transnational sex work is also widespread between neighboring countries in the Global South. For example, the women working in *barras-bars* and brothels in Ecuadorian coastal cities are largely Peruvian and Colombian. Their life situations range between conditions resembling slavery to a high degree of autonomy. Just like, one might add, the conditions for male workers in many parts of the Global South. At the same time, female migrants are often in a structurally different position from their male counterparts. They are vulnerable to sexual abuse and violence from men, and many are domestic and service workers in subservient positions with no real possibilities for upward mobility. Male migrants, by contrast, often form communities and strong ties with others from their place of origin, frequently at the workplace. Moreover, men usually have easier access to the public sphere than do women. This is clearly the case in the gender segregated societies of the Arabian Peninsula, but immigrant clubs and associations tend to be male-dominated elsewhere as well.

Nostalgia

When we observe that something moves, simple dialectical negation suggests that we should ask what does not move. Quite obviously, most of the world's inhabitants stay put, even if the circumstances of their lives change because of globalization's direct or indirect impact. This is what Bauman (1999: 77) means when he says that "we are all on the move these days." At the same time, the age of fast transnational movement has also proven to be the age of nostalgia and traditionalism, which could be defined as a modern ideology promoting tradition. As Giddens (1991) says, complex contemporary societies tend to be "post-traditional." This does not mean that they have done away with all tradition but that traditions must be defended actively since they can no longer be taken for granted. In the post-traditional world, dormant traditions are resurrected, adapted to fit new circumstances, commercialized, and politicized.

As I write these lines, Norway has just celebrated its Constitution Day (May 17), and never before have there been as many folk costumes in town as this year. More than 90 percent of the population celebrate May 17, and more than half of the women wear folk dresses (*bunader*: Eriksen 2004). The number of men who wear traditional dress for the occasion is also on the rise—although much lower. In my childhood, three decades ago, which unfolded in a less intensively globalized world, folk dresses were rarely seen in the urban centers of southeastern Norway. Now, consider the fact that a short while before the annual May 17 celebrations, Norwegians had, like other Western Europeans, been debating the question of whether or not to legislate against the use of headscarves (*hijabs*) among Muslim immigrant women. Again, a couple of decades ago, *hijabs* were hardly ever seen among Muslim immigrant women in Europe. Even today, many young Muslim women wear the *hijab* against their parents' wish.

In all likelihood, few of the very many women (and men) sporting neotraditionalist garb on Constitution Day would have reflected on the parallel between the rise of visible identity markers among minorities and in the majority. And one would have to be a social scientist interested in globalization to see these markers of difference not as a natural expression of a natural identity, nor as a simple reaction against globalization, but as one of its most common reflexive forms. If anything, globalization at the level of social identity is tantamount to a renegotiation of social identities, their boundaries, and symbolic content. Nobody can give an unequivocal, uncontroversial definition of what it means to be a Berliner, a Malaysian, or a Norwegian any more, but this does not necessarily mean that these identities are going away. Some of them are, in fact, strengthened, invested with new or old symbolic content, some wane to the benefit of others, some are enlarged or shrunk, some become transnational, and others remain attached to place. Just as a fish is totally uninterested in water as long as it swims happily around—it is even unlikely to be aware of the existence of water—most people don't think twice about those of their identities that can be taken for granted. But the moment you drag the poor creature out of the sea, be it on a hook or in a net, it immediately develops an intense interest in water; what the water means to it, how it is essential for its survival, and—not least—the peculiar nature of water. Had fish been equipped with an ability to ponder, a great number of short-lived (and doubtless poststructuralist) theories about water would have been sketched in haste, in maritime surroundings, every day. In the case of humans, not only are the national, regional, and local identities contested and challenged, but it is becoming increasingly difficult to defend absolutist views of gender and kinship identities as well. Place— that is to say a fixed, stable, meaningful space—is becoming a scarce and flexible resource. Maintaining a predictable and secure group identity is hard work in a world of movement, but it is being undertaken, very often successfully.

- Globalization involves accelerated and intensified movement of people, objects, and ideas, not only from north to south, but in every direction.
- Movement nonetheless reflects and tends to reproduce global power discrepancies.
- Although there is currently enormous attention to migration in the West, a far greater percentage of humanity were migrants a hundred years ago than today.
- Contemporary migration is not a finite process but usually involves enduring transnational ties.
- Forms of human mobility enhanced by and contributing to globalization include, among other things, migration, tourism, business travel, student mobility, crime, and even forms of transhumance, which includes the seasonal migrations of the wealthy in cold climates to warmer places and seasonal migrant labor.

Questions

- In which ways are transnational links involving migrants economically important?
- How would you describe the global grammar of tourism? What are its main homogenizing features?
- What are the main differences between the tourist and the refugee, and how do the differences shed light on global power discrepancies?
- What is long-distance nationalism, and how can it pose problems to democracy?
- Why does movement make it difficult to establish firm, stable group identities, and what are some of the ways in which this challenge is being met?

Further Reading

Castles, Stephen, and Mark J. Miller (2009) *The Age of Migration: International Population Movements in the Modern World*, 4th edition. London: Palgrave Macmillan. Probably the most authoritative and comprehensive overview of migration, with historical and contemporary perspectives equally represented. No theoretical bells and whistles, but a sound and trustworthy guide to a central form of mobility.

Mathews, Gordon, Gustavo Lins Ribeiro, and Carlos Alba Vega, eds. (2012) *Globalization from Below: The World's Other Economy*. London: Routledge. A fascinating and original collection of articles describing in great ethnographic detail the flow of cheap and often pirated goods from China around the world, with petty traders, hawkers, and small-scale capitalists in the informal sector at the forefront.

6

Mixing

The battleground of the twenty-first century will pit fundamentalism against cosmopolitan tolerance.

—ANTHONY GIDDENS, *RUNAWAY WORLD*, 4

There is no such thing as a pure culture, and the cultural history of humanity may well be written as a history of borrowing and lending, inspiration and imitation, amalgamation and hybridization of cultural skills and meanings. Yet, the extent and scope of cultural mixing have accelerated and intensified in the current era, owing to the processes identified in earlier chapters. As a result, new cultural forms emerge continuously—bhangra music in the United Kingdom, Spanglish in U.S. inner cities, crossover food, and Melanesian reggae—but these tendencies are counteracted by various forms of cultural puritanism, from the French concern with their language to religious revitalization.

Many years ago, I had the pleasure of interviewing the author Vikram Seth, who had then just published his epic novel from the early 1950s in India, *A Suitable Boy*. As it happened, we spoke extensively about cultural mixing—his main characters were, to varying degrees, Westernized, yet remained distinctively Indian in their values and way of life. As we spoke, our server arrived with a tray, pots, and cups. Taking his first sip, Seth sputtered and exclaimed that he had been served a mixture of tea and coffee! Must be horrible, I opined, but Seth insisted that he saw the concoction as a new, exciting mixture.

Mixing is always a result of mobility and movement, but repulsion, obliteration, and encapsulation are also possible outcomes of cross-cultural encounters. This chapter looks at both sides of the coin—cosmopolitanism and hybridity on the one hand, withdrawal and boundary-marking on the other. First of all, we should make it clear that just as the other dimensions of globalization are multifaceted, the cultural dynamics of globalization cannot be seen as Westernization *tout court* but must be understood as a multidirectional and genuinely complex process (Amselle 2001; Appadurai 1996; Hannerz 1996). Second, we should keep in mind that there is no such thing as a pure culture. Mixing has always occurred, but its speed and intensity are much higher today than before. Cultural mixing must therefore be seen as a key dimension of globalization.

In earlier chapters, I have presented views on globalization that suggest there is a drive towards homogeneity, but I have also emphasized that (1) there is reflexive resistance to this, resulting in glocal forms blending the particular and the universal or even withdrawing completely from the globalizing forces, (2) globalization processes are partial and are unable to transform local cultures totally, and besides, (3) large segments of the world's population are affected only indirectly or not at all by globalization processes.

Yet, nobody denies that mixing takes place, in language, food habits, customs, and so on, in many ways and in every country of the world. Sometimes, cultural impulses from two or several distinct groups mix to create something new; sometimes, the universalist drive of globalization processes mixes with local cultures to produce a glocal version of the universal. Arguing against the belief in a fast global integration in the sense of homogenization, Jean-François Bayart says:

[it] is the Islamists who introduced intellectual categories of the economy into the Muslim world. It is the healers, sorcerers, and kin who speak the market in Central Africa. It is the families of the Chinese diaspora who unify the economic space of East Asia. (2003: 334)

Arguing against the theorists who see hybridity and creolization as products of globalization, Jean-Loup Amselle (2001: 22) favors a view according to which cultures have always mixed and proposes that "all societies are mixed and thus that mixing is the product of entities which are already mixed, thus sending the idea of an original purity to oblivion" (my translation).

However, as every serious anthropologist working within the emerging globalization paradigm would stress, "no total homogenization of systems of meaning and expression has occurred, nor does it appear likely that there will be one any time soon" (Hannerz 1990: 237). According to Ulf Hannerz, global culture is marked by the following:

an organization of diversity rather than by a replication of uniformity. . . . But the world has become one network of social relationships, and between its different regions there is a flow of meaning as well as of people and goods. (1990: 237)

Elsewhere, Hannerz has also said that the "recent confluence of separate and quite different traditions" does not "mean that these . . . cultural currents in themselves have been 'pure', or 'homogeneous', or 'bounded" (1996: 67).

This is important. Accelerated mixing does not imply a prior pristine state of clearly bounded cultures. Granted that cultural mixing is a common, usually undramatic phenomenon in the contemporary world, we need to look more closely at some of the concepts used to describe the process of mixing. They do not necessarily refer to the same thing.

Variation within any group is considerable, and cultural flows across boundaries ensure that mixing, in the contemporary world, is a continuous possibility or reality. However, the impression sometimes given that everything seems to be in continuous flux, that an infinity of opportunities seem to be open, and that no groups, cultural identities, or ethnic categories are fixed is caused by a conflation of discrete phenomena:

First: Strong identities and fixed boundaries do not preclude cultural mixing. Ethnic variation may well exist without significant cultural variation. Therefore, processes of cultural mixing say little about group identities and degrees of boundedness.

Second: Fluid identities, conversely, do not preclude cultural stability or continuity. Cultural variation can exist without ethnic variation or other kinds of strong group boundaries. Culture is an implication of varying degrees of shared meaning, while group identities result from clear, if disputed, social boundaries.

Third: The political manipulation with and cynical exploitation of cultural symbols do not mean that the people in question do not necessarily have anything in common. Historiography, it has been shown time and again, is necessarily a selective and biased discipline simply because far too many events have taken place in the past for any historian to give all of them a fair treatment. Yet, its slanted narratives may become self-fulfilling prophecies in that they give the readership (often schoolchildren) a shared frame of reference. Besides, the people described by nationalist historians or ideologists of group boundedness may not have that in common which their ideologists ascribe to them, but they may have other important cultural elements in common, such as shared jokes or ideas about kin relatedness. What has interested writers on cultural mixing are the situations where these frames of references cease to be taken for granted, where they are contested, nonexistent, or are being continuously rebuilt. But it may just happen to be the case, in other words, that ethnic boundaries coincide with certain cultural ones. (Moreover, the fact that something is socially constructed does not imply that it is unreal.)

This means that the ambiguous grey zones, which can be located within the space between categories and boundaries under pressure, are privileged sites for studying the interplay between culture and identity. This is not because all boundaries eventually disappear, but because they are made visible through their negotiation and renegotiation, transcendence, transformations, and reframing.

Forms of Mixing

There are a number of different outcomes from long-term encounters between distinct groups. Sometimes, one group is eventually absorbed into the other; sometimes, it is absorbed culturally but not socially (the ethnic boundaries remain intact); sometimes, the groups merge to create a new entity; sometimes, a hierarchical complementary relationship or a symmetrical competitive relationship occurs; sometimes, again, one group eventually exterminates the other.

The anthropologist Olivia Harris (1995), writing on cultural complexity in Latin America, and particularly the Andean area, has proposed a typology depicting six possible ways of conceptualizing long-term, regular contact between originally discrete groups.

First, she describes a model she simply calls "mixing" (in Latin America often spoken of, both in racial and cultural respects, as *mestizaje*). This model shows how new meanings are generated from the mixing of diverse influences. It corresponds to common usage of the terms hybridity and creolization.

The second model is the one of "colonization," which in the South American context implies European dominance, exploitation, and violence towards Indians, including the enforced introduction of Christianity and the Spanish language. This model is strongly dualist and somewhat mechanical in its notion of power and, in Harris's view, draws a rather too strict line between European and Indian culture, reifying (freezing) both in the act. This may be true, but it remains a fact that the social boundaries (if not the cultural ones) between Indians and Europeans have remained largely intact, notwithstanding the emergence of intermediate categories, such as the mestizo.

Third, an alternative to the rigid model of colonization implies the attribution of "more agency to the colonized" and a phrasing of "the relationship in terms of borrowing" (Harris 1995: 112). The traditions remain discrete, but Indian elites (Harris refers particularly to Incas and Mayas) borrow knowledge from the Christians. This is classic *diffusionism*.

The fourth model is "that of juxtaposition or alternation, where two radically different knowledge systems are both accepted without a direct attempt at integration" (Harris 1995: 114). Since, for example, Maya and Christian cosmologies entailed fundamentally different conceptualizations of time and of the past, they could not be mixed, but actors could draw situationally on either. This is a variety of *multiculturalism*.

The fifth way of conceptualizing the meeting is "that of imitation, assimilation or direct identification," whereby persons self-consciously reject their own past and adopt a self-identity and knowledge system they perceive as better or more beneficial to themselves. A conversion from Indian to mestizo identity in the Andes, Harris notes, "usually involves wholesale rejection of Indian identity, in favour of and identification with what is seen as white or Hispanic" (1995: 115).

The sixth and final mode discussed by Harris is that of "innovation and creativity," where "attention is firmly removed from contrasted knowledge systems and priority is given to autonomy and independent agency" (1995: 117). Unlike the five other models sketched, this kind of conceptualization does not focus on origins.

All these models refer to mixing either at the level of identity, at the level of symbolic meaning, or both, but they are clearly distinctive from one another. All can be used to make sense of contemporary encounters between different cultural systems.

Let us now look more closely at two of the most common concepts used to describe cultural mixing today.

Hybridity and Creolization

The concept of *cultural creolization*, owing its influence in anthropology largely to Ulf Hannerz (1987, 1992; but see also Drummond 1980; Stewart 2007), refers to the intermingling and mixing of two or several formerly discrete traditions or cultures. In an era of global mass communication and capitalism, creolization, according to this usage, can be identified nearly everywhere in the world, but there are important differences as to the degrees and forms of mixing. As mentioned above, this perspective has been criticized for essentializing cultures (as if the merging traditions were pure at the outset, cf. Friedman 1994). Although this critique may sometimes be relevant, the concept nevertheless helps in making sense of a great number of contemporary cultural processes, characterized by movement, change, and fuzzy boundaries.

Creolization, as it is used by some anthropologists, is an analogy taken from linguistics. This discipline in turn took the term from a particular aspect of colonialism— namely, the uprooting and displacement of large numbers of people in the plantation economies of certain colonies, such as Louisiana, Jamaica, Trinidad, Réunion, and Mauritius. Both in the Caribbean basin and in the Indian Ocean, certain (or all) groups who contributed to this economy during slavery were described as creoles. Originally, a *criollo* meant a European (normally a Spaniard) born in the New World (as opposed to

Postcolonialism and the Power of Definition

For a newly independent country, taking over ownership of factories, mines, and fields is fairly straightforward, argues the Kenyan author Ngugi wa Thiong'o; what is much more difficult is decolonizing the mind (1986). In his essays, Ngugi relates how he, as a boy growing up in colonial Kenya, was taught about daffodils and snowflakes, Shakespeare and the Tudors, but nothing about African geography or history. Liberating oneself from such an involuntary appropriation of worlds other than one's own is a chief concern in the body of fiction and theory called postcolonial.

Colonialism was a global enterprise, the British Empire a political entity "where the sun never set," and postcolonialism is global as well, but moving in the opposite direction, from south to north, in a series of attempts to reclaim some of the power of definition that was lost through generations of colonialism.

Postcolonial studies, a new academic subdiscipline, is often traced to the publication of Edward Said's *Orientalism* (1978), a hugely influential book, which criticized European scholars and writers in the colonial era for depicting the Orient in stereotypical and prejudiced ways. However, the debt to the Martiniquan doctor Frantz Fanon and his *Black Skin, White Masks* (1986 [1952]) is usually acknowledged. Fanon showed how imperialism affected the mentality and desires of black people, making them reject their own histories and experiences and yearn for "a little bit of whiteness."

The project of postcolonialism consists, simply put, in developing and promoting the worlds of experience silenced by the dominant or hegemonic groups. Some postcolonial writers, like Ngugi and the Kurdish author Mehmed Uzun, even strive to develop vernaculars as literary languages, but many write in the metropolitan languages, thereby creating a dilemma often discussed: how can the imperialist vehicles of communication be used to denounce imperialism?

Many contemporary writers see a link between the quest for liberation and autonomy among the dispossessed of the world and the need to tell new stories depicting hitherto silenced experiences and rehabilitating life-worlds and social milieu, which have formerly either been ignored or depicted as backward and primitive. A global democratization of communication must arguably include not only equal access to technology but also a fair distribution of the right to speak and the right to be heard.

peninsulares); today, a similar usage is current in the French *département* La Réunion, where everybody born on the island, regardless of skin color, is seen as *créole* as opposed to the *zoreils*, who were born in metropolitan France. In Trinidad, the term creole is sometimes used to designate all Trinidadians except those of Asian origin. In Suriname, a creole is a person of African origin, while in neighboring French Guyana, a creole is a person who has adopted a European way of life. In spite of the differences, there are some important resemblances between the various conceptualizations of the creole, which resonate with the theoretical concept of creolization: Creoles are uprooted, they belong to the New World, they are the products of some form of mixing, and they are contrasted with that which is old, deep, and rooted.

A question often posed by people unfamiliar with the varying uses of the term is: "What is *really* a creole?" They may have encountered the term in connection with food or architecture from Louisiana, languages in the Caribbean, or people in the Indian Ocean. Whereas vernacular uses of the term creole vary, there exist accurate definitions of creole languages in linguistics and of cultural creolization in anthropology. There are nevertheless similarities, although there is no one-to-one relationship between the ethnic groups described locally as creoles in particular societies and the phenomena classified as creole or creolized in academic literature (Stewart 2007).

Hybridity is a more general concept than creolization, and it may be used to refer to any obviously mixed cultural form. World music, various forms of contemporary crossover cuisine, and urban youth cultures borrowing elements from a variety of sources, including minority cultures and TV, are typical examples of phenomena explored under the heading hybridity.

Generic terms like creolization, hybridity, or simply mixing are often adequate to describe cultural phenomena and processes resulting from the increased contact of globalization. Sometimes, more precision is needed, especially when cultural processes are connected with social ones.

Different parts of a cultural environment and of people's life-worlds are being affected by influence from outside at different speeds and to differing degrees. Sometimes people are acutely aware of changes taking place in their immediate environment and take measures to stop it, to enhance it, or to channel it in their preferred direction. At other times, people may be unaware of these processes, even if foreign influences and cultural mixing may change their cultural environment profoundly. These are some of the intricacies of contemporary cultural processes that need disentangling if we are to be successful in studying them accurately. Merely stating that mixing is an inherent feature of contemporary culture is no more enlightening than saying that cultural diffusion is a fact. Thus:

Cultural pluralism directs the attention of the researcher towards the relative boundedness of the constituent groups or categories that make up a society. It is a close relative of multiculturalism.

Hybridity directs attention towards individuals or cultural forms that are reflexively, or self-consciously, mixed—that is, syntheses of cultural forms or fragments of diverse origins. It opposes multiculturalism seen as nationalism writ small.

Syncretism directs attention towards the amalgamation of formerly discrete worldviews, cultural meaning, and, in particular, religion.

Diasporic identity directs attention towards an essentially social category consisting of people whose primary subjective belonging is in another country.

Transnationalism directs attention, rather, to a social existence attaching individuals and groups not primarily to one particular place but to several or none.

Diffusion directs attention towards the flow of substances and meanings between societies, whether it is accompanied by actual social encounters or not.

Creolization, finally, directs our attention towards cultural phenomena, which result from displacement and the ensuing social encounter and mutual influence between two or several groups, creating an ongoing dynamic interchange of symbols and practices, eventually leading to new forms with varying degrees of stability. The term *creole culture* suggests the presence of a standardized, relatively stable cultural idiom resulting from such a process. *Cultural decreolization* occurs when, in the case of group-based power differentials and inequalities, the subordinate group is socially or culturally assimilated into the dominant one (e.g., *cholos* becoming *mestizos* in Latin America) or when a creolized idiom is purified and made similar to a metropolitan or high culture form.

World Music

One of the most intensively studied areas of cultural mixing is that to do with music. Although music has, perhaps more easily than language, always been influenced by impulses from afar—Mozart's famous "Turkish March" speaks for itself, Bártok's string quartets were influenced by Gypsy music, Grieg's "Peer Gynt Suite" took elements from Scandinavian folk music—the most famous contemporary example of cultural mixing in music is that of so-called world music: jazz musicians borrow from Indian ragas, rock musicians borrow from African percussive music, house and techno technicians borrow from the Javanese gamelan, and Jamaicans borrow from, and lend to, everybody. There are large-scale festivals devoted to world music (the oldest, and most famous, in Europe being Peter Gabriel's WOMAD festival, founded in 1980); the genre (if it is a genre) has its own categories in music shops whether online or offline, its own labels, and its own charts.

The term world music, as it has been established in everyday language since the late 1980s, testifies to an increased mobility of musicians, especially from the Third World, a greater intensity in the networks engaged in between musicians of diverse origin, and a faster flow of musical impulses across the globe. The mixed musical forms labeled world music are thus a prime example of intensified globalization.

In a critical assessment of the genre entitled "A Sweet Lullaby for World Music," the anthropologist and ethnomusicologist Steven Feld (2003) describes how "any and every hybrid or traditional style could . . . be lumped together by the single market label *world music*" (195), adding that this signified not only the triumph of the commercial but also a disquieting *banalization of difference*. The mixing represented in this kind of world music, as it is described by Feld, is a surprisingly close relative of the "globalization of nothing" phenomena analyzed by Ritzer (cf. Chapter 4). However, Feld notes that this tendency is counteracted with a yearning for authenticity and the noncommercial. He also adds that the discourse about world music, academic and nonacademic alike, is, "like globalization discourse more generally, . . . equally routed through the public sphere via tropes of anxiety and celebration" (Feld 2003: 198).

But the analysis does not stop there. Taking as an example a song, "Rorogwela," composed by Afunakwa, a Baegu woman from the Solomon Islands, Feld goes on to show how oral and indigenous music is being transformed and recreated by Western musicians, and he describes the difficulties involved in giving the original composers recognition and their rightful part of the revenues generated. In discussing this topic, Feld touches upon a much larger family of issues—namely, those to do with IPRs (intellectual property rights). In an era where the cultural production of traditional peoples is being repackaged as commercially palatable exotic products, it has become a question of key importance to many, especially indigenous peoples themselves, to be able to defend their legal rights to their music, literature, and handicrafts (see Kasten 2004).

Contrasting a UNESCO series of authentic recordings of traditional music with the commercial adaptation of similar (sometimes identical) music, Feld ends his lullaby with a remark about the way in which "world music participates in shaping a kind of consumer-friendly multiculturalism, one that follows the market logic of expansion and consolidation" (2003: 213). Although many forms of musical mixing exist in our era of intensified globalization, and musicians from the Third World occasionally get their share of the profits and recognition, the commercial dimension of mixing—the world of Benetton—can rarely be disregarded altogether.

The flows of musical influences often have paradoxical effects. Ted Lewellen (2002) describes the development of the Congolese rhumba from the 1920s to the 1940s, a guitar-based style borrowing from Cuban music. By the 1970s, the influence from soul was also apparent: Partly African in origin, Cuban music and American soul returned to Africa, to be merged with locally developed styles. Later, a variant of Congolese popular music, the *soukouss*, became popular in Europe, where it was regarded as *la vraie musique africaine*. However, *soukouss* was hardly listened to in Africa itself, where the lyrics sung in local languages, often strongly political, were as important as melody and rhythm.

A Mixed Family in Mauritius

Writings on the globalization of culture tend to be full of anecdotes revealing the disembeddedness of cultural signs or connections between the local and the global, but it is also necessary to pay close attention to the wider implications of such processes at the level of everyday life. I shall now provide a brief example, a main purpose of which is to emphasize the continued relevance of anthropological fieldwork in a world where the small-scale work of ethnography may seem incapable of grasping the global forces at work.

Rose-Hill is a Mauritian town of some forty-five thousand inhabitants, according to the census. However, boundaries between Mauritian towns are unclear, and it would probably be most accurate to describe Rose-Hill as one of five or six nodes along the nearly continuous urbanized stretch from Port-Louis to Curepipe, where more than half of the ethnically diverse Mauritian population of slightly over a million live.

The quarter of Roches-Brunes, located on the western outskirts of Rose-Hill, is dominated by a municipal housing estate (*cité ouvrière*), and most of the

Rushdie and Naipaul: Two Views on Mixing

Among the many novelists who have depicted the cultural complexities and dilemmas in postcolonial societies, V. S. Naipaul and Salman Rushdie are possibly the most famous in the English-speaking world. Naipaul, born in Trinidad in 1932, is the grandson of Indian immigrants, and he migrated to Britain in 1949, publishing novels, travel writing, and essays since the mid-1950s. Among Naipaul's most celebrated books are *A House for Mr Biswas* (1961) and *The Enigma of Arrival* (1987). Naipaul received the Nobel Prize for literature in 2001. Rushdie, born in Bombay (now Mumbai) on the eve of Indian independence in 1947, grew up in England and had a major breakthrough with *Midnight's Children*, an epic novel about the first years of Indian independence. In 1988, with the publication of the very complex and allegorical novel *The Satanic Verses*, Rushdie was accused of blasphemy against Islam, and the Iranian ayatollah Khomeini proclaimed a *fatwa*, a death sentence on the writer.

Both Rushdie and Naipaul describe the intensive cultural mixing taking place in postcolonial cities such as Bombay (Rushdie) and in the Caribbean (Naipaul) as well as through the migration experience. Interestingly, they seem to represent diametrically opposed views on cultural mixing: Rushdie (1991: 394) is an optimist, seeing the enriching and liberating power of "mongrelization," as he once called it, while Naipaul is wary and deeply critical of what he sees as inauthentic mimicry and superficial cultural forms unable to anchor the individual in a strong tradition.

Naipaul's early, comic novels are satires of what he sees as Trinidadian vulgarity, the "carnival mentality" where Trinidadians, in noisy and superficial ways, mix cultural impulses they have done nothing to deserve in order to create an identity consisting of shiny surfaces with no intimation of depth or coherence. Members of an impure, hybrid creole culture, Trinidadians are mimicking metropolitan culture in Naipaul's view: In the late 1950s, he described how all the men leaving a cinema in Port-of-Spain after viewing *Casablanca* had immediately adopted Humphrey Bogart's style of walking. After Biswas, Naipaul's novels were increasingly melancholy, sometimes bitter depictions of thwarted or dishonest attempts at creating secure, firm identities. He is at his most cynical and devastating when he writes about Asian Muslims (in *Among the Believers*, 1981, and *Beyond Belief*, 1998)—converts, he calls them, even if they, strictly speaking, have been Muslims all their lives and can refer to centuries of Islamic faith in their countries.

Rushdie has no time for cultural purism. "A bit of this and a bit of that; that is how newness enters the world," he writes in *Imaginary Homelands* (1991), in a celebration of the hybridization and cultural mixing caused by international migration, the global flows of ideas, and the spread of a worldview that is open to change and ambivalent to tradition and inherited identities. In *Fury* (2001), Rushdie satirizes a postmodern identity movement in a lightly concealed version of Fiji, which dons clothes and code names from *Star Trek*; in *The Satanic Verses* (1988), arguably a literary masterpiece, he lashes out against all attempts to close the world and fix its boundaries, from orthodox religion to xenophobic nationalism. Even Rushdie's language, quite unlike Naipaul's economic, sober English, is exuberant and full of neologisms and expressions from Hindi and Indian English.

Naipaul and Rushdie exemplify two views of cultural purity and mixing, but also two views of creativity. Is it through mixing existing material in new ways, or through writing from a well-defined vantage point embedded in a tradition, that human creativity is given the most fertile conditions? Such questions are characteristic of many debates about the globalization of culture, and they have several possible answers.

approximately one thousand people living in the area are working-class creoles or blacks. The more imposing dwellings belonging to a few affluent families are located away from the more monotonous *cité ouvrière*. Apart from the creoles, some coloreds (light-skinned creoles with middle-class aspirations) and Chinese live in the area, as well as a few Hindus and a single Muslim household. Roches-Brunes is not representative of Mauritius with regards to ethnicity, since the largest community island-wide is Hindu.

In describing the relationship between the global and the local, I shall focus on the Rioux household, and this ethnographic snapshot is from the early 1990s (note the absence of cell phones and Facebook accounts in the following). It is what is commonly described as a matrifocal household, consisting of Mme Rioux, her daughter Aline (twenty), her two sons, François and Jean, both in their mid-twenties, Aline's baby daughter, and a lodger, a young student from the neighboring island of Rodrigues. Their income is average by local standards. Aline works as a shop girl in the town center; her elder brother François is a carpenter's apprentice, and her younger brother Jean is unemployed. The household sometimes receives remittances from other relatives, notably a married daughter who lives in the neighboring French *département* La Réunion, and the student from Rodrigues pays a monthly rent.

The living-room in the Rioux's home contains several objects signifying links with distant places. Two posters depicting pop stars (one English, one American) are prominently displayed; so is a cupboard with glass doors, behind which are souvenirs from Paris, Bombay, and London (gifts from foreigners). There is a radio cassette and a black-and-white TV set. On the floor next to the TV set, there is a small heap of foreign magazines, some of them in English, which is a language none of the household members has mastered. Images of Europe are powerful and persuasive in Mauritius; an opinion poll carried out in the mid-1970s indicated that half of the population wished to emigrate if they could, but the number declined sharply following the economic boom of the 1980s and 1990s (Eriksen 1998).

The mass media consumed in the household confirm the common stereotype of life in the Western world as an easy, glamorous life. Local knowledge of Europe generally suggests it is a continent of affluence and excitement. Many Mauritians have emigrated, the majority to France and Britain. Aline Rioux says she wouldn't emigrate; she has heard too many ugly stories of girls who were forced into prostitution, or who were married to old men living in the countryside. There has, in other words, been a certain feedback from other parts of the global system. She reads *romans-photo*, "photo-novels" of French origin and occasionally a local magazine. She is fond of French pop music.

François Rioux plays soccer and follows world politics in the local newspapers; he frequently discusses global issues with his friends. The whole family watches American soap operas on TV; the younger generation goes to the cinema to see largely American films dubbed in French about twice a month. They are devoted Catholics and go to Mass every Sunday (actually, Aline goes somewhat more rarely).

The members of the household agree that education is important for a person's opportunities, unless he or she has relatives in high places. François, Jean, and Aline are all prepared to compete for jobs and promotion. None of them has completed secondary school.

Seen superficially and in a fragmented way, as I have done now, the world-structures and patterns of consumption of the Rioux household seem comparable to—similar to—that of working classes in many other countries. The globalization of culture seems predominant in Roches-Brunes, which, to an untrained observer like Claude Lévi-Strauss of *Tristes Tropiques* (1989 [1955]), must seem like a squalid backyard of civilization. Scrutinized more closely, however, the lives and world-structures of the Rioux and the others in the *cité* have a distinctively local character and cannot at all be understood outside of their local context.

Soccer and pop music may credibly be seen as prime instances of global culture. Soccer in Roches-Brunes follows the same rules as in Britain. Unlike World Cup soccer, however, it is entirely local in character. François Rioux owes much of his reputation in the neighborhood to his skills as a soccer player. As a result, he is popular with the girls, makes friends with the boys, and in fact, he got his present job at least partly because of his personal popularity. Concerning pop music, so arrogantly despised by most anthropologists who encounter it in the field, a similar local context applies. It is played at local parties and in rum shops, and may evoke sentiments and stimulate social relations quite different from its effects in other environments. Among Afro-Caribbeans, for example, the late Michael Jackson (the singer) was controversial already in the late 1980s because he was considered not sufficiently black; in the black Mauritian working-class, he was second only to God, not least because he was considered black.

The Rioux family comment on American TV shows (dubbed in French) incessantly. Very often, they compare the characters with people they know; when commenting on rich and miserly men, they might make remarks to the effect that "Hey, that's just like Lee Foo used to treat my friend," referring to a neighborhood Chinese merchant. They always compare the plots and social milieu on the screen with contexts with which they are familiar. It should also be noted, significantly, that for a Mauritian creole, European culture is attractive partly because it is reflexively being contrasted locally with Mauritian Hindu culture. Films and magazines describing middle-class life in Europe or North America, for example, thus make sense and are popular partly because they can be interpreted into a local dichotomous schema depicting Indian culture as inferior. Overcommunicating what is locally perceived as Europeanness indicates a culturally valued air of superiority compared with the local Indians. In their selective interpretations of aspects of global culture, the inhabitants of Roches-Brunes appropriate them and transform the global into something local.

There are sound reasons that the thesis of globalization, in its most general and sweeping forms, should be treated with great caution. For one thing, local life-worlds are produced and reproduced locally, and there are social fields where the globalization of culture has little or no effect—for example, in the socialization of children, where Mauritian creole custom is strikingly different from that of the hegemonic white Franco-Mauritians. For another, there are large parts of the world where the globalizing agencies hardly enter. *Poverty*, it needs to be mentioned, functions as an efficient antiglobalization mechanism in these matters. The very poor have scant access to the shared interfaces of modernity, and the agencies of modernity are not particularly interested in providing them.

A Model

The politics of identity, this chapter has suggested, is interwoven with cultural mixing in complex ways. There is no one-to-one relationship between cultural mixing and political cosmopolitanism or tolerance, nor can it be assumed that a yearning for cultural purity necessarily goes together with a xenophobic or nationalist political attitude. However, as will be made clear in Chapter 8, an ideology of cultural purity very often accompanies an identity politics, which stresses the virtues of the in-group and, by implication, stereotypes outsiders.

As mentioned on several occasions, whenever you have discovered something, you should look for the opposite or its negation. This piece of advice is perhaps especially important in studies of globalization because of the many tensions involving what we may call, in a broad and general sense, the global and the local, or the universal and the particular. Cultural puritanism, which literally implies the purging of impurities and contamination, is a widespread reaction to forms of mixing entailed by globalization. It is partly in this sense that several authors (Gray 2003; Steger 2008) have argued that the militant Islamic fundamentalists of al-Qaeda are produced by modernity; the perceived need to purify a religion comes only after a period of mixing and contamination, and the antimodern rhetoric of the Salafist movement of which al-Qaeda, ideologically, is part, would not have been possible without modernity. A negation is totally dependent on that which it negates.

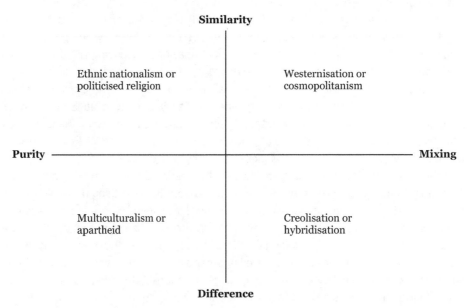

FIGURE 6.1 *Some possible positions in discourses about culture and identity (from Eriksen 2007a).*

Let us consider some possible options for people living in societies exposed to a variety of cultural influences, both from the inside and from the outside—in a word, fairly typical societies in our present age.

At the ideological level, some promote mixing, while others are favorable to purity. At the level of social integration, some emphasize the need for similarity within a given society, while others are happy to accept considerable diversity or difference. These dimensions can be combined in altogether four ways (see Figure 6.1).

Cultural purity and similarity are championed by nationalism and politicized religion. The outside world is seen as a source of contamination.

Mixing and similarity would typically be defended by groups and persons who either see Westernization as a good thing (associated with progress, education, etc.) or who argue that society ought to rest on the shared values of cosmopolitanism, the view that differences must exist, but they must be tolerated, and dialogue across cultural divides bring people more closely together.

An emphasis on purity along with an acceptance of differences within society seems to be a recipe for segregation. South African apartheid is an obvious example, but there are also forms of multiculturalism in the contemporary North Atlantic world that fit this description: different groups with different values and customs should coexist without enforced contact or missionary activity.

Finally, a favorable attitude towards both mixing and difference sets the stage for a society where hybridity, or, in societies like Mauritius, creolization is considered unproblematic and virtuous. The absence of clear boundaries is not seen as a problem, and the emphasis is on the individual's freedom to adapt or adopt the values and practices that he or she deems valuable.

The four corners of the figure are not mutually exclusive in practice (the real world tends to muddy neat models). In most societies, these options coexist, often in conflicting ways, sometimes in precarious equilibrium. In many coastal hamlets in northern Norway, where there has been a revitalization of Sami (Lappish) identity since the 1980s, families are split over which identity to choose. These families are of mixed origins and were for generations subjected to a policy of Norwegianization as a result of which many consider themselves Norwegian and not Sami. When some family members choose to return to the Sami identity of (some of) their ancestors and others refuse to have anything to do with Sami culture or identity, one can only imagine the silences during Sunday dinner. It could, moreover, be argued that the 1990s wars in Yugoslavia were, at the ideological level, fought between a model of ethnic nationalism and a model of cosmopolitanism or multiculturalism. Less violently, but seriously enough, French language policy has in recent decades sought to purge French of English loanwords, at the same time as the descendants of Arab immigrants devise their own forms of hybridized French influenced by Arab and Berber syntax and vocabulary, novel verbal forms labeled by sociolinguists, not sociolects or dialects but *multiethnolects*.

Mixing is rarely uncontroversial, but it takes place continuously. A task for researchers is to discover and analyze the forms of mixing not commented upon, those which are endorsed and those which are actively resisted or fought over. Every society has its own peculiar debates about cultural mixing, and one of their elements is always globalization.

- The cultural mixing resulting from globalization takes many forms, usually indicating power discrepancies between the groups involved.
- Mixing at the cultural level does not preclude strengthened group identification.
- Cultural mixing does not create homogeneity but new configurations of diversity.
- An important objection against theories of hybridity and creolization is that cultures have never been pure and bounded.
- The cultural diffusion associated with globalization cannot simply be described as Westernization but usually is better depicted as a form of cultural glocalization.

Questions

- What are the main arguments against the view that cultural hybridity is a product of globalization? Do you agree?
- What are the main possible outcomes of long-term encounters between culturally different groups?
- Mention, and define, four concepts used to describe cultural mixing, emphasizing their mutual differences.
- How can world music be described as a vessel of the "banalization of difference"?
- The author makes a sharp contrast between cultural mixing and social identification. Explain the significance of this distinction.

Further Reading

Hannerz, Ulf (1996) *Transnational Connections*. London: Routledge. A selection of essays by an anthropologist who has contributed to shaping the field, concerning itself with cultural complexities, creolization, and the emergence of new forms of cultural diversity.

Marling, William H. (2006) *How "American" is Globalization?* Baltimore: Johns Hopkins University Press. Very thought-provoking and entertaining book showing, through examples from popular culture, that globalization is somehow both less and more American than commonly believed.

Said, Edward (1978) *Orientalism*. New York: Vintage. A foundational text in postcolonial studies, Said's book criticizes Western scholarship for being ideologically biased and creating an image of the Orient based on prejudices masquerading as scientifically informed depictions.

7

Risk

We joined Europe to have free movement of goods . . . I did not join Europe to have free movement of terrorists, criminals, drugs, plant and animal diseases and rabies and illegal immigrants.

—MARGARET THATCHER, CITED IN DAVID MORLEY, *HOME TERRITORIES*, 226

At the local level, globalization creates both opportunities and constraints, and globalizing processes also entail new kinds of risk and uncertainty. Rapid changes perceived—usually correctly—as being instigated outside the community, including changes in the economy, culture, or the environment, are interpreted and dealt with in a variety of ways in different parts of the world. In a more fast-paced, interconnected world, everything flows more easily, including contagious diseases, weapons, and invasive species that may wreak havoc with local ecosystems. Two main forms of globalized risk are climate change and terrorism, which in different ways highlight why risk and vulnerability must be considered key concepts in globalization.

The terrorist attacks on the United States on September 11, 2001, followed by attacks on Madrid and London in 2004 and 2005, respectively, signaled a new phase in the public awareness of what globalization was about. The upbeat optimism of the 1990s, when globalization was above all associated with the Internet, political freedom, individualism, and democracy among intellectuals and the general public alike, was now suddenly replaced by a heightened awareness of globalization as a volatile, anarchic, and dangerous state: It signaled the loss of control. While freedom, seen as an individual right, had been the main template for globalization in the 1990s, its close relative, insecurity, now came to the forefront. To millions of people, the new insecurity does not just refer to abstract climate change or debatable challenges to identities, but to their material livelihoods. A growing part of the world's workforce can be described as a *precariat* (Standing 2011), a precarious part of the proletariat, with few or no union rights, weak job security, and short-term contracts. The Swiss-owned transnational company Adecco, which hires out people temporarily, had 700,000 employees worldwide in 2010 and "has become one of the world's largest private employers" (Standing 2011: 33). As an increasing proportion of the global workforce are hired in temporary positions, as independent consultants, or in the informal sector, it may be the case that new job opportunities arise due to increased flexibility, but so does uncertainty and risk.

Although people may in a traditional past have been no more secure in their lives than members of the contemporary global middle class are—in many cases, they were far less secure—at least they tended to belong to a community by default. Nobody challenged their group membership, whether it was based on kin, religion, or locality; they knew who to turn to in times of need and scarcity, and they had a clear notion of the moral universe within which they lived. When contemporary social theorists speak of our era as somehow more insecure than the past, this is roughly what they tend to have in mind. Zygmunt Bauman's concept "liquid modernity" (2000) concerns the floating, shifting qualities of values and social structure in our era; Ulrich Beck's "risk society" (1992 [1986]) refers not to increased objective risks but to a heightened awareness of risks, and Anthony Giddens's term "post-traditional society" (1991) describes a society where a tradition can no longer be taken for granted, but must actively be defended vis-à-vis its alternatives, which now appear realistic.

These and many other concepts used to describe an era of increased inter-connectedness suggest that globalization makes people more vulnerable since the conditions for their existence are no longer locally produced and cannot be controlled.

Climate change, AIDS, terrorism, avian influenza, sudden economic downturns, invasive plant and animal species, and unpredictable waves of migration—there is a widespread feeling of vulnerability, easily translatable into a subjective sense of insecurity and powerlessness, in an overheated era of accelerated change, when conditions for local life are often felt to be defined elsewhere, at an abstract global level.

A term often preferred to vulnerability is risk. Risk can be defined as a function of probability and consequences. If the probability is high and the consequences negligible, the risk is estimated to be low. Conversely, even if the probability is minimal, the risk is considered high if the consequences are enormous. Of course, it is rarely possible to estimate risk objectively, but risk assessment is still important and can trigger action in many widely different areas, from financial investment to climate change.

As Beck writes, risks are in a sense both real and unreal: some risks have visible consequences already today (from terrorist attacks to deaths caused by water pollution), but "on the other hand, the actual social impetus of risks lies in the *projected dangers of the future*" (1992 [1986]: 34). Beck's seminal *Risk Society* and many later books on risk are concerned with issues like environmental destruction and climate change, AIDS and other transnational diseases, terrorism, and deterritorialized conflicts. Although

Beck's original statement was concerned with what he saw as a transformation of modernity, towards a less self-confident, less secure situation, the insights from the sociology of risk can easily be transposed onto the transnational canvas.

Natural and Manufactured Risks?

Sometimes, a distinction is made between *natural* and *manufactured* risks (e.g., Giddens 1999). Natural risks include snakebite and shark attacks, tsunamis and earthquakes, while the manufactured ones might have been avoided with the proper use of the foresight entailed by the precautionary principle, a notion that is widely used in the transnational environmentalist or green movement. However important it may be to indicate which risks and dangers can be avoided by human agency, there can be no sharp distinction between the two. If you know the whereabouts of sharks, being attacked is not a purely natural event if you choose to go into a shark-infested sea.

A more complex and more interesting example is that of the tsunami, which struck coastal areas in several Asian countries on Boxing Day, 2004. Thousands were killed, mostly locals, but also a considerable number of tourists perished. The material damage was enormous in Thailand, Malaysia, and Sumatra (Indonesia). In an important sense, the tsunami was a natural accident. The cause was an underwater volcanic eruption; it had nothing to do with the depletion of fish stocks, global warming, or pollution. At the same time, it was argued that with proper precautionary measures, such as an efficient early warning system, much of the damage could have been avoided.

There is an interesting parallel between the tsunami and the Lisbon earthquake in 1755. The latter was seen all over Europe as a horrible disaster. Some believed it was caused by the wrath of God; others saw it as an example of the amorality of nature and the lack of a higher meaning; yet others argued that the consequences were partly a result of poor foresight. The philosopher Jean-Jacques Rousseau, in particular, argued that if the Portuguese had been less urbanized and lived in a different kind of housing, the number of casualties would have been much lower. Voltaire, on the contrary, saw the earthquake as a meaningless event signifying the death of God and the futility of an overly optimistic belief in progress. Rousseau, in this way, represented the voice of those who called for proper early warning systems in 2004 and also showed that the distinction between natural and manmade risks can be misleading since many risks have elements of both.

By an uncanny coincidence, a major academic book on risk and vulnerability (Wisner et al. 2004), published on the eve of the Southeast Asian tsunami, uses a Japanese painting of a tsunami as its cover image. Ben Wisner and his co-authors make a powerful argument against the idea that certain forms of vulnerability, or risk, are purely natural, while others are manufactured. Following a similar line of argument to Rousseau, they argue that urbanization has led to a great increase in vulnerability in the poor parts of the world. The high population densities of cities makes it easy for disease to spread, and settlers in urban areas often have no other option than to "occupy unsafe land, construct unsafe habitations or work in unsafe environments" (Wisner et al. 2004: 70).

Although many risks and vulnerabilities are produced locally and can be alleviated through domestic policies, there can be no doubt that many different forms of vulnerability have been globalized, the most obvious being those that affect the poorest. Structural adjustment programs (SAPs), aiming to improve the economic performance of countries in the Global South, have led to cuts in public expenditure on health and education and have led to large-scale unemployment in many countries. The rich North Atlantic countries continue to protect their own agricultural sectors through subsidies and import tariffs while encouraging poor countries to open up their economies. Dependence on export earnings, typical of many agricultural sectors in the South, increases vulnerability because reliance on one or a few products reduces flexibility. If the cocoa crop fails or the price of cocoa declines, the consequences for the Ivorian economy are very serious indeed. In a past when agricultural production was largely intended for the local market or even the domestic sphere (the household), agriculture was more diverse and flexible and better able to withstand temporary setbacks affecting one or a few crops.

Although droughts and floods are natural occurrences (which may nonetheless be linked to global climate change), their consequences are anything but natural, and the causes of those consequences may often be traced to transnational economics (enhancing vulnerability) and the world of development aid (preventing some of the most horrible consequences). Thus, Rousseau was right in his unwillingness to blame disasters on God or nature alone. Even natural hazards are to some extent socially manufactured.

The Ethnic Elite

In Western Europe and North America, it is customary to think of ethnic minorities in terms of discrimination and deprivation. However, in large parts of the world, ethnic minorities constitute elites. Some of the standards imposed on countries by global agencies (like the IMF [International Monetary Fund]) and powerful states (like the United States) have created new tensions pitting the majorities against the ethnic elites. Within a dominant mode of thought, a multiparty democratic political system is favored, as is market liberalism. These entities, it is widely believed, will make the world a better place. This is assumed in the foreign policy of the rich countries, in trade agreements, and in leading development organizations.

On this background, the American law professor Amy Chua's book *World on Fire* (2003) deserves attention. Her argument is that the competence, networks, and work ethic of ethnic elites in many countries contribute to added value to the benefit of all of society. When society is pressured to introduce multiparty democracy and ideas about equality are allowed to spread, frustrations and hatred are directed towards the "market dominant minorities." The outcome may be riots and ensuing economic chaos.

It is easy to find examples that seem to confirm this general description. In Chua's country of origin, the Philippines, 1 percent of the population (the Chinese) control 60 percent of the economy. The Tutsi in Rwanda and Burundi may also be seen as a market dominant minority—at least that is how they were seen by the Hutu. Chua also speaks of Jews in Russia, Lebanese in West Africa, Indians in East Africa, Chinese in Southeast Asia, and whites in southern Africa. She also has interesting views on Latin America, where a conspicuous proportion of the elites are of purely European descent.

The tensions and riots described by Chua, which doubtless create economic chaos, not to mention massive loss of life, in many countries, are connected to transnational processes in at least two ways: The conditions for the targeting of successful ethnic elites are transnational—ideas about rights and equality and transnational business engaged in by the elites. Moreover, many ethnic elites participate modestly in domestic politics and make moderate contributions to the domestic economy. They often invest overseas and have strong obligations towards co-ethnics elsewhere.

Chua's solution consists in delaying the introduction of democratic rights until basic welfare provisions are in place. Another alternative might be to regulate the huge income differences between the elites and the majority through progressive taxation, and to create incentives for members of the majority to engage in the businesses controlled by the ethnic elites.

Towards the end of her book, Chua notes that the U.S. government's "ethnic policy for Iraq was essentially to have no ethnic policy. Instead, U.S. officials seemed strangely confident that Iraq's ethnic, religious, and tribal division would dissipate in the face of democracy and market-generated wealth" (2003: 291). She here indicates a main source of vulnerability in the contemporary world caused by the tensions wrought by globalization.

Perceived Risk and Real Consequences

Perceived vulnerability has increased in the rich countries too. The complexity of global systems precludes a proper overview and makes it difficult to make decisions on the basis of sound knowledge. The extent of a given risk or danger is difficult to estimate. Most of the readers will recall the global anthrax scare in the autumn of 2001. Appearing just after the 9/11 terrorist attacks on the United States, the appearance of deadly anthrax spores in letters sent to a few individuals on the East Coast was widely believed to be an alternative form of terrorism, and many believed that the terrorist network al-Qaeda was behind it.

Less than a dozen received letters contained anthrax spores, all of them on the East Coast. Yet, the perceived risk of being killed by a seemingly innocent white powder lacing a letter was huge worldwide. Postal servicemen were instructed to treat suspicious letters and packages with special caution, and commentators in the media feared that the world had only seen the beginning of a large-scale campaign.

Many of those who did not believe in the al-Qaeda hypothesis speculated that an Iraqi scientist (she was named, her picture published in newspapers worldwide) was the evil genius behind the campaign.

Interestingly, although no letters containing anthrax spores were found outside the United States, where seventeen persons were infected and five died, heightened security surrounding mail deliveries was imposed in many countries. Thousands of false alarms led to the careful opening, by authorized personnel wearing airtight uniforms, of letters and packages worldwide. In a few cases, entire office buildings were evacuated where suspicious letters had been identified.

Although the anthrax crime has, at the time of writing, not been solved, it has been ruled out that the letters had anything to do with either Iraq or al-Qaeda.

The example nicely sums up the argument so far: Perceived risk is a result of anticipated consequences rather than scientific probability, contemporary risks travel easily across and between continents, and there are enormous uncertainties involved in risk assessment. The fact that many risks are proven to be much less significant than commonly believed—what we fear is rarely that which kills us—the sociologist Frank Furedi (2002) has spoken of the contemporary obsession with risk as "a culture of fear." His argument is that the benefits from genetically modified foods, genetic research, and mobile phones, to mention three of his examples, are far greater than the risks involved, and that policy should therefore be based on optimism rather than anxiety. This rejoinder from a colleague of Giddens, Beck, and Bauman—three leading theorists who speak gravely of increased risk—should be kept in mind throughout this chapter. Since risks are largely psychological, their relationship to reality can always be disputed. It is nevertheless difficult to dispute the fact that some of the key issues of global politics in the early twenty-first century are to do with vulnerability and risk, both in rich and poor countries, although in different ways. Let us consider a few examples.

Invasive Species

An environmental problem, which has increasingly entered the political agenda in many countries, is that of introduced plant and animal species, which create imbalances, sometimes severe ones, in local ecosystems. Like so many other risks, the problems associated with alien species have recently grown in importance owing to accelerated and intensified globalization.

Many of the species, which are today considered invasive and damaging, were originally introduced voluntarily, often during colonialism. The possibly most famous example is the rabbit in Australia, introduced by the First Fleet in 1788 for food and kept in cages. In 1859, twenty-four rabbits were released for hunting purposes. They soon spread, bred like rabbits, and began to cause serious damage on crops. Rabbits have also contributed to the extinction of many indigenous plants.

Also in Australia, the Caribbean cane toad was introduced in 1937 to eat insects that caused damage to the sugarcane. The toad, first introduced in eastern Queensland, is now widespread in most of northern Australia. Being poisonous, the toad has perhaps been especially damaging to predators, but it has also outcompeted other amphibians in the area. A third example could be the Burmese python in Florida, originally brought to the state as pets, but some individual snakes must have been released or escaped from homes, quickly establishing a healthy breeding population and threatening a broad range of native species with no evolved defense methods against this alien invader, including deer, rodents, and even alligators.

One of the most infamous examples of invasive species causing havoc is that of the Nile perch in Lake Victoria, Africa's largest lake. This large and tasty fish was introduced into the lake in the 1950s and has since then caused the extinction or near extinction of several hundred native species of fish. It can easily be fished by large operators but has forced thousands of smaller fishermen out of business. In the award-winning film *Darwin's Nightmare* (2004), the filmmaker Hubert Sauper tells an even more complex story, demonstrating not only the ecological and economic consequences of Nile perch dominance in the lake but also that the same transport planes that are used to ship fresh fish on their way up (to Europe) bring weapons on their way down, thereby fuelling armed conflict in the region. The repercussions of the ecological changes wrought by this big, confident, and fast-breeding fish are, in other words, felt in several other subsystems, from security to economy and local organization.

Species have always spread, but the speed and compass of current dissemination of nonendemic species lacks precedent. Many marine species are introduced unwittingly through ballast brought by ships, while plants can spread just because someone brought a single specimen or a handful of seeds home for the garden.

Measures are being taken to limit or even eradicate invasive species. Yet, precisely the qualities that led to their becoming invasive make them difficult to catch. To many people whose livelihoods, leisure activities, or physical environment have been affected by destabilization caused by invasive species, the spread of unwanted plants or animals in one's immediate surroundings may appear as a condensed image of globalization gone mad, with the risks and disadvantages far outweighing the advantages. The example of invasive species, moreover, calls attention to the unintentional side effects of well-intentioned interventions—this is a general sociological phenomenon, but one that gains tremendous importance when crossing borders is made easier.

Climate Change

In 2008, a formal request was made to the Geological Society of London to create a new division in the world's geological history. Conventionally, the latest and current epoch is known as the Holocene, the comparatively warm period that began at the end of the last Ice Age around twelve thousand years ago, but some scientists felt that the last couple hundred years, beginning with the Industrial Revolution, deserve to be singled out as a separate era, the *Anthropocene*. The reason was that human activities now made their mark on the entire planet—its ecology, its surface, even its climate—

to such an extent that the only appropriate term for this period of growth, acceleration, connectedness, and overheating in its exploitation and use of natural resources, such as fossil fuels, would be a concept that tied it to our species.

The term "the Anthropocene" is taken seriously by many scientists, although it has not (yet?) been made an official label for our time. The key factor in its acceptance consists in the effects of human activities on the world's climate. Of course, it is complex. When asked to illustrate what they mean by irreducible complexity, theorists sometimes evoke two examples of systems that are complex in such a way that they cannot be described properly in a simplified manner: the fluctuations in the global financial market and the global climate. It comes as no surprise, therefore, that geophysicists and other climate experts disagree about the causes, likely effects, and political implications of contemporary climate change. Indeed, the U.S. government failed to ratify the 2002 Kyoto protocol, an attempt to commit all countries to reduce their CO_2 emissions, ostensibly because its representatives did not trust the scientific findings underpinning the treaty.

This much said, the vast majority of experts have long been convinced that the Earth's climate is changing and that human activity—notably the massive emission of greenhouse gases from deforestation and the use of fossil fuels—is a main cause. The scientific thinker James Lovelock, originator of the "Gaia hypothesis," according to which the planet can be studied as a self-regulating organism, once compared the present situation to a fever. In his 2006 book *The Revenge of Gaia*, Lovelock describes the narrow limits within which crucial parameters need to be for the Earth to be a livable place for a great variety of plants and animals. If the temperature increases with 5 degrees (Celsius), the entire tropical belt becomes desert. If the proportion of oxygen in the atmosphere rises a few percentage points above the current 21 percent, a mere spark will lead to a fire, but if it declines to 15 percent, it becomes hard to breathe and impossible to light a fire.

Lovelock's book, which shows how icebergs and glaciers shrink, how deserts grow, and how the development of the global temperature of the last hundred years can be mapped on a graph resembling a hockey stick, expresses an alarmist sense of vulnerability. With a population of a billion around 1800, he seems to argue, humanity could have done pretty much what we wanted; it would not have inflicted permanent damage on the precarious ecological equilibrium of the planet. With a global population of over seven billion (and growing—it was just over six billion when the first edition of this book was published in 2007), and a widespread technology based on fossil fuels, irreversible consequences are bound to occur.

A fascinating aspect of climate change is the way in which small changes may lead to enormous consequences, often on a global scale. In this way, climate change illustrates, better than most other global phenomena, the butterfly effect. Let us consider one brief example.

If the sea temperature in the tropical Pacific rises only 1 degree Celsius (1.8 degrees Fahrenheit) above the average, it results in the phenomenon known as El Niño in South America, leading to flooding in Peru and drought in Australia. As far away as the

Amazon basin, the effects of El Niño are felt through dry and hot weather, which may last for months. Forest fires are likely in Indonesia. Along the western coast of South America, fish becomes less abundant because of the higher water temperatures, and this in turn leads to a decrease in the guano production (fertilizer based on bird droppings). El Niño events also affect coral reefs adversely. During the 1997–98 El Niño, the enormous rainforest fires in Indonesia fed particles and smog into the ocean west of Sumatra. After the fires, the coastal seawater appeared to turn red, an effect caused by the proliferation of a tiny organism living off the iron in the smog particles. However, these organisms (dinoflagellates) produce toxins, which kill coral organisms. The naturalist Tim Flannery (2006: 107) comments that "it will take the reefs decades to recover, if indeed they ever do."

El Niño (and El Niña, which is caused by cooling and has different consequences) has been a regularly recurring phenomenon forever, but many scientists believe that El Niño-like events are now becoming more common because of the overall effects of humanly induced global warming.

There are visible signs of climate change elsewhere as well. Some indigenous Alaskan villages have been relocated because of rising sea levels, and the inhabitants of the low-lying Carteret Islands off New Guinea have been relocated to the higher-lying Bougainville Island (Orlove 2009).

Climate Change and Global Democracy

Describing the complexities of local responses to climate change in Greenland, where there are clear indications that the ice sheet is shrinking, Mark Nuttall (2009) describes sheep farmers at the southern tip of the island who "shake their heads in wonder as they dig potatoes from the ground and pluck their first harvests of broccoli, cauliflower, and cabbage" (296). Summers have become perceptibly longer and warmer in the Arctic area over the last few decades. As a rule, under conditions of global warming, temperatures rise fastest near the poles, and many Greenlanders see more opportunities than difficulties in this development. However, as is well known, the warmer conditions in Greenland entail warmer conditions elsewhere as well. Only a few degrees separate the Mediterranean from a semidesert state, and when glaciers melt in the Arctic, the influx of freshwater into the North Atlantic is believed to have adverse consequences for the Gulf Stream. Consisting of salt water, heavier than the freshwater of the shrinking glaciers, the Gulf Stream may already have been considerably weakened. However, there have so far been no perceptible consequences for the temperatures of northwestern Europe. Some scientists now argue that the contribution of ocean currents to climate has been exaggerated and that wind systems are more important. Others point out that when the Gulf Stream has slowed in earlier periods, the temperature has dropped by as much as 10 degrees Celsius in a decade.

The term environmental refugee has increasingly been used in recent years to describe displaced persons fleeing an environment destroyed by human activity. Used in a wide sense, the term might encompass many of the world's slum dwellers—ex-farmers whose fields were destroyed by highways, ex-fishermen facing dwindling returns because of water pollution, and so on. More dramatic are stories about entire communities that have been displaced because of recurrent flooding or the thawing of the permafrost on which their villages were built.

In 2004, Inuit organizations appealed to the Inter-American Commission on Human Rights for a legal ruling concerning alleged damages to their livelihood caused by climate change. There has been a sharp decline in the numbers of the animals traditionally hunted by the Inuit (bear, seal, caribou), and villages are becoming uninhabitable because of thaw (Flannery 2006). On the other side of the Bering Straits and in northern Scandinavia, indigenous reindeer herders are facing serious problems because of recurrent mild periods in winter. Reindeer survive in winter by digging through the snow for lichen, but melted snow becomes solid ice when refrozen. It cannot be dug through, and the animals frequently suffer fractures when they slip and fall.

The committee appealed to by the Inuits has no legal powers, but its ruling could make it possible to sue either the U.S. government or U.S. corporations. One can only imagine the complexities involved in suing transnational corporations for damages inflicted over perhaps a century and contributing to climate change with locally harmful consequences.

In some ways, the consequences of climate change illustrate George Monbiot's (2003: back cover) view that "everything has been globalized except democracy." It is difficult to see any international body, or organization, taking full responsibility for an entire nation forced to flee because of rising seawaters. Several Pacific states, along with the Maldives in the Indian Ocean, are flat coral atolls, which would be wiped out if the water were to rise a couple of meters.

Things can even get much worse, as Lovelock, Flannery, and many others are wont to point out. Many of the world's greatest cities, from Hong Kong to Calcutta and London, are located to flat landscapes at sea level. Some even believe that it is by now too late to reverse the tendency towards global warming and climatic instability. The world thermostat is sluggish and has taken a severe beating to be brought onto the present course, they argue, and even with a dramatic reduction in greenhouse gas emissions, the turmoil continues.

Wavering Trust in Expert Systems

A minority of climatologists have argued that the main cause of current climatic instability is the high solar spot activity, which has been noticed in recent years. Nonspecialists—that is, the vast majority of people, can only trust their own intuitions and what they are told by the experts, when they make up their minds. Faced with expert systems of knowledge, trust is essential, but when experts disagree or are proven wrong, that trust begins to erode. This is a central argument in Beck's sociology of modernity (1992 [1986], 1999) and in Giddens's writings on late modernity (1990, 1991), while Furedi (2002) has argued that the experts—scientific and technological— have in fact been right much more often than not.

The fact nevertheless remains that a strong reliance on the pronouncements of experts, which feed into policies, depends on widespread trust to be efficient, and environmental issues have to some extent jeopardized the trusting relationship between experts and the public. The expert system, one of Giddens's main forms of disembedding (discussed in Chapter 1), is an abstract and arcane body of knowledge, which is inaccessible to the vast majority of people.

Experts are sometimes wrong. Financial experts have routinely been unable to predict stock market crashes. The strategic experts of the FBI and the CIA were unable to predict and prevent the terrorist attack on the United States in 2001. Experts on marine life disagree about the numbers of minke whales in the North Atlantic. Few, if any, experts on Eastern Europe were able to predict the rapid demise of Soviet-style Communism, and nobody predicted, in 1991, that Fidel Castro would still be alive and exerting his power in Cuba in 2013. Predictions about the spread of contagious diseases, such as HIV-AIDS, Sars, Ebola, and avian influenza (bird flu), vary wildly.

In the world of computers and fast information networks, even some of the major predictions have been proved wrong. In 1943, the IBM CEO Thomas Watson pronounced that there might be a world market for about five computers. In the early 1980s, when personal computers became common, pundits predicted the advent of the paperless office. A decade later, as advanced telecommunications made video conferences and telephone meetings possible and affordable, many predicted that this would reduce air travel. Finally, at the end of the twentieth century, there was global anxiety around the so-called Y2K issue (the millennium bug), and billions were spent in attempting to prevent disaster.

The issue consisted in the fact that most of the world's mainframe computers, which ran elevators, ATMs, greenhouse thermostats, traffic lights, airspace controlling systems, and so on, had their basic programming done in the 1960s and early 1970s, when bytes were expensive. For this reason, programmers skipped the first two digits of the year, typing 79 rather than 1979. Because of the ambiguities arising on January 1, 2000, it was widely believed that computers worldwide would refuse to cooperate and break down. Even microcomputers, like the one I am using now, were believed to be at risk, since their software contained traces of the old software from the era before the cheap gigabyte.

Belief in Y2K overshadowed all other concerns associated with the turn of the millennium in the most computerized (richest) countries. Experts went on television stating that they had filled their basements with tinned food and water containers, their garages with firewood. Retired programmers were taken out of retirement to help in reprogramming the software. India's IT sector took off partly (some would say largely) because of the massive demand for programming expertise in the last couple of years of the twentieth century.

In the event, as everyone will recall, nothing dramatic happened to the world's computer driven systems as the century grinded to a halt, although it was reported that some Australian bus ticket validation machines failed to operate after the turn of the millennium.

The faith placed in the reality of the Y2K problem by governments, enterprises, and individuals all over the world suggests that the belief in expert systems can sometimes be regarded as blind faith. Lacking criteria for evaluating the predictions, many invoked the precautionary principle.

In a more serious vein, it should be noted that the expert knowledge systems used by transnational financial institutions, such as the World Bank and the IMF, have demonstrably failed to create economic stability and prosperity in the Third World countries who followed them (Gray 1998; Scholte 2005; Stiglitz 2002; Rodrik 2011, and many others have documented this). The economic crisis affecting parts of Europe since 2010, often dubbed the Euro crisis, can similarly be attributed, at least partly, to a faith in economic models developed by recognized experts, but which did not correspond satisfactorily to the local realities.

The feeling that one cannot even trust the experts, more pronounced in the rich countries than elsewhere, since the demotic political discourse in these countries presupposes that experts are to be trusted, has led many to abandon faith in technological progress and social engineering. Some have turned to religion, thereby falsifying the secularization thesis popular among twentieth-century sociologists, according to which rationalization would slowly erode the basis for religion. On the contrary, demand for religious meaning seems to be rising. In addition to many other things, religion can alleviate a sense of insecurity and meaninglessness. The revival of religion in the wake of partial or failed modernization is a global—and globalized—trend. Islam has become the main identity marker for many, if not most, Muslims in the world. Pentecostal missions across the world, often surprisingly coordinated in their activities, enjoy substantial success in countries as diverse as Ghana, the Philippines, and Brazil. New age religions—that is, eclectic mixtures of a variety of religious impulses, have many followers in the rich world. Through a curious recursive movement, new age religion, much of which had its origins in India but was Westernized and adapted to modern society and lifestyles in the United States, has enjoyed a recent popularity in India itself. (Rhythmic music has made a similar cyclical movement from Africa to the New World and back.)

Religion, often poorly understood by the secularized academic elites, is a widespread alternative to the confusion, uncertainty, and sense of vulnerability created by faltering expert systems in a world of fast movement, deterritorialization, and uncontrolled change. It offers a coherent world and a meaning of life, usually including a mission in life, which has become increasingly difficult to deliver by the prophets of modernity.

Dealing with Global Risks Locally

Local communities around the world are not only affected in different ways by both the discourse around and the effects of climate change, but they also respond very differently. As pointed out by Jonathan Ensor and Rachel Berger (2009), "just as some cultures may be deeply and narrowly defined and thereby resistant to change (or certain forms of change), in others adaptation and flexibility are or have become part of life" (237). They go on to mention Kenyan pastoralists and sand-bank dwellers in Bangladesh as examples of peoples who are accustomed to adjusting and adapting to ecological fluctuations.

In the most diverse settings around the planet, people develop notions about global crises and the ways in which they affect local conditions. The concept of global climate change has spread almost as fast as the concept of universal human rights and is referred to in local settings in many parts of the world. Yet, perceptions of climate change, its causes, and possible remedies, vary considerably. Besides, struggles to mitigate environmental degradation are usually local. In a country such as Nepal, for example, there is little talk of climate change outside of certain international NGOs (nongovernmental organizations) and elite groups, but people around the country make considerable efforts to clean up rivers, prevent soil erosion, and save trees.

Quite often, however, the link between the local and the global is perceived and understood to be important. In the Indonesian environmental movement described by the anthropologist Anna Tsing in her book *Friction* (2005), several concerns blend and several lines of conflict—or friction—emerge. The environmental movement in Kalimantan (Borneo) depends on collaborating with and linking up with indigenous village leaders on the one hand and student activists on the other hand. The former's concern to save a way of life is distinctive from but compatible with the latter's educated concern with biodiversity and saving the lungs of the planet.

The environmentalist movement in Kalimantan faces formidable opponents. An ideology of development, combining technological optimism and—from the early 1990s—a strong belief in the blessings of deregulated markets, has dominated Indonesian politics. Resource extraction, from logging to mining, took place in both legal and illegal ways, as "big and small operators advanced privatization through military and political force, displacing earlier residents' resource rights" (Tsing 2005: 21). Following the Asian crisis of 1997–98, however, there was a considerable openness to alternative paths, and in the early 2000s, "Al Qaeda competed with Bollywood and Marx in shaping local visions" (Tsing 2005: 215). In this space, the environmental movement, already relatively strong not least because it was supported by some powerful state bureaucrats, saw opportunities for a different, nonmarket driven kind of globalization. Some had heard the story about Chico Mendes, the leader of the Brazilian rubber tapper movement who was killed in 1988, and found inspiration in the Brazilian movement for workers' rights and local autonomy. Similarly, the story of the Chipko movement in the Himalayas, where an ecological movement led by women and combining ecological and indigenous concerns served as a source of inspiration for the Indonesian activists. Tsing tells a complex story of alliances between environmental activists, religious groups, indigenous Dayak leaders, and national and transnational NGOs in opposing the standardizing, centralizing, and profit-maximizing companies. Their motivations may differ, but the cause is the same: "For the village head, it [keeping the timber company away] is a consolidation of her village territory; for Kompas Borneo [sustainable tourism organization], it is the growing legitimacy of environmental politics regionally; for WALHI [the Indonesian forum for the environment], it is the practice of grassroots support against government coercion and corporate land grabs" (Tsing 2005: 259). What these and others opposing the companies had in common was not a shared worldview but a common understanding of the right of local people to autonomy. Although the environmental challenges facing humanity are global, they can only be dealt with in concrete localities. Globalization creates new risks and vulnerabilities, but they are only perceived locally.

The AIDS Epidemic and Globalization

Epidemic diseases have played a major part in human history, not least in periods when there has been large-scale contact between formerly mutually isolated groups (Diamond 1998; McNeill 1977). Diseases that were trivial to Europeans, who had lived in close contact with domestic animals for millennia, were deadly to many Native Americans.

The AIDS epidemic is deadly everywhere, but its consequences vary geographically. Believed to have originated in central Africa, AIDS was first diagnosed in a group of homosexual men in Los Angeles in 1981. Soon found to exist in the Caribbean (Haiti) as well, AIDS had been reported in eighty-five countries by the end of 1986. Today, it is estimated that seventy thousand to one hundred thousand persons had been infected with the disease before it was named.

Since the mid-1980s, AIDS has spread quickly, but unevenly, throughout the world. In the North Atlantic, it remains a disease associated with syringe users and homosexual men. In the Middle East and North Africa, it remains a rare disease, clearly in large part owing to strong cultural restrictions on extramarital sex. In certain parts of Asia, notably India, China, and some Southeast Asian countries like Thailand, the disease is spreading quickly. Finally, in many countries in sub-Saharan Africa, the social and economic consequences of AIDS are, and have for some years been, disastrous. By 2013, eleven countries in this region had lost more than a tenth of their labor force because of AIDS. In a handful of African countries, the reduction in the labor force may reach 20 percent by 2020.

The uneven spread of AIDS illustrates a general fact about globalization: ideas, things, and people move faster than before, but not indiscriminately. Factors affecting their uneven movement are cultural, economic, and political. Yet, it must be pointed out that in a nonglobalized world or even in a slower, globalized world, the AIDS epidemic would have spread much more slowly if at all.

The varying impact of the AIDS epidemic also shows how vulnerability is contingent on many factors. In the rich northern countries, antiretroviral drugs now make it possible to live with HIV indefinitely without contracting AIDS. In most Muslim countries, transmission of the disease is slow and inefficient for cultural reasons. In Thailand and India, sex workers are a main source of transmission, whereas the pattern is different in many African countries, where casual sex is widespread, and women account for roughly half of the infected. In Botswana, Lesotho, Swaziland, Malawi, and Zimbabwe, the adult HIV prevalence rate is estimated at over 20 percent. Life expectancy has plunged. Millions of children are orphaned. Economic growth is set back. Some leaders even deny the connection between HIV and AIDS.

However, some African countries have been successful in containing AIDS, notably Uganda, where the prevalence has fallen from 15 percent in the early 1990s to less than 5 percent in 2012. The general explanation is that the Ugandan state, supported by international NGOs, has successfully taught the population how to avoid being infected. Monogamy and premarital abstinence have been key factors here, while condoms have been less important, partly because certain Christian aid organizations take a negative view of contraception. The antiretroviral drugs, which prevent HIV from developing into AIDS, are expensive, and transnational lawsuits are fought over the right to develop cheaper generic drugs for the benefit of Africans and others in poorer countries.

The HIV/AIDS epidemic illustrates the interwoven character of the contemporary world. It spread and grew thanks to the increased mobility of people, it has varying consequences locally because of important cultural, economic, and political differences between countries, and it can only be fought efficiently through transnational cooperation with a local resonance.

Globalization and Wars on Terror

Tsing mentions that the environmental activists in Indonesia seemed to become more pious during and after the 1990s, women covering themselves up in ways they did not do before. If we now move to another globalized risk, we soon notice that religion can be significant in other ways too. To what extent the 9/11 terrorists were ultimately motivated by religious sentiment is debated, but it is a well-documented fact that politicized religion has come to the forefront in many parts of the world in recent decades. The first example that comes to most readers' mind is that of political Islam, but political Hinduism has played a central role in Indian politics since the mid-1980s, and Christian interest groups have enjoyed growing influence on politics in the United States. On a more local scale, the number of witchcraft accusations has grown rapidly in many parts of Africa since the early 1990s.

This is not the place to give a thorough treatment to religion in globalization (see Beyer 2006), but the religious element in the ongoing conflict between Jihadists and secular forces, including the United States and its allies, is clearly very important, probably on both sides. In the present context, however, I should like to emphasize the effects of deterritorialized warfare on perceived vulnerability.

The terrorist attacks that destroyed the World Trade Center and damaged the Pentagon on the morning of September 11, 2001 were difficult to classify with conventional criteria. The American president would soon denounce them with a declaration of war on terrorism, but war is normally declared on another country, not on an ideology or a deterritorialized political practice. The uncertainty concerning whether to see the terrorist acts as a very large crime or as a military attack implied a threat to the boundary between the outside and the inside of American society (Eriksen 2001a). Had it been interpreted as a crime, the federal police would have been charged with finding the surviving terrorists, collaborating with police elsewhere through the transnational police organization Interpol, and involving intelligence personnel when necessary. Since the government interpreted the attack as military, however, military retribution would be required. A temporary result of this interpretation was the presence of heavily armed soldiers at the entrances of public transport hubs, such as the Grand Central Station in New York.

Enemies of a sovereign state are usually abroad and could traditionally be identified as other states. However, these enemies seemed to be neither outside nor inside. Unlike terrorists in other locations, they were not just opposed to the political regime of the state but to its very existence and that of its inhabitants (according to a declaration made by Osama bin Laden in 1998).

Some of the state's enemies were physically inside it. The suicide bombers were themselves bona fide residents of the United States, several of them—infamously— students at a flight school (but curiously uninterested in learning how to land a plane). However, the network of militant Islamists of which they were a part, al-Qaeda, was decentralized and to a great extent deterritorialized. This meant that the enemy was neither a group of insurgents or revolutionaries wishing to overthrow the regime in Washington, nor a resentful alien state.

As is well known, the reactions of the United States to the terrorist attack were comprehensive and wide ranging. A war was waged against the Taliban regime of Afghanistan, which had sheltered and supported al-Qaeda, and many of their leading officers were believed to hide in the country. The Taliban removed from power in Kabul (and left to fight a perpetual guerilla war against what some continue to perceive as a puppet regime installed by the Americans), the United States went to war against Iraq in 2003, following undocumented (and later disproved) claims that Iraq's secular dictator Saddam Hussein had a collaborative relationship with al-Qaeda and that the country had developed weapons of mass destruction. It was only in 2011 that Osama bin Laden was finally tracked down and killed.

Human Rights and Security

In the same period, in the words of human rights scholar Richard A. Wilson (2005: 6), "the Bush Administration advanced a formulation of international security that detached [human] rights from security concerns." The prison camp in the American Guantánamo base in Cuba, for example, is operated outside, and in violation of, international law. It remains operative in 2013, years after President Obama promised to close it down. The United States has also tried to undermine "the ICC [International Criminal Court] through bilateral agreements which grant a special exemption from prosecution for U.S. soldiers" (Wilson 2005: 6). Enhancing all forms of security associated with civilian air travel, the United States has also fortified embassies overseas, sometimes moving them from city centers into locations easier to guard. The impression given to the outside world is that of a society under siege at home and at war abroad.

The failure of the United States to destroy al-Qaeda and associated groups illustrates a contrast introduced early in this book between the territorial power and the decentralized network. Any number of fighter planes, commandos, and warheads is insufficient to destroy a versatile, flexible, and mobile network of committed adversaries. At a structural level, the war on terror has some resemblance to the attempts to remove child pornography from the Internet. States deploy their territorial power and may be able to find and catch users and some producers of child pornography, but since the actual material is located on servers overseas, which can be moved quickly and easily to new locations, the offending pornography as such can scarcely be removed.

A survey commissioned by *Foreign Policy* in September 2006 indicated that eighty-six of the one hundred experts surveyed believed that the world was now more dangerous than it was five years earlier, and eighty-four believed that the United States was losing the war on terror. A significant majority believed that the country was becoming less safe as a result of the draconian measures, unpopular in large parts of the world, Muslim and non-Muslim, taken against terrorism.

The war on terror is instructive as a lesson on globalization.

First, it shows that the boundary between a society's inside and outside is relative.

Second, it confirms the hypothesis that in a global information society, flexible networks are a superior mode of organization to the territorially based hierarchy.

Third, it is an example of a truly transnational, deterritorialized conflict. Terrorist suspects (and perpetrators) have been caught in Spain, France, Denmark, Germany, Pakistan, and many other countries.

Fourth, it gives many examples of the global repercussions of transnational processes. In the remote northern Norwegian port of Tromsø, for example, an unbeautiful fence has been built along the formerly picturesque seafront, for the sake of the security of foreign, mostly American cruise ship passengers. A taxi driver in New York, originally from El Salvador, told the British writer Tariq Ali (2002) that he supported al-Qaeda because the United States, in his view, had destroyed his own country and forced him to migrate. Other wars, such as Israel's attack on Lebanon in the summer of 2006, are indirectly connected to this transnational campaign.

Fifth and lastly, but not least importantly, the war on terror indicates that the attention of others, and their respect, are in short supply in an era of global communication. Osama bin Laden and his ideological allies rarely spoke of imperialism and global capitalism as their adversaries but often use words like respect, dignity, and humiliation. Many non-Americans have been struck by the ease with which the United States accidentally kills large numbers of civilians during their campaigns against a particular government or a particular terrorist group. This has led many to conclude that a Muslim life has a much lower value than an American one.

* * *

Writing a few years before the 9/11 attacks, Manuel Castells (1998) prophesied that international terrorism would be the main security threat in the rich countries in the global network society. At the time of writing, he seems to have been proven right, notwithstanding the fact that the number of people killed by terrorists remains very low compared with almost any other cause of death. As Furedi rightly points out (2002), what we fear is rarely that which actually kills us. Besides, it should be pointed out that the majority of terrorist attacks are carried out by individuals other than Muslim fundamentalists. The terrorist attacks in Norway on July 22, 2011, which left seventy-seven dead and dozens injured, were carried out by a single right-wing extremist resentful of immigration and Muslims in particular.

Did September 11, 2001 represent a turning point in the short history of the post-Cold War world? I have suggested, at the outset of this chapter (and, at greater length, in Eriksen 2001a), that while the 1990s was chiefly an optimistic decade where globalization was generally associated (in the rich North Atlantic societies) with openness, communication, prosperity, human rights, and peace, the world entered a paranoid phase of globalization with the terrorist attacks. Suddenly, the Internet was not the main metaphor for globalization—it was terrorism. Everything travels more freely in a globalized era, including hatred and resentment.

This, one may be allowed to hope, is too bleak a prospect. It should be kept in mind that globalization is not a process with a particular direction; it is not directed towards a specified end. Ideas about human rights and democracy continue to spread; the battle against some dreadful diseases is successful; migration gives new hope to millions of people; and global communication makes global solidarity and a cosmopolitan outlook possible in ways that were unthinkable two generations ago. At the same time, globalization also entails the spread of deadly diseases, destructive ideas and practices, fundamentalism, and paranoia, drugs, and weapons. It brings us closer to each other through instantaneous communication and travel, but it also brings us further from each other by continuously reminding us of the deep differences in values, lifestyle, and opportunity that continues to divide us, probably more painfully than ever before.

- Globalization changes the risk environment because of increased interdependence and ensuing vulnerability.
- Risk perception rarely corresponds with objective risk: what we fear rarely kills us.
- Climate change is simultaneously a result of (economic and technological) globalization and an example of a truly global risk.
- Transnational terrorism contributes to breaking down the boundaries between a society's inside and outside.
- Common policy dilemmas in the context of serious perceived risk consist in the tension between security and rights.

Questions

- A distinction is often made between natural and manufactured risks. What is the main limitation of this perspective?
- What could be some of the social and economic consequences of climate change, and how is it that cause, effects, and remedies must be seen as global in character?
- Give a few examples of false alarms resulting from fear of unmanageable global processes. Why are they so widespread?
- What is the role of experts in assessing risks, and why do many feel that they have failed?
- How can politicized religion be a possible result of a heightened sense of risk and vulnerability?
- In what way did the 9/11 terrorist attacks break down the inside/outside boundary of American society, and how does this relate to globalization?

Further Reading

Adger, W. Neil, Irene Lorenzoni, and Karen O'Brien, eds. (2009) *Adapting to Climate Change: Thresholds, Values, Governance.* Cambridge: Cambridge University Press. This very comprehensive, interdisciplinary reader covers both historical and (mostly) contemporary examples of societies' ways of adapting—or not adapting—to climate change.

Tsing, Anna Lowenhaupt (2005) *Friction: An Ethnography of Global Connection.* Princeton, NJ: Princeton University Press. This book by an anthropologist demonstrates the enormously complex networks and links creating alliances and frictions around logging and environmentalism in Borneo. It shows who the actors are, what is at stake for them, why conflict is inevitable, and how the global is connected with the local.

8

Identity Politics

*Neo-tribal and fundamentalist tendencies, which reflect and articulate
the experience of people on the receiving end of globalization, are
as much legitimate offspring of globalization as the widely acclaimed
"hybridization" of top culture—the culture at the globalized top.*
—ZYGMUNT BAUMAN, *GLOBALIZATION—THE HUMAN CONSEQUENCES*, 3

*Globalization is fundamentally dual: It simultaneously leads to homogenization and new
forms of diversity, and its large-scale processes are recontextualized and embedded in
preexisting local realities and practices. It can even be said that a characteristic feature
of globalization is resistance to globalization, often by globalized means, such as new
information technology and transnational networking. The field of identity politics is
a particularly apt domain for studying this kind of dynamics: While such movements
rest on assumptions of cultural uniqueness and rootedness in a tradition, they have to
present and promote their interests in ways that have been standardized at a global
level. At the same time, identity politics represents a concerted effort to reembed
something under threat of being disembedded—namely, collective identity.*

An important insight from recent studies of globalization and modernity is the fact
that modernization and increasing scale in social organization are marked by a
complex process of simultaneous homogenization and differentiation. Some differences
vanish, whereas others emerge. As the anthropologist Jonathan Friedman puts it:

> Ethnic and cultural fragmentation and modernist homogenization are not two
> arguments, two opposing views of what is happening in the world today, but two
> constitutive trends of global reality. (1990: 311)

Phrased more generally, *disembedding* is always countered by *reembedding*. The more abstract the power, the sources of personal identity, the media flows, and the commodities available in the market become, the greater will the perceived need be to strengthen and sometimes recreate (or even invent) local foundations for political action and personal identity, locally produced books and songs, products with the smell, the sound, the taste of home. We cannot generalize bluntly about this. Many people are perfectly happy to live in a disembedded world, and hundreds of millions are so poor, disenfranchised, and marginalized that the problem never occurs to them—or if it does, it appears as a dream of slick affluence. Yet, reembedding processes are sufficiently comprehensive, varied, and influential to defend its place as we approach the end of this journey through some of the main dimensions of globalization. This chapter looks at identity politics as a means to reembed, while the next chapter presents some of the social movements previously described as the antiglobalization movement, currently more often described as alterglobalization movements.

While, as a postgraduate student in the mid-1980s, I was planning my first fieldwork in Mauritius, recognizing the ethnic plurality of its population and the mixed composition of settlements, I imagined Mauritians to have a profoundly reflexive, negotiable, and ambivalent attitude to cultural practices and ethnic identity. Being confronted with a bewildering array of options, epitomized in the everyday lives of their neighbors, I expected them to treat group identification with ironic distance. This did not turn out to be the case. In fact, the majority of Mauritians took their own notions and conventions for granted, more or less ignoring what their neighbors were up to. Moreover, the social universe inhabited by most Mauritians was much simpler than an assessment of the actual ethnic diversity of the island would lead one to expect. Categories were lumped and taxonomies were simplified, and group identification was usually taken for granted. This reminds us of the trivial but often forgotten fact that cosmopolitan societies do not necessarily create cosmopolitans, that globalization does not create global people. "The social thickness of the global" spoken of by Sassia Sassen (2003: 262) refers to the webs of commitment, sometimes spanning thousands of kilometers, cultivated by denizens of transnational space (see Lien and Melhuus 2007).

In other words, millions of people are transnational, not in the sense of being uprooted and free-floating agents, but in the sense that they maintain important ties of moral obligations across vast distances. Upon close examination of these transnational ties, it often turns out that they resemble the old ties in the sense that they build on similar commonalities and obligations (see Eriksen et al. 2010).

The Globalization of the Insult

Today, messages travel instantaneously and unpredictably across the globe. As a result, they risk being taken out of context, misunderstood, or exaggerated in significance. It should also be pointed out, however, that the globalization of communication makes a truly global conversation among humanity possible for the first time in history.

Does such a global conversation make self-censorship necessary in order to avoid offending the sensibilities of others, or does increased openness rather enable a deeper mutual understanding and empathy across countries and continents? The Danish cartoon affair may shed light on this question.

The largest subscription newspaper in Denmark is the conservative *Jyllands-Posten*, based in the second largest city of the country, Aarhus, in the center of Jutland. In the summer of 2005, Flemming Rose (2006), the culture editor of the newspaper, decided to invite the leading newspaper cartoonists of the country to make cartoons depicting the Prophet Muhammad, ostensibly in order to demonstrate that the freedom of expression was nonnegotiable and absolute in liberal Denmark, or in his own words, to "find out how far the self-imposed censorship had gone." The resulting twelve cartoons were published in the weekend edition of *Jyllands-Posten* on September 30, 2005.

The cartoons were diverse in their intentions and capability to enrage (although the general ban on depicting the Prophet in Sunni Islam must be kept in mind, indicating that any drawing of Muhammad might in principle be seen as offensive). The most infamous one is the depiction of Muhammad wearing a bomb in the shape of a turban on his head.

Soon after the publication of the cartoons, and following a petition from Danish imams, the ambassadors of eleven Muslim countries requested a meeting with Prime Minister Anders Fogh Rasmussen, who declined, responding by letter that it was not the Danish government's business to interfere with the freedom of expression and the press. A few months later, two Danish imams travelled to Egypt and Lebanon, carrying with them a dossier, which not only contained the cartoons, but also several other pieces of alleged evidence of discrimination against Muslims in Denmark. They met with politicians and religious leaders, asking for support in protesting to the Danish state, and were able to present their case at the summit of the Organization of the Islamic Conference in Mecca. In Denmark, the Muslims who went to the Middle East were roundly denounced as traitors by some, including the leader of the right-wing Danish People's Party, Pia Kjærsgaard.

By the beginning of February 2006, protests in a number of countries had turned violent. Embassies were burnt down in Damascus and Beirut; Libya closed its embassy in Copenhagen, armed men stormed the EU offices in the Gaza Strip, and there were angry demonstrations in many countries with substantial Muslim populations. During the riots in early February, people were killed in Gaza, Libya, Pakistan, and elsewhere (but, ironically, not in Europe); in Nigeria alone, thirty-eight people were reported killed during anticartoon riots.

At the same time, the cartoons were reprinted as an act of solidarity in several other countries; *Die Zeit*, the *Times of India*, *France-Soir*, *La Stampa*, *El Periodico*, and *El Mundo*, to mention a few, printed them—even the BBC showed the cartoons on TV. This transnationally coordinated publication could be seen as a defense of the freedom of expression, but it could equally well be seen as an oblique critique of Islam and Muslims. Many other Western newspapers did not publish the cartoons, seeing their inflammatory potential.

This was not merely a case of Western liberalism against Muslim censorship. The Egyptian newspaper *El Fagr* actually reprinted six of the cartoons in October 2005.

The question of a boycott of Egyptian goods was, naturally, not raised at the time. A Jordanian weekly, *Al-Shihan*, published three of them in February 2006, along with the rhetorical question: What harms Islam the most, these pictures or images of violent hostage-takers in Iraq? (The editor was dismissed, and the newspaper was removed from the kiosks.)

Opinion remained divided, both in the West and in Muslim countries, about the cartoons. Clearly, *Jyllands-Posten* was legally entitled to publish them, but many argued that it was unwise and a deliberate provocation. Others insisted that the freedom of expression should entail the right to offend. There is no neutral, objective solution to this kind of dilemma, but the case demonstrates that the insult (and, perhaps, the misunderstanding) is globalized along with everything else (Eriksen 2013).

The Politicized Concept of Culture

Culture, Raymond Williams has written (1976: 87) in a much quoted passage, is one of the two or three most complex words of the English language. The meaning of the word, Williams shows, has gone through many changes since the original Latin *colere*, which referred to the cultivation of the soil. Today, the word has several, if related, meanings.

One of the most common meanings of culture posits it as synonymous with the way of life and worldview the members of a particular group or community have in common, which distinguishes them from other groups. This definition may at first seem plausible, but it does not survive closer scrutiny. Within nearly every group or people there are varying ways of life and worldviews; the rich differ from the poor, the men from the women, the highly educated from the illiterates, the urban from the rural, and so on. Additionally, as shown above, it is often extremely difficult to draw boundaries between cultures. If one argues that a Norwegian culture exists and is by default different from Danish culture, one will need to show what it is that all Norwegians share with each other but not with a single Dane. That is not an easy thing to do. Finally, culture is not naturally a solid object, even if the word unhappily is a noun. Culture is something that happens, not something that merely exists; it unfolds through social process and therefore also inherently changes. It should have been a verb.

Problems of this kind have made such a conceptualization of culture difficult to manage, and many scholars have ceased to use it, while others insist on using culture in the singular sense, as that which all humans have in common, defining them as a species as opposed to nature in general and other species in particular.

However, ideologists and political entrepreneurs of many shades have embraced this Romantic concept of culture. In recent decades, culture and cultural identity have become important tools for the achievement of political legitimacy and influence in many otherwise very different societies—from Bolivia to Siberia. It is used by political leaders of hegemonic majorities as well as by the spokespersons of weak minorities.

Indigenous peoples all over the world demand territorial rights from the states in which they live, emphasizing their unique cultural heritage and way of life as a crucial element in their plea. Immigrant leaders in Europe occasionally present themselves as the representatives of cultural minorities, demanding, inter alia, special linguistic and religious rights. The hegemonic elites of many countries also refer to their national culture in justification of warfare or oppression of ethnic minorities. Cultural pleas are, in other words, put to very different political uses.

A frequently mentioned paradox concerning the breakup of Yugoslavia in the 1990s and subsequent wars is the fact that the fighting parties, Serbs, Croats, and Bosnian Muslims, were culturally very similar, yet justified their mutual animosity by claiming that they were actually profoundly different. This kind of situation, where ethnic relations between groups that are culturally close take on a bitter and antagonistic character, is more common than widely assumed. In Trinidad, in the southern Caribbean, the following development has taken place in recent decades: The two largest ethnic groups, Africans and Indians (originally from India; they are not American Indians), have gradually acquired more and more in common, culturally speaking in terms of language, way of life, ambitions, and general outlook. At the same time, they have become ever more concerned with expressing how utterly different they are; culture and cultural differences are spoken about more often, and cultural differences are brought to bear on daily life, public rituals, and political organization to a greater extent than what was earlier the case. Partly, this is because the groups are in closer contact than earlier and compete for the same scarce resources; but it is also partly because members of the two groups feel that their cultural boundaries are threatened by tendencies towards creolization and therefore feel an acute need to advertise their cultural differences.

The groups have simultaneously become more similar and more different. This paradox is characteristic of globalization processes, whereby differences between peoples are made comparable and therefore come to resemble each other and where small differences are enlarged. It could, in line with this, be said that the entire Western discourse over multiculturalism is embedded in a shared cultural framework encompassing, and bringing out the contradictions between, the Romantic notion of culture and the Enlightenment notion of individual rights. To put it somewhat more crudely: To make demands on behalf of a self-professed culture indicates that one subscribes to a shared global political culture. The logic of multiculturalism and ethnopolitics shares its dual origins with the logic of nationalism in the Enlightenment and Romantic thought of early modern Europe.

Perhaps it could be said, somewhat simplistically, that because people everywhere become more similar due to the forces of globalization, they try their best to be different. However, the more different they try to be, the more similar they become— because everybody tries to be different in the same ways. Deep cultural differences, which still exist in the realms of religiosity, the conceptualization of the person, kinship, and so on, are less likely to be politicized.

Identity Politics as a Response to Globalization

Recent years have witnessed the growth, in societies in all continents, of political movements seeking to strengthen the collective sense of uniqueness, often targeting globalization processes, which are seen as a threat to local distinctiveness and self-determination. A European example with tragic consequences is the rise of ethnic nationalism in Croatia and Serbia from the 1980s, but even in the more prosperous and stable European Union, strong ethnic and nationalist movements grew during the 1990s and into the new millennium, ranging from Scottish separatism to the anti-immigration Front National in France, nationalist populism in countries like Austria, Denmark, and the Netherlands, and, even more recently, neo-Nazis in Greece and the fervent nationalists of Jobbik in Hungary. In Asia and the Middle East, two of the most powerful examples from recent history were the rise of the Taliban to power in Afghanistan and the meteoric success of the Hindu nationalist BJP (Bharatiya Janata Party, Indian People's Party) in India towards the end of the last century; many African countries have also seen a strong ethnification of their politics since the late 1980s. To this could be added the rise of political Islam in the Sahel and the north of the continent. In the Americas, various minority movements, from indigenous groups to African Americans, have with increasing success demanded cultural recognition and equal rights. In sum, politics around the turn of the millennium has to a great extent meant identity politics.

This new political scene, difficult to fit into the old left–right divide, is interpreted in very different ways by the many academics and journalists who have studied them. This is partly because identity politics comes in many flavors: Some are separatist nationalist movements, some represent historically oppressed minorities, which demand equal rights, some are dominant groups trying to prevent minorities from gaining access to national resources, some are religious, some are ethnic, and some are regional. At the very least, identity politics from above (the state) must be distinguished from identity politics from below (popular movements).

Many writers see identity politics in general as an antimodern counterreaction to the individualism and freedom enhanced by globalization, while others see it as the defense of the weak against foreign dominance, or even as a strategy of modernization using the language of tradition to garner popular support. Some emphasize the psychological dimension of identity politics, seeing it as nostalgic attempts to retain dignity and a sense of rootedness in an era of rapid change; others focus on competition for scarce resources between groups; some see identity politics as a strategy of exclusion and an ideology of hatred, while yet others see it as the trueborn child of socialism, as an expression of the collective strivings of the underdog.

Neither of these interpretations and judgments tells the whole story, both because the concrete movements in question differ and because the phenomenon of identity politics is too complex for a simple explanation to suffice. What is clear, however, is that the centripetal, or unifying, forces of globalization and the centrifugal, or fragmenting, forces of identity politics are two sides of the same coin, two complementary tendencies that must be understood well for anyone wishing to make sense of the global scene at the turn of the millennium.

A Grammar of Identity Politics

For a variety of reasons, globalization creates conditions for *localization*—that is, various kinds of attempts at creating bounded entities: countries (nationalism or separatism), faith systems (religious revitalization), cultures (linguistic or cultural movements), or interest groups (ethnicity). For this reason, a more apt term is glocalization. Let us now move to a general description of some features that the glocal identity movements of the turn of the millennium seem to have in common—the rudiments of a grammar of identity politics.

First, identity politics always entails *competition over scarce resources*. Successful mobilization on the basis of collective identities presupposes a widespread belief that resources are unequally distributed along group lines. Resources should be interpreted in the widest sense possible and could, in principle, be taken to mean economic wealth or political power, recognition or symbolic power. What is at stake can be economic or political resources, but the *recognition of others* has been an underestimated, scarce resource, as well as meaningful social attachments where one is in command of one's own life to an acceptable degree.

Second, *modernization and globalization actualize differences and trigger conflict*. When formerly discrete groups are integrated into shared economic and political systems, inequalities are made visible, since direct comparison between the groups becomes possible. Friction occurs frequently. In a certain sense, ethnicity can be described as the process of making cultural differences comparable, and to that extent, it is a modern phenomenon boosted by the intensified contact entailed by globalization. You do not envy your neighbor if you are unaware of his existence.

Third, *similarity overrules equality ideologically*. Ethnic nationalism, politicized religion, and indigenous movements all depict the in-group as homogeneous, as people of the same kind. Internal differences are glossed over, and for this reason, it can often be argued that identity politics serves the interests of the privileged segments of the group, even if the group as a whole is underprivileged, since it conceals internal class differences.

Fourth, *images of past suffering and injustice are invoked*. To mention a few examples: In the 1990s, Serbs bemoaned their defeat at the hands of the Turks in Kosovo in 1389; leaders of the Hindu BJP have taken great pains to depict Mughal (Muslim) rule in India from the 1500s as bloody and authoritarian; and the African American movement draws extensively on the history of slavery. Even spokesmen for clearly privileged groups, such as anti-immigrant politicians in Western Europe, may argue along these lines.

Fifth, *the political symbolism and rhetoric evokes personal experiences*. This is perhaps the most important ideological feature of identity politics in general. Using myths, cultural symbols, and kinship terminology in addressing their supporters, promoters of identity politics try to downplay the difference between personal experiences and group history. In this way, it became perfectly sensible for a Serb, in the 1990s, to talk about the legendary battle of Kosovo in the first person ("*We* lost in 1389"). The logic of revenge is extended to include metaphorical kin, in many cases millions of people. The intimate experiences associated with locality and family are thereby projected onto a national screen.

Sixth, *first-comers are contrasted with invaders*. Although this ideological feature is by no means universal in identity politics, it tends to be invoked whenever possible, and in the process, historical facts are frequently stretched.

Finally, *the actual social complexity in society is reduced to a set of simple contrasts*. As Adolf Hitler already wrote in *Mein Kampf*, the truly national leader concentrates the attention of his people on one enemy at the time. Since cross-cutting ties reduce the chances of violent conflict, the collective identity must be based on relatively unambiguous criteria (such as place, religion, mother-tongue, kinship). Again, internal differences are undercommunicated in the act of delineating boundaries towards the frequently demonized Other.

Identity politics is a trueborn child of globalization. The more similar we become, the more different we try to be. Paradoxically, however, the more different we try to be, the more similar we become—since most of us try to be different in roughly the same ways worldwide.

Against the view that identity politics is somehow anachronistic, it has been argued many times, always correctly, that although it tends to be dressed in traditional garb, beneath the surface it is a product of modernity and its associated dilemmas of identity. The strong emotions associated with a tradition, a culture, or a religion can never be mobilized unless people feel that it is under siege.

Viewed in this way, the collective emotions that identity politics depend on reveal themselves to be deeply *modern* emotions associated with the sense of loss experienced in situations of rapid change, disembedding, and deterritorialization. The need for security, belonging, and enduring social ties based on trust is universal and cannot be wished away. Ethnic nationalism, minority movements, and politicized religion offer a larger share of the cake as well as a positive sense of self, and these movements are bound to remain influential in large parts of the world.

Indigenous Strategies

Indigenous peoples are usually defined as ethnic groups associated with a nonindustrial mode of production and a stateless political organization (Eriksen 2010). The identity politics engaged in by such groups differ from that of nations and migrant minorities in that territorial autonomy and cultural self-determination are their main political goals. Engulfed by dominant states and increasingly incorporated into the global economy, indigenous groups fight legal battles on many fronts, claiming rights to land and water, language, their own artistic production, and political autonomy.

The forms of resistance engaged in by indigenous movements are diverse, ranging from institutional politics among the Sami of northern Scandinavia, who have separate parliaments with real but limited legislative power, to the armed uprising among peasants of Chiapas in southern Mexico, and less spectacular forms of everyday resistance. However, as Thomas Hall and James Fenelon (2004) point out in an important review of indigeneity and globalization, indigenous struggles against globalized external dominance tend to differ from class-based struggles through their emphasis on the following:

> local community, identity politics, land claims, and rights to a variety of traditional practices, which include alternative family organizations such as matrilineality and/ or polygyny, communal ownership of resources such as land, the use of land for sacred ceremonies, and indigenous knowledge, that occasionally includes use of psychoactive substances. (156)

Although indigenous groups may occasionally profit economically from global integration, their identity depends on a certain degree of political autonomy. Following Hall and Fenelon (2004), we may say that states have traditionally subdued indigenous groups through genocide (extermination), ethnocide (their enforced assimilation into the majority), or culturicide (the destruction of group culture, if not necessarily group identity). In defending their group identity as well as the cultural content of this identity, indigenous groups run into a broad range of problems, some of them to do with human rights, national law, and the universal rights and obligations of citizenship, and some simply to do with the brute force of the state and capitalism— indigenous peoples usually reject private property in favor of the communal ownership or stewardship of resources. A final set of problems pertain to the character and nature of indigenous culture, which is, like all other culture, influenced and transformed by reflexive modernity. What exactly does it mean to be a Lakota, a San, or an Inuit? Such issues are discussed vividly among scholars and indigenous peoples alike, but it must still be stressed that their main struggle is over land rights with accompanying political autonomy. Paradoxically, perhaps, many indigenous peoples have been assisted in their quest for self-determination by transnational agencies and even global organizations, such as the WCIP (World Council of Indigenous Peoples), leveling pressure on nation-states from a transnational or supranational point of leverage.

A recent development in indigenous identity work is the tendency, which can be observed in many areas, of shifting the emphasis from political rights claims to commercial ventures: Rather than portraying the ethnic community as a political entity, it becomes a kind of commercial organization. John Comaroff and Jean Comaroff (2009) have studied this process, drawing on examples from all over the world but with a particular emphasis on South Africa, seeing it as a feature of the global spread of neoliberalism. Let us consider a short example.

The Sami of northern Scandinavia have been obliged to relate to the state and Christian missions for more than two centuries, and since the Second World War, their organizations have worked politically to promote their ethnic and cultural interests. This struggle has mainly involved claims to land, political autonomy, and language rights. In recent years, like in the examples described by the Comaroffs, there has been a perceptible shift in the predominant Sami approaches to identity. Increasingly, Sami territories are being marketed with a view to increasing tourism, and the market for Sami handicrafts has likewise grown steadily, especially in the high designer end. One Sami woman, who now receives tourists in her home, serving traditional foods and entertaining the visitors with Sami tales and myths, explains that this activity brings her in contact with her origins in ways that feel more authentic than political activity would (Flemmen and Kramvig 2008). Now, she says, people voluntarily pay to hear her stories, to familiarize themselves with the Sami way of life, and to eat Sami food. This in turn has made it necessary for her to relearn her half-forgotten heritage. She contrasts her commercial venture with standard identity politics, which in her view represents a more negative approach, where the state or county would eventually give in to pressure, not because they see the intrinsic value of Sami culture, but because they feel they have to. At the same time, this kind of revitalization is individualized, unpolitical, and framed by a narrative of self-realization and personal achievement.

Attempts among indigenous peoples around the world, from Siberia and the Pacific to the Americas and South Africa, to achieve copyright to their immaterial cultural products and handicraft techniques, in order to prevent piracy and economic loss, have similarly become a pressing concern recently. Whereas this kind of identity work can be effective in strengthening collective pride and boosting self-esteem within the group in question, it can also be controversial, precisely because it moves the project of maintaining a cultural identity in an individualized, goal-rational, and commercialized direction. Many spokespersons from indigenous groups reject the logic of the market and the commercialization of their cultural identity, and this leads to frictions within the groups not dissimilar to the ones resulting from the tension between cultural purification and mixing, which will be considered below.

Indigenous Cosmopolitans

Globalization and indigeneity are two words that seem to sit uneasily together: Globalization refers to the spread of modernity, intensified contact across boundaries, cultural impurities (and reactions to it), uprooting, and creolization—while indigeneity is associated with a nonindustrial, nonmodern way of life, usually denoting historically stateless peoples with an oral cultural tradition rooted to a specific locality, landscape, or area.

It may, accordingly, be assumed that when indigenous peoples become urbanized and begin to enjoy the mixed blessings of modernity, which may include formal education, wage work, and life in a consumer society, they somehow cease to be indigenous. Yet, the lives of the small, stateless peoples of the world have been influenced by their contact, voluntary or not, with the outside world, before contemporary globalization and in most cases even before colonialism. Some of these groups have perished, some were assimilated and swallowed up by larger and more powerful entities, while a great many indigenous groups have survived into the twenty-first century, albeit not in unchanged form, and some are indeed experiencing a boost in their identity projects precisely in an age characterized by accelerated, intensified, and sometimes overheated transnational contacts. The transnational indigenous movement, which includes peoples from southern Africa, North and South America, northern Europe, and the Pacific, is itself made possible by globalization, as are some forms of cultural expression enabling contemporary indigenes to define and negotiate their identities in new ways.

Writing from the vantage point of North America, Craig Proulx (2010) notes that it is a common non-Aboriginal perception (Aboriginal is used as a synonym for indigenous) that "Aboriginal people become somehow less authentically Aboriginal when they move from reserves to cities and beyond" (39). He then moves on to describe a hybrid cultural form that has become popular among some First Nation and Inuit peoples in Canada, as well as among young Australian Aborigines—namely, rap and hip hop, a musical subculture with origins in Jamaica and among city-dwelling African Americans.

Speaking of his use of rap to express his cultural identity, MC Wire, a Gumbaynggirr man from New South Wales, explains that he cannot become a traditional man. Instead, as a "modern-day black fella," he uses hip hop as a "lyrical healin," enabling him to establish contact with the worldview and dreaming of his ancestors. Moreover, Proulx notes, hip hop has contributed to preserving some indigenous languages in Australia, as when the rapper Munki Mark raps in his grandmother's language Jardwadjali (from western Victoria).

In Canada, the indigenous Tribal Wizdom cooperative based in Vancouver uses hip hop as a means to raise consciousness about political issues, helping to "translate indigenous oral traditions into youth-friendly contemporary forms at a time when youth tend not to have time to sit and listen to elders or grass roots leaders" (Proulx

2010: 46). Other native rappers are more concerned with cultural identity than with political rights, and yet others do not emphasize their ethnic origins at all. The point is, nonetheless, that just like everybody else, indigenous people do not necessarily become less authentic by appropriating globalized, hybrid cultural forms. The conclusion may be that it is not where it comes from that matters but what you do with it.

Reembedding in Diasporas

National and other modern identities founded in traditionalist ideologies (they claim, persuasively, to be premodern) have proved to be extremely resilient. The enthusiasm for the proposed European Constitution in the EU member states is very modest, and the Constitution has failed to get a majority in any of the countries that have held referendums. With the emergence of the Euro crisis since 2010, affecting southern European countries in particular, both the common currency and the very project of European integration have been challenged forcefully in many countries, revealing that the common European identity may be a thin veneer above deeper and stronger national and local identities. Moreover, identification with national soccer teams in Europe and South America remains very strong, ethnic networks giving career opportunities for members of the in-group in polyethnic societies are thriving in many parts of the world, religions demanding the undiluted loyalty of their followers are on the rise, and everywhere, most people seem to prefer to watch locally produced programs on TV.

The human need for secure belonging in a community, however abstract (such as a nation or a religion of conversion), seems to be an anthropological constant, but it can be satisfied in many different ways and dealt with politically in different ways, too. Commitment to a group, which forms part of a larger, plural social universe, does not necessarily lead to xenophobia and conflict; it may equally well result in cosmopolitan tolerance (see Appiah 2006 on cosmopolitanism; Hannerz 1989 on "the global ecumene").

Creating a sense of security in an environment that changes rapidly can be hard work, and it seems particularly difficult for transnational migrants and their descendants, who are confronted with opposing pressures from their immediate surroundings. The states in which they live may demand their full and undivided loyalty, or they may do quite the opposite and deny them citizenship and political rights. Both alternatives create stress and ambiguity among migrants. The classic modern notion of citizenship as the sole key to political identity is difficult to maintain at a time when dual loyalties, exile, and movement are widespread.

Solutions to dilemmas of identity and belonging among uprooted people vary. Some seek to be assimilated in the new country and effectively to change their group identity. This has to a great extent happened over the last 150 years with Poles in Germany and

Swedes in Norway, but not with Irish in Britain. With transnational migrants who may have a different skin color and religion than the majority, full assimilation does not seem to take place anywhere, although New World countries like the United States and Canada have a more open-ended national identity than most Old World countries, from Ireland to Japan. As a rule, migrants and their children remain attached to their country of origin. The tie tends to be weakened in the second generation, whose members have invested more in the new country than their parents, but what happens in the third generation depends to a great extent on the ability of the host country to expand its national identity to encompass the descendants of relatively recent migrants.

Whether or not full assimilation is possible, most migrants and their children retain important transnational ties (see Cohen 1997 for a wealth of historical and contemporary examples) and draw extensively on ethnic or religious networks in the new country. Far from being the fragmented and alienated people one might expect migrants to be, given their ambiguous political and cultural position, they tend, broadly, to reproduce important aspects of their original culture in the new setting. This is often met with animosity in sections of the majority population, who may insist that the newcomers do their best to adapt to the host society; but at the same time, this option is often closed to immigrants who face discrimination and differential treatment from the majority. A connection to a homeland, be it the tiny Caribbean island of Nevis (Olwig 2003) or a future independent Kurdistan, gives a sense of attachment, which can otherwise be difficult to develop in alien surroundings. The cultural conservatism often witnessed in migrant populations, not least among Muslims in Europe, is understandable as a reaction to hostility and indifference in the majority population. Moreover, as James Rosenau has argued in a number of works (e.g., 1990), the authority of the state has become increasingly problematic, not only with respect to immigrants, but in general, because of increased turbulence and uncertainty—what we might call effects of globalization (cf. Croucher 2004: 51–52). The sociologist Daniel Bell, writing as early as 1973, spoke prophetically of the nation-state as being too small for some tasks and too large for others; it was too small to solve the problems facing humanity and too large to give the individual a secure sense of identity.

Trust and Social Capital

A successful immigrant entrepreneur in Oslo explained on television in 2004 that the secret of his success consisted in employing only people from his own ethnic group. He knew their fathers, their cultural idioms, and their norms. He could exert moral pressure on them in a way that would have been impossible with ethnic Norwegians. This kind of practice is typical of ethnic entrepreneurs everywhere. As John Gray (1998: 182ff.) notes, the *guanxi* ethos of reciprocity and mutual trust is a key element in the economic success of Chinese businessmen overseas, much more important than formal agreements.

It is also known that interest-free loans among relatives are common among many moral communities consisting of migrants, as is the kind of transaction typified through the *hawala* transmission of money via middlemen from refugees to kinspeople in Somalia. First-generation Tamil migrants may, in some respects, be poorly integrated into greater Norwegian society, but they are tightly integrated among themselves and, in important ways, in their Sri Lankan communities, through kin and caste-based loyalties with economic, political, and social dimensions.

The burning question is what or who to trust. In the classic sociology of Weber, Tönnies, and their supporters, it was believed that trust tended to be interpersonal in the *Gemeinschaft*, or traditional society, while it would be linked to abstract institutions in the *Gesellschaft*, or modern society. The citizen of a modern state is expected to trust the state, while the tribesman supposedly trusts his relatives and covillagers. In fact, things are less simple. The networks of the "network society" (Castells 1996) are often interpersonal, and what keeps them going is trust. A Manhattan banker or a Danish bureaucrat depends crucially on informal networks enabling him to do his work and to feel part of a community, just as a Turkish immigrant in Germany depends on ethnic networks to satisfy his needs, of which the sense of security is one.

Informal interpersonal networks continue to exist side by side with the formal organization of any society, and interpersonal trust continues to be crucial. In a society with a great deal of mobility and few historically based communities—namely, the United States—scholars and commentators have for years been deeply engaged in a discussion on the future of community. The sociologist Robert Putnam argued in *Bowling Alone* (2000) that civil society and the webs of commitment and trust that made up American communities were eroding—in effect that the moral communities (*Gemeinschaften*) of the United States were being weakened. Putnam's perspective, and not least his concept of *social capital*, has been taken on by scholars in many countries trying to investigate the extent of trust in our changing, complex societies.

Trust presupposes familiarity, and familiarity presupposes regular contact. The amount of work invested into networks just to keep them going is tremendous in the informational network society. Think of yourself as a student or scholar. Responding to e-mails, sending and receiving SMS messages, or talking on the phone to people in conversations where the main objective consists in reminding them of your existence, is likely to take up a major proportion of your precious time. The vulnerability of moral communities based on trust and reciprocity thereby made tangible is chronic. This does not mean that they no longer exist or no longer exist in the West but that keeping them operative requires continuous effort when society is complex (i.e., does not consist of a single moral community) and especially so when one's personal network is partly transnational. In this sense, Anthony Giddens (1991) is right in claiming that our era is post-traditional. Tradition no longer recommends itself—it must be defended actively; similarly, communities of trust and commitment no longer perpetuate themselves through convention but must be guarded and nurtured. Yet, they remain powerful attractors—the first place to look for ordering instances in a world of teeming movement.

The vision of the individual as a hybrid, moving, unstable entity engaging in networks of variable duration, dominant in the anthropological globalization discourse, is limiting and exaggerated. Moral commitments in relationships, cultural conservatism, and coercive pressures to conform remain extremely powerful everywhere. However, they no longer encompass all of society. This is why life on the New York streets is so unsafe; the reason is not that individuals are not full members of moral communities based on trust and reciprocity, but that the people they are likely to encounter in dark alleys belong to other moral communities. If I may make a brief comparison to traditional societies, this situation resembles that of intertribal encounters in highland New Guinea as described by the anthropologist Marshall Sahlins (1972). Within the tribal group, generalized reciprocity is the norm—that is, sharing based on trust. Among neighboring people, the main kind of relationship is exchange in the market place. With total strangers, however, any kind of action, including theft ("negative reciprocity"), is legitimate. Similarly, interpersonal trust and moral commitment in plural, complex societies are unlikely to encompass everybody. The single mother of Somali origin living in Amsterdam is likely to find a sense of security among other Somalis, but not in greater Dutch society.

Transnational networks are interpersonal, imbued with trust and intimacy, and these qualities form the moral basis for exchange. In order to understand globalization, it is far from sufficient to look at macro processes; we must also pay attention to the webs of trust and reciprocity that create transnationalism at the micro level—and towards the situations where reciprocity fails, creating unpayable and humiliating debts of gratitude, silencing at the receiving end of unidirectional systems of exchange, exclusion from dominant circuits, and a lack of respect. When the late Osama bin Laden spoke about the United States or Israel, he sounded almost like a disenchanted ragamuffin: as mentioned in the last chapter, there is nothing about economic domination or world imperialism in his rhetoric, but words translated as arrogance and humiliation recur. The implications of not being seen and respected are clearly an underestimated affliction in the contemporary world and are a main cause of such forms of reembedding as political Islam and nationalist ethnopolitics.

Neonationalism and Islamism: Two Sides of the Same Coin?

As I have shown in Chapter 6, hybrid cultural forms are often counteracted by quests for purity and authenticity, which may be, but are not necessarily, politicized in situations of increased ethnic diversity due to immigration. What is, nevertheless, clear is that one main effect on the public sphere of the forms of mixing engendered by globalization is a heightened polarization and a strengthened conflict potential around group identities. Although few in the Western world today subscribe to the fiction of cultural purity, neonationalist movements reacting to the impurities and unpredictable changes taking place by insisting, often in militant ways, on the authenticity and moral superiority of that which is rooted and local. Neonationalism, often targeting immigrants and especially Muslims as the unwanted other, is on the rise in many Western countries. In Greece, the openly neo-Nazi party "Golden Dawn" has grown steadily and was in 2012 for the first time represented in the Greek parliament, while the extreme right-wing Jobbik party in Hungary rose from 2 percent in 2006 to 16.7 percent of the votes in 2010. In these cases, it is easy to see the xenophobic right as a reaction to economic hardship, unemployment, and uncertainty. However, Islamophobic and ethnonationalist tendencies have also been on the rise in countries relatively unaffected by economic crises, such as Denmark, Norway, Australia, and the United States.

Muslims are the main enemy of the new right, and in particular, Muslim immigrants, but ostensibly multiculturalist national elites are also targeted. It is therefore a matter of some interest that the ideology and rhetoric of these movements are closely paralleled by the militant identity politics among Muslims attempting to redraw a clear boundary between us and them, purifying Islam and positing the Western world as the Other.

One main form of ideological polarization, thus, seems to be that obtaining between two emerging forms of identity politics—namely, nationalism and Islamism. However, the two share the same underlying logic, trying to stem the tides of global hybridization by withdrawing into something rooted, old, and clearly bounded. It may thus be more accurate to speak of a polarization between, on the one hand, various forms of antagonistic localism (nationalism, Islamism, etc.) and on the other hand, celebrations of—or at least acceptance of—hybridity and impurity.

In this way, neonationalism and Islamism can be seen as two sides of the same coin. Apparently starkly different from each other, they conform to the same grammar and represent very similar reactions to the turmoil and impurities generated by globalization.

Let us tentatively ask, then, if globalization at the end of the day leads to homogenization or to heterogenization—do we become more similar or more different owing to the increase in transnational mobility and communication? In one sense, people worldwide arguably become more similar. Individualism, the belief that individuals have rights and responsibilities regardless of their place in wider social configurations, is a central feature of global modernity. It is also easy to argue that similarities in consumer preferences indicate a certain flattening or homogenization. Yet, at the same time, local adaptations of universal or nearly universal phenomena show that global modernities always have local expressions and that the assumed similarities may either conceal real differences in meaning or that they may be superficial with no deep bearing on people's existential condition. Although neonationalism and Islamism share many of the same formal features, their content varies, not only mutually, but also from locality to locality.

Human Rights and Identity Politics

In earlier chapters, I have spoken of standardization in the domains of exchange (money), communication (language), political organization (the state), and a few aspects of everyday life (consumption). However, the flattening, or leveling, forces of standardization on a global canvas can be studied from other points of view as well. In fact, it may well be argued that the spread of human rights ideas and practices was one of the most spectacularly successful forms of globalization in the twentieth century.

First established as a global ethics when the embryonic United Nations passed the Universal Declaration of Human Rights in 1948, human rights are invoked frequently in politics at the domestic, local, and transnational level worldwide. A main critique of transnational business practices (see Klein 1998) has been their failure to respect the human rights of their workers. Debates about immigration into Western Europe are often concerned either with human rights violations within immigrant groups (especially with respect to women) or with transgressions on the part of the majority. Powerful North Atlantic aid donors now use good governance, which includes the implementation of human rights, as a criterion for giving aid to poor countries. Rebel groups, petitioners, and political minority groups worldwide use claims of human rights violations as their main claim to be heard.

The transnational monitoring of and canvassing for an extension of human rights has grown tremendously. NGOs (nongovernmental organizations), governments, and UN agencies invoke human rights regularly. Specializations, such as human rights and gender, or human rights and the environment, or human rights for indigenous groups, are firmly established in the global discourse about justice and ethics.

In its report on culture and globalization, *Our Creative Diversity*, the UNESCO (United Nations Educational Scientific and Cultural Organization, 1995) simultaneously favors cultural diversity and the protection thereof, and a global ethics based on a shared recognition of human rights. While the possible contradictions in this position have been pointed out (see Eriksen 2001b), the aim for the UNESCO is to ensure the universal respect for some shared values while simultaneously resisting global cultural homogenization. In other words, standardization at the level of morality is good but not at the level of expressive culture.

It has often been shown, not least by anthropologists, that human rights are always implemented in a particular local context (Cowan et al. 2001; Goodale 2009; Wilson 1997), meshing the universal with the particular in a glocal way. Human rights have to be interpreted, contextualized, and sometimes prioritized in order to be useful. Limitations on the use of freedom of expression, for example, vary internationally. Whether to put the greatest emphasis on social and economic rights, for example, or civil and political rights, is a political issue. In some countries, governments make efforts to reduce income disparities and see this as a human rights question; in others, free competition (with ensuing disparities) is interpreted as conforming to human rights. In some societies, the freedom of the individual is seen as the highest value, while in others, the integrity of the family, which gives the individual security, is deemed more important.

Human rights are thus universal principles, which, translated into practice, always have a local element. However, and this is important, they give most of the world a set of benchmarks, or a shared language of comparison, in which to frame their differences.

The notion of a *shared grammar* may be a very fruitful one when we consider various transnational flows and practices. Ethnicity, it could be said, is a means of rendering cultural differences comparable. There has evolved a global discourse about ethnicity, which entails a great number of formal commonalities between ethnic groups struggling for recognition everywhere. The emphasis on cultural heritage, shared customs, and a history of oppression is shared by ethnic minorities everywhere. To a great extent, they have learned from each other, even if their battles are local and unique. We shall consider this in greater detail in the last chapter.

At a different level of identity politics, it could be argued that global communication makes it easier both to try to implement standardized forms of religion and to resist such attempts. In a slower era, Islam would, from Morocco to Indonesia, appear in distinctly local forms without this posing a problem, Sunni Islam being a decentralized religion. In Morocco, saints were revered (like among the neighboring Spanish Catholics); in Pakistan, the influence from Hinduism has been perceptible; in Indonesia, the articulation of Islam with *adat* (traditional custom) in its time led to the development of a local blend of Islam. With the increased mobility and instantaneous communication of the present age, the pressure to conform to certain standards is more perceptible than formerly. Puritan movements, which have grown in significance in Pakistan, attempt to purge Pakistani Islam of Hindu elements, and the *hijab* (headscarf), rare in Malaysia some decades ago, is now seen almost universally among Malay Muslim women. The tensions between purity and impurity, or hybridity (mixing) and multiculturalism (separate cultures), highlights not only identity politics as a reembedding strategy, but also shows that there are frictions and indeed contradictory processes taking place within the social fields affected by the disembedding and destabilizing forces of globalization.

- Identity politics—religious, nationalist, ethnic, or regional—is a typical form of resistance to globalization, especially in its economic dimension.
- Paradoxically, identity politics insisting on the primacy of the local and unique tends to draw on globalized resources, such as international NGOs and computer networks.
- Indigenous and migrant identity politics tend to pursue different goals: autonomy from and recognition by greater society, respectively.

Questions

- In which ways does the author claim that globalization is dual?
- What are some of the typical forms of reembedding?
- What are some of the elements of a grammar of identity politics proposed by the author?

- What are some central differences between the reembedding engaged in by diaspora populations and the identity politics of indigenous peoples?
- What are the main differences between commercialization and politicization of identity?

Further Reading

Chua, Amy (2003) *World on Fire: How Exporting Free Market Democracy Breeds Ethnic Hatred and Global Instability*. London: Heinemann. Strikingly written, provocative, and wide-ranging study (by a law professor, but there isn't much law here!) of the tense relationship between ethnic elites (like Chinese in Indonesia, Lebanese in West Africa, etc.) and majorities in democratizing societies.

Comaroff, John L., and Jean Comaroff (2009) *Ethnicity, Inc.* Chicago: University of Chicago Press. In a wide-ranging, critical, but also often entertaining way, this book explores contemporary commercialization of identity, presenting examples ranging from Native American casinos to Zulu cultural tourism and attempts to patent indigenous knowledge for commercial purposes.

9

Alterglobalization

Disembedding inspires reembedding in the form of identity politics, but it also leads to other reactions. Notably, the forms of disembedding created by global neoliberalism (the Washington Consensus, deregulation of markets, etc.) have inspired strong, diverse reactions worldwide. The Occupy movement, the World Social Forums, and the millions demonstrating in Spain are familiar in the Global North, but grassroots globalization in the Global South can be even more effective in demonstrating that "a different world is possible," as a rejoinder to the so-called TINA maxim: "There Is No Alternative."

In several significant ways, the human world is presently more tightly integrated than at any earlier point in history. In the age of the jet plane and satellite dish, the age of global capitalism, ubiquitous markets, and transnational mediascapes, it is time and again claimed that the world is rapidly becoming a single place. Yet, a perhaps even more striking development of the post-Cold War world is the emergence—seemingly everywhere—of political movements whose explicit aim is the restoration of rooted tradition, religious fervor, or commitment to ethnic or national identities, majoritarian as well as minoritarian. Identity politics seen as a reaction to globalization was the topic of the last chapter. This chapter deals with a different kind of critical reaction to neoliberal globalization, a different form of reembedding, consisting of a broad family of social movements and strategies for change, which may be subsumed under the general label of *alterglobalization*. Literally, the globalization of the others or the other globalization, the term is preferred to antiglobalization by most activists and theorists in the field as being less negative and more accurate. The movements and initiatives described in this chapter are not opposed to interconnectedness, information technology, transnational trade, or mobility, but argue in favor of a more equitable, democratic, and decentralized form of globalization. Included in this chapter is also a brief review of some important controversies over information, surveillance, and openness. While the groups and individuals who fight against centralized control over information do not necessarily share all the objectives of the social movements associated with alterglobalization, they share their concern to strengthen local autonomy and political accountability in the face of powerful governments or corporations.

Globalization is always *glocal* in the sense that human lives take place in particular locations—even if they are transnational, on the move, dislocated. Anthropologists have written about the "indigenization of modernity" (Sahlins 1994), showing how modern artifacts and practices are incorporated into preexisting worlds of meaning, modifying them somewhat, but not homogenizing or flattening local realities. Many of the dimensions of modernity seen as uniform worldwide, such as bureaucracies, markets, computer networks, and human rights discourses, always take on a distinctly local character, not to mention consumption: A trip to McDonald's triggers an entirely different set of cultural connotations in Amsterdam from what it does in Chicago, not to mention Beijing or Moscow.

Some writers on globalization have argued that the shrinking of the world will almost inevitably lead to a new value orientation, some indeed heralding the coming of a new kind of person (e.g., Anderson 1999). These writers, who seem to proclaim the advent of a new man, or at least new set of uprooted, deterritorialized values, are often accused of generalizing from their own North Atlantic middle-class habitus. The influential sociologist John Urry, lending himself easily to this criticism, argues in the final chapter of his *Global Complexity* (2003) that globalization has the potential of stimulating widespread cosmopolitanism (however, he does not say among whom). But, as Urry readily admits in an earlier chapter in the same book, the principles of closeness and distance still hold—for example, in viewing patterns on television, where a global trend consists in viewers' preferences for locally produced programs.

In other words, the disembedding characteristic of globalization creates global cultural homogeneity only at a very superficial level. It creates a global grammar of comparison enabling communication and exchange to be channeled relatively easily across borders. It thereby stimulates an awareness of difference, precisely because it entails a language of comparison. At the same time, homogenization clearly does take place at the level of formal organizations, such as transnational NGOs (nongovernmental organizations), the formal economy of neoliberal capitalism, and in a number of other areas. Yet, even here, at the operative level of practice, even ostensibly identical forms, such as educational systems or banking, are infused with local content and adjusted to fit local ways of doing things.

Globalization is dual and operates, we might say, through dialectical negation: It shrinks the world by facilitating fast contact across former boundaries, and it expands the world by creating an awareness of difference. It *homogenizes* human lives by imposing a set of common denominators (state organization, labor markets, consumption, etc.), but it also leads to *heterogenization* through the new forms of diversity emerging from the intensified contact. Globalization is *centripetal* in that it connects people worldwide, and it is *centrifugal* in that it inspires a heightened awareness of, and indeed (re-) constructions of local uniqueness. It centralizes power and prompts movements among indigenous peoples, small nations, and others, fighting for local autonomy and self-determination. Finally, globalization makes a universalist *cosmopolitanism* possible in political thought and action because it reminds us that we are all in the same boat and have to live together in spite of our mutual differences, but it also encourages *fundamentalism* and various forms of missionary universalism as well as parochial localism because global integration leads to a sense of alienation threatening identities and notions of political sovereignty.

Protest Movements

Third ways or third alternatives are often created through the working out of these tensions. They represent attempts to find a balance between openness and closure, between the near and the distant, the local and the global, whose parameters are not defined by powerful corporations or states. These alterglobalization movements range from the Italian-origin slow food movement to the transnational Occupy movement, the Spanish *indignados* (the indignant), and a dazzling range of grassroots initiatives aiming to regain control of local life-worlds without delinking from modernity or, for that matter, the globalized world. Indeed, the anthropologist David Graeber, himself a key figure in the Occupy movement, argued in 2001:

> if one takes globalization to mean the effacement of borders and the free movement of people, possessions and ideas, then it's pretty clear that not only is the [anti-neoliberalist] movement a product of globalization, but that most of the groups involved in it—particularly the most radical ones—are in fact far more supportive of globalization in general than supporters of the International Monetary Fund or World Trade Organization. (12)

Neoliberalism necessarily creates both winners and losers. Central to this doctrine (and practice) is the concept of comparative advantage: If it is cheaper and more efficient to grow bananas in Costa Rica than in Dominica, one should; as a result, banana growers in Dominica suffer since they cannot effectively compete. If South Korea can build supertankers at a lower price than Norway, they should; as a result, Norwegian shipyards are closed down and hundreds lose their jobs. (This, in fact, is exactly what happened in my hometown in the 1980s.) A world economy based on such principles of competition and free markets (although the markets of the rich countries tend to be protected, particularly in the realm of food production) leads to an overall growth in the world economy, but in highly uneven ways. Social inequalities have grown steadily in most countries since the early 1980s, and global competition renders virtually every producer everywhere vulnerable. It is against this kind of uncertainty and powerlessness, coupled with disgust at the greed and undeserved wealth of a few superrich persons, as well as deep global inequalities, that these social movements direct their efforts. It has been estimated that the 225 richest individuals in the world have a combined wealth equal to the income of the poorest 47 percent of the entire world's population. The richest fifth of the world's population consumes 86 percent of all goods and services, while the poorest fifth consumes just 1.3 percent.

The heterogeneous groups that were for years called the new social movements or antiglobalizers first came to prominence during the protests at the WTO (World Trade Organization) meeting in Seattle in 1999. Demonstrators protested against global inequalities, a world economic order, which was inimical to human values and autonomy at the national or local level, and one that had plunged previously well-functioning countries like Argentina into disarray and crisis. As Marianne Maeckelbergh (2009) has shown, this coalition of students, environmental activists, trade unionists, indigenous organizations, women's rights groups, and many others did share some values, but most importantly, they were united in their opposition to the Washington Consensus, which saw unfettered markets as a main recipe for prosperity. The alterglobalizers began to come together, not only in large-scale demonstrations, but also at the annual World Social Forums, a convention first organized in Porto Alegre, Brazil in 2001. Against the so-called TINA doctrine ("There is no alternative" [to global neoliberalism], a quote from the late Margaret Thatcher), these meetings were founded in the conviction that "another world is possible." Participation in these meetings included political parties, mostly left-wing, but was dominated by a broad range of organizations with little in common, perhaps, except the conviction that global neoliberalism was a bad idea for humanity as a whole. They included:

> trade unions, farmers, and other workers' organizations; ethnic organizations representing both native populations and migrant groups; consumers associations challenging multinational companies; religious organizations and church groups; environmental groups; women's associations; radical autonomous youth centers (Italy's "centri sociali"); and the like. (Della Porta and Diani 2006: 4)

Yet, protest against a flawed global order tends to be more pronounced than the elucidation of alternatives. The indignation of *los indignados* in Spain, a movement that emerged in the spring of 2011, was not primarily motivated by a sense of global injustice but by the mismanagement of Spain. Hundreds of thousands of young people protested against austerity measures and mass unemployment, organizing mass demonstrations in dozens of Spanish cities. A heterogeneous coalition between otherwise quite different groups, this movement is united through a concern with jobs, welfare, and a more transparent, accountable political system.

"Another World is Possible"

The global financial crisis beginning in 2008 has had repercussions worldwide (see Tett 2010 for an excellent overview and critical analysis) and has been linked to the subsequent Euro crisis and the mounting unemployment numbers and social unrest in countries like Greece and Spain. However, the beginning of the contemporary alterglobalization movement can be traced to another financial crisis—namely, the Asian crisis of 2007, which led to major economic setbacks in several Southeast and East Asian countries. While the causes of this economic crisis were complex, it was clearly exacerbated by currency speculation leading to the destabilization of several of the region's currencies.

During the Asian crisis, the editor of the renowned French monthly *Le Monde Diplomatique*, Ignacio Ramonet, wrote a lengthy editorial where he proposed the establishment of an organization committed to fighting currency speculation through the introduction of a small tax (the Tobin tax, named after the economist James Tobin) on all international currency transactions. In 1998, ATTAC was formed in France, later to spread to several dozen countries.

ATTAC, an acronym for *Association pour la taxation des transactions financières et l'aide aux citoyens*, was among the first transnational organizations to champion a globalization from below where ordinary people were benefactors instead of being overrun and asked to pay the bill. Although it started with a specific aim—namely, the introduction of a Tobin tax, ATTAC soon evolved into a more wide-ranging organization targeting, in particular, corporate power and trade agreements (e.g., through the WTO), which seemed to favor the rich countries disproportionately. ATTAC have taken part in protests at WTO meetings (the first being in Seattle in 1999) and function as a lobbying group at G8 summits. On its official website, ATTAC declares that they "fight for the regulation of financial markets, the closure of tax havens, the introduction of global taxes to finance global public goods, the cancellation of the debt of developing countries, fair trade, and the implementation of limits to free trade and capital flows" (ATTAC n.d.). Their main slogan is "Another World Is Possible."

Decentralized in its structure, ATTAC suffers from the same problems and is faced with similar challenges to other sprawling, transnational groups trying to develop viable alternatives to global neoliberalism. Although everybody in the movement believes that another world is possible, they do not agree about the details of this world. Politically, ATTAC comprises a great variety of interest groups, from communists to liberals and anarchists, trade unionists to environmentalists, indigenous activists to farmers' organizations. They all nonetheless share the conviction that unfettered, corporation-driven global capitalism is good news for the few and bad news for the many. In this, ATTAC comes across as the archetypical alterglobalization movement, indicating that although local understandings of the good life and the good society vary, their criticisms of the dominant economic system in the world can be surprisingly similar.

The Transnational Occupy Movement

Protests against austerity measures, increasing inequalities, mismanagement, and a loss of democratic accountability as results of globalized neoliberalism have emerged in many parts of the world in recent years, perhaps most interestingly in the very heart of global financial capitalism—namely, New York City. The Occupy movement, starting in New York as Occupy Wall Street in September 2011, but soon spreading to other Western countries, directed its attention chiefly to corporate greed and the kind of financial wizardry that a few years earlier had created huge fortunes for a few very rich persons and corporations, before showing its inherent instability with the meltdown of markets and ensuing financial crisis starting in 2008. Interestingly, the inspiration for Occupy Wall Street came from as diverse sources as British student protests against higher tuition fees, the beginning of the Arab Spring in Tunisia, and the satirical magazine *Adbusters* (Bolton et al. 2013).

While the richest percentage of the U.S. population had disposed of 10 percent of the total national income in 1980, the figure in 2010 was 23.5 percent. Using slogans such as "We are the 99%," referring to the disproportionate wealth and power held by the top 1 percent in society, thousands of Americans staged a demonstration in the Wall Street area on September 17, 2011. Within just a few weeks, similar demonstrations were organized in more than ninety cities in and outside the United States. The broad aim of the Occupy movement is to contribute to the creation of a world with less inequality and injustice, but its spokespersons (being a flat structure, it has no formal leadership) also emphasize the need for alternative political organization, based more on cooperative principles than on hierarchical and formal structures.

While some main objectives within Occupy are broadly shared by the activists, there is also disagreement over key questions, as vividly documented by Susan Kang (2013), concerning the role of markets in the economy and the desired political model. A proposed mission statement, which "included a criticism of corporate domination over politics, culture, and social life, promoted greater democracy within major institutions, and urged others to join in occupying Wall Street" (Kang 2013: 63) was voted down at an early meeting. There has even been disagreement as to whether or not the movement should in fact voice clear demands, since their shared commitment to reduce corporate power should be the overarching goal.

The Occupy movement, a latecomer in the family of alterglobalizing social movements, is part of a complex network of likeminded groups, such as the critical media hub Indymedia, the French-origin movement ATTAC, some of the protesters in Arab-speaking countries (see boxed text on the Arab Spring), environmentalists, and socialists. Interestingly, several politicians in high positions, from Brazil's president Dilma Rousseff to the British ex-prime minister Gordon Brown and U.S. President Barack Obama himself, have expressed sympathy with some of the criticisms of corporate power and greed coming from the Occupy movement.

These and other protest movements continue to question global neoliberalism and may soon be a political force to be reckoned with. As pointed out by Geoffrey

Pleyers (2010), the growth in participation at World Social Forums has been staggering, reaching a peak in 2005 with 170,000 participants.

Alterglobalizing Strategies in the South

An economically and politically marginal area, the southern Pacific coast of Colombia was for many years—until the 1950s—only partly integrated into the state. The largely Afro-Colombian population developed viable life strategies, sometimes autonomously, sometimes under conditions of servitude. Towards the latter part of the twentieth century, state power, capitalism, and the armed conflicts haunting Colombia increasingly encroached the area, leaving the local population in a difficult situation. In a complex and rich study of a network of local organizations known as the PCN (*Proceso de Comunidades Negras*—Process of Black Communities), the anthropologist Arturo Escobar explores how these communities are "attempting to reinvent themselves through a new relation to the state, themselves, the environment, and global forces" (2008: 309). Far from wishing to withdraw from the state and the market economy, the PCN is creating an economy based on local needs and resources but involved in external trade, a politics emphasizing direct democracy and a relationship to the environment based on the values of diversity and sustainability. Escobar argues that the peculiar form of modernity evolving on the southern Colombian coast is better equipped to meet the challenges of the twenty-first century—environmental crisis, centralization of power, racism, and intolerance, to mention a few—than the dominant neoliberal model. A long-standing critic of conventional theories of development, Escobar (see 1992) describes numerous examples of local economic enterprises, such as the Coagropacífico cooperative, which are profitable without creating huge disparities or environmental destruction locally. He also describes local cosmologies as positing a dynamic unity between humans and the environment rather than seeing them as opposed forces, intimating that Westerners have many lessons to learn from the communities organized through the PCN. What they represent is a genuine form of alterglobalization, founded simultaneously in locally embedded life-worlds and a reflexive positioning in large-scale, ultimately global networks. Their refashioning of their economy and social lives to meet local needs rather than satisfying systemic demands, incidentally, can be seen as a tangible exemplification of Karl Polanyi's (1957 [1944]) aforementioned, classic critique of market dominance, where he argues that society will tend to be resilient and resistant to being taken over completely by the anonymous, disembedded market logic.

In another part of the world—namely, Maharashtra state in India—Arjun Appadurai (2013) has explored a different kind of reembedding strategy, or alterglobalization movement. Unlike Escobar's site, Mumbai is a bustling world city, a commercial hub with major industries in or near the city and, of course, the undisputed capital of Bollywood movies. It is also a crowded and polluted city with severe infrastructural problems, ranging from housing to sewage. Most of Mumbai's inhabitants can rightly be described as urban poor.

The movement investigated by Appadurai consists of a coalition, or alliance, between three partners focusing on different issues pertaining to slum dwellers and disenfranchised inhabitants of the city. Like Escobar in Colombia, Appadurai sees the work of the alliance through the lens of the post-Cold War world—that is to say the world of deregulation and neoliberalism, economic globalization, and transnational networking. Eschewing divisive party politics as well as expert-driven projects, the alliance insists on the slow and cumbersome "mobilization of the knowledge of the poor into methods driven by the poor and for the poor" (Appadurai 2013: 161). Flexible in its organizational structure and capable of working both with long-term plans and urgent issues, the alliance embodies some of the same features as the PCN in Colombia: a democratic form of decision making, reliance on local skills and knowledge, and commitment to the principles of grassroots activism. At a transnational level, the alliance takes part in the Shack/Slum Dwellers International (SDI), visiting and exchanging experiences with slum dwellers in South Africa, Thailand, and elsewhere in India. At the time of writing, the SDI is working to develop a funding mechanism that would both liberate member organizations from unpredictable local and private sources and strengthen the global cooperation between the constituent local movements.

As these two examples indicate, grassroots globalization, or alterglobalization, shares some formal traits with neoliberal or state-driven globalization but differs crucially in insisting on the right to local autonomy and engagement with the global system on one's own terms, as an equal actor, and not as a recipient of charity.

Satire against Neoliberalism

"Ours is the age of billionaires. From a mere dozen in the early 1980s to more than a thousand today, their numbers have surged along with their influence." Thus begins anthropologist Angelique Haugerud's book *No Billionaire Left Behind: Satirical Activism in America* (2013), a study—part hilarious, part critical, part analytical—of a group of comedian activists who target corporate greed, tax evasion, dithering politicians, and mounting inequalities in American society. The group, variously named "Billionaires for Bush" (2004), "Billionaires for Plutocracy" (2011), and "Multi-Millionaires for Mitt" (2012), tend to dress in cocktail dresses or expensive suits and top hats, more often than not with the additional props of a large cigar and a champagne flute, rally under slogans such as "Taxes Are Not For Everyone," "It's A Class War—And We're Winning," and "Widen The Income Gap!" Their preferred sport seems to be badminton.

The tenor of the Billionaires' rhetoric is captured well in its self-presentation on the still open (but historically obsolete) Billionaires for Bush website (2004): "Billionaires for Bush is a grassroots network of corporate lobbyists, decadent heiresses, Halliburton

CEOs, and other winners under George W. Bush's economic policies. Headquartered in Wall Street and with over 60 chapters nationwide, we'll give whatever it takes to ensure four more years of putting profit over people. After all, we know a good president when we buy one."

In satire, the message is by definition implicit. As pointed out by Haugerud, the Billionaires demonstrate, by lampooning the neoliberal rhetoric of free markets and liberty, that there are always socially defined rules regulating both economies and societies, that there is no natural law stating that it is acceptable for individuals to amass unlimited wealth in a society and a world of scarcity, and that a different politics would distribute the world's assets more equitably.

Adopting names like Iona Bigga Yacht (Alice Meaker) and Phil T. Rich (Andrew Boyd) and using hyperbole (exaggeration)—slight or outrageous—to get their message across, the Billionaires are firmly anchored in a long tradition of political satire, which may be traced at least to the European carnival tradition. During carnival, it was legitimate to turn hierarchies on their heads with a comic intent, but the function of carnival performances could often be subversive and critical of the powers that be. But there appears to be a greater universality to satire and parody as political instruments. The anthropologist Max Gluckman (1952), writing about rituals and politics in South Africa in the 1950s, described "rituals of rebellion" as events where hierarchies were turned on their heads and social roles inverted: Women dressed and behaved like men, and men behaved as if they were entitled to the throne. However, Gluckman (1952) sees these rituals, at the end of the day, not as inherently subversive but rather as confirmations of the status quo. By posing as the king, he argues, the "rebels" confirm their support of the institution of kingship. Gluckman, in other words, sees this form of satire as a security valve. The Billionaires' message is different: Their aim is to expose the shallowness and callousness of the microculture of the superrich and to call for a politics that puts ordinary people first—they ask politicians to focus on the possibilities of a human economy rather than basing policies on figures on a spreadsheet.

The Slowness Movement

A less visible and less overtly political form of political resistance to globalization than the alterglobalizers is offered by the transnational slow movements (see Honoré 2005), notably Slow Food and Slow Cities (*città slow*). Favoring traditional alternatives to the transnational and standardized, these movements emphasize the value of locally produced food and not least local food traditions, slowness as a value superior to speed in lifestyle questions, and a politics that puts the quality of life before material standards of living.

Typical Western middle-class phenomena, the slow movements first emerged in northern Italy, where they are associated both with the preservation of medieval towns and with local specialties, such as Culatella ham, wine, and *lardo di Colonnata* (yes, it sounds like lard, and lard it is, cf. Leitch 2003). To use the distinctions suggested by George Ritzer (2004), the slow movements fit the category of "the glocalization of something" since they play by the rules of global capitalism but try to fill it with something local and nonscalable.

The initiative to the Slow Food movement came following a concerted attempt in 1986 to prevent the opening of a McDonald's restaurant near the famous Spanish Steps in Rome. The people behind the initiative felt that the homogenizing and flattening aspects of globalization were profoundly at odds with not only historical traditions and the unique character of historical Rome but also—in the case of McDonald's—represented a trivialization of food and an affront to traditional cuisine. The movement was founded by Carlo Petrini (2007), a former left-wing activist who had written about food for the Communist newspaper *L'Unitá* since the 1970s. It attempts to combine an attention to lifestyle and quality of life with a systemic criticism of large-scale agribusiness using food—in particular, food that has been produced on a small scale in a local setting where it has a long tradition. Ecological arguments about unintentional consequences of industrial farming as well as the importance of preserving genetic diversity are also emphasized by the movement, which—appropriately—uses a garden snail as its symbol.

Slow cities, or *Cittaslow*, is aligned with the Slow Food movement and was also founded in northern Italy, but a decade later (in 1999). Concerned—like Slow Food—with the preservation of the local character and unique ambience of urban spaces, it is a membership organization associating the quality of life with a slower, more humane pace compatible with environmental preservation. Existing chiefly in Europe and Asia, *Cittaslow* and the entire Slow movement can be criticized for representing an affluent middle-class community concerned chiefly with self-realization and personal well-being. However, the aims of the slowness movements are by and large compatible with those of other social movements fighting global neoliberalism, as well as local or regional initiatives in the Global South, such as the Colombian example described above. The key viewpoint is that profit-driven, globalized neoliberalism represents a threat to local autonomy, social justice, and the environment.

From the Arab Spring to the Snowden Affair

One of the most obvious features of contemporary globalization is the information revolution. The proportion of the world's population who are online in one way or another, who use cell phones, and who make Google searches and online purchases has soared since the 1990s, and the technology itself has also evolved. For years, scholarly attention to the new information technology was mainly directed towards understanding its consequences for everyday life and work, knowledge production, and social networking from below. In recent years, a different aspect of the information revolution has become increasingly apparent—namely, its potential political uses.

Electronic information can both be used from below, to criticize and expose powerful agents, and from above, to monitor citizens. Social scientists have also discovered big data of the kind that is produced through millions of Google searches and other online activities, as a new source of insight into key social and cultural processes (Mayer-Schönberger and Cukier 2013).

Three examples reveal, in very different ways, the potential of the new information technology to challenge power or to wield it:

First, the so-called Arab Spring, beginning in Tunisia in December 2010, would have been difficult to organize without cell phones and internet connectivity. The series of protests and demonstrations, both peaceful and violent, stretching across the Arab-speaking world from Morocco to Oman, leading to the downfall of four governments and major reforms in several countries, plus a dreadful civil war in Syria, were generally illegal or semilegal. In most of the countries in question, the press and other media were subjected to state censorship, and open protest against mounting social inequalities, corruption, and the lack of democracy was often dangerous. Through innovative use of inexpensive communication technologies, mostly cell-phone-based, protesters were able to coordinate their efforts without being intercepted by state authorities, and—not least important—to report about events in real time as they unfolded, prompting reactions from the international community.

Second, the much-publicized revelations of diplomatic secrets by WikiLeaks, a nonprofit organization relaying information brought to them by anonymous sources, demonstrates the vulnerability of a system whereby classified and sensitive information is communicated electronically. Since 2007, WikiLeaks have published secret files, private e-mail correspondence, and significant documents, which have often revealed a discrepancy between official statements from governments and actual practices. Targeting the United States in particular, WikiLeaks have publicized material about conditions in the prison camp at Guantánamo Bay and about the wars in Afghanistan and Iraq, but they have also relayed evidence of corruption in a number of countries and many other kinds of information that the organization argues deserves to be made known to the public. The founder of WikiLeaks, the Australian activist Julian Assange, has risked prosecution in the United States since 2010 (and, for alleged sexual offenses, in Sweden). He was granted political asylum by Ecuador, and he moved into the Ecuadorian embassy in London, refusing to leave for fear of extradition, since June 2012. The U.S. soldier Bradley Manning, who was convicted in 2013 for revealing military secrets about the American wars abroad, had been a major source for WikiLeaks until his arrest in 2010.

The third example concerns the NSA (National Security Agency) and Edward Snowden and reveals the other side of the coin—namely, how government authorities may collect massive amounts of data about citizens based on their Internet use, in order to monitor possible threats to the integrity and security of the state.

While WikiLeaks strives to make information that would otherwise have been secret available to the greater public, the NSA has for years collected information about ordinary people, both Americans and foreigners, in the hope that this might help them to identify potential terrorists and other enemies of the country. Using the techniques developed to analyze big data fast and inexpensively, they use algorithms that, for example, look for combinations of certain search terms on Google or other forms of suspicious behavior. Whereas the research methods using big data have been used for other purposes, such as locating recent outbreaks of the flu or tracking down cybercriminals, the U.S. state's usage of data believed by most users to be confidential and private, in order to spy on its own citizens (and foreigners!), was immediately perceived as highly problematic when it became widely known in 2013.

As an active user of the Internet, you continuously leave electronic traces behind. Anyone with access to data from my bank, Facebook, Amazon, Google, and (god forbid) my e-mail, would easily patch together a fairly accurate depiction of my personal economic situation, my literary and musical interests, my intellectual orientation, political views, and social networks, regardless of my citizenship or country of residence. If you read books on a Kindle, data on which sentences you've highlighted will be stored electronically in cyberspace and linked directly to you. In the past, nobody would be able to know what kind of seditious and subversive literature you indulged in—least of all the government.

Most users of various Internet-based information and communication services have presumably assumed that the information they left behind was safe and confidential, although many have speculated about its possible usefulness to an unfriendly government. Few, however, suspected that the NSA secretly collected massive amounts of information about ordinary citizens, among other things intercepting telephone calls and searching for pernicious terms in e-mails—and that Google had given them access to their enormous databanks. It was only after the computer specialist Edward Snowden, who had worked for the CIA and the NSA, leaked information about these and other mass surveillance programs to the *Guardian* in May 2013 that the extent of these activities began to be known. Facing prosecution for espionage and theft of government property, Snowden fled to Hong Kong and subsequently to Russia.

At the time of writing, it is still unknown whether Assange and/or Snowden will eventually be sentenced and imprisoned. Public opinion is divided on both. What makes their stories analytically interesting is the way in which they demonstrate the connection between information and power, by revealing the existence of secret mass surveillance programs even in a country like the United States. The examples also indicate that interpersonal communication through electronic networks makes it easier not only for people to stay in touch with each other and get the information they need from anywhere in the world but also facilitates the task for governments who wish to monitor people's movements and activities.

All the examples of alterglobalization discussed in this chapter confirm the fundamental duality, or dialectics, of globalization emphasized throughout this book. There is a continuous tension, sometimes expressed as conflict, between the standardized and scalable on the one hand and the locally unique and nonscalable on the other hand, sometimes expressed as a tension between state power and civil society. This kind of contradiction, or friction, is not going away: it is a defining feature of globalization and of the contemporary world.

- The disembedding forces of globalization are complemented by reembedding projects seeking to retain or recreate a sense of continuity, security, and trust.
- Even disembedded institutions take on local meanings and flavors in different societies.
- The alterglobalization movement consists of thousands of locally embedded or transnational organizations that have little in common except a common rejection of global neoliberal capitalism.
- Any belief in TINA ("There Is No Alternative") is disproved by the myriad forms of reembedding and resistance engaged in worldwide, but also by the exclusion of millions from global networks.

Questions

- How can globalization simultaneously lead to increased cosmopolitanism and increased fundamentalism?
- What was the ideological background of the Occupy movement?
- In what ways are social movements such as *los indignados* and ATTAC products of globalization?
- Is the Slow movement a critical force interrogating global neoliberalism, or is it mainly focused just on changing middle-class lifestyles in the affluent countries?

Further Reading

Appadurai, Arjun (2013) *The Future as Cultural Fact: Essays on the Global Condition.* New York: Verso. This collection of essays by one of the foremost interpreters of globalization emphasizes its dual nature as an uneven process of connectedness taking place equally from above and from below. With great erudition and tempered optimism, Appadurai identifies tendencies in urban living, design, finance, and thought, which may define our common future.

Maeckelbergh, Marianne (2009) *The Will of the Many: How the Alterglobalisation Movement is Changing the Face of Democracy.* London: Pluto. An ethnography of the transnational protest movements written by a scholar-activist, who is equally skilled as an observer and analyst as she is an engaged participant in many of the conventions and demonstrations she describes.

Afterword

An Overheated World

Disembedding, acceleration, standardization, connections, mobility, mixing, globalized risk: It is easy to conjure up a vision of the world as being in constant flux. In this book, I have argued against simplistic versions of this view, and even if one is fascinated by the idea of a world in continuous movement, one has to keep in mind that different social and cultural fields are moving at different speeds and even in different directions.

Truly global processes affect the conditions of people living in particular localities, creating new opportunities and new forms of vulnerability. Risks are globally shared in the era of the nuclear bomb, transnational terrorism, and potential ecological disasters. On the same note, the economic conditions in particular localities frequently (some would say always) depend on events taking place elsewhere in the global system. If there is an industrial boom in Taiwan, towns in the English Midlands will be affected. If oil prices rise, that means salvation for the oil-exporting Trinidadian economy and disaster for the oil-importing, neighboring Barbadian one.

Patterns of consumption also seem to merge in certain respects; people nearly everywhere desire similar goods, from cell phones to ready-made garments. A precondition for this to happen is the more or less successful implementation of certain institutional dimensions of modernity, notably that of a monetary economy— if not necessarily evenly distributed wage work and literacy. The ever-increasing transnational flow of commodities, be they material or immaterial, creates a set of common cultural denominators, which appear to eradicate local distinctions. The hotdog (*halal* or not, as the case may be), the pizza, and the hamburger (or, in India, the lamburger) are truly parts of world cuisine; identical pop songs are played in identical discotheques in Costa Rica and Thailand; the same Coca-Cola commercials are shown with minimal local variations at cinemas all over the world, volumes by Dan Brown and E. L. James are ubiquitous wherever books are sold, and so on. Investment capital, military power, and world literature are being disembedded from the constraints of space; they no longer belong to a particular locality. With the development of the jet plane, the shipping container, the satellite dish, and more recently, the Internet, distance no longer seems a limiting factor for the flow of influence, investments, and cultural meaning.

Yet, disembedding is never total, and it is always counteracted by reembedding attempts. Sometimes, reembedding does not even seem to be required—if one cares to look, the social world in which most of humanity live remains embedded in important respects, notwithstanding decades of intensive, technology-driven globalization. The impact of globalization—or, rather, its significance for the lives we lead—is considerable, but every one-sided account is ultimately false. Warning against the view of globalization as somehow the outcome, or the end product of modernity, James Mittelman (2001: 7) writes that if "globalization is a contested and political phenomenon, then it cannot have a predetermined outcome. A political agenda of inevitability overlooks the fact that globalization was made by humans, and, if so, can be unmade or remade by humankind." It is far-reaching and consequential, but globalizing processes are always full of contradictions, which are not likely to go away soon. Some are globalizing, some are just being globalized, and many are scarcely affected by globalization.

John Gray (2005) puts it even more strongly in a critique of a book mentioned in the preface of this book, so it seems appropriate to end with some reflections from his essay. In a review of Thomas Friedman's *The World is Flat*, polemically entitled "The world is round," Gray compares Friedman's belief in the "levelling of the world" with the belief in "unfettered" global capitalism underpinning Marx and Engels's 1848 *Communist Manifesto*, and concludes that both have been proven wrong, Friedman incidentally much faster than Marx and Engels. Gray (2005: 22) reminds his readers, as an antidote to Friedman's optimism on behalf of the power of global capitalism to spread prosperity worldwide, that for two hundred years, "the spread of capitalism and industrialization has gone hand in hand with war and revolution."

Gray further argues that Friedman conflates two notions of globalization:

the belief that we are living in a period of rapid and continuous technological innovation, which has the effect of linking up events and activities throughout the world more widely and quickly than before; and the belief that this process is leading to a single worldwide economic system. The first is an empirical proposition and plainly true, the second a groundless ideological assertion. Like Marx, Friedman elides the two. (2005: 23)

However, Gray remarks, communication technology affects the everyday lives of people less than petroleum and electricity did. And globalization does not necessarily lead to a global free market, nor does it make the world more peaceful or more liberal.

Many of the examples in this book lend support to Gray's view. One typical consequence of globalization has been the rise or rekindling of various forms of identity politics. To Gray, al-Qaeda is just as typical a product of globalization as the World Trade Organization (see Gray 2003). Transnational capitalism creates both wealth and poverty. Millions of people—indeed hundreds of millions—will never have access to the wealth because they are simply ignored and squeezed into increasingly marginal areas, like hunter-gatherers encountering armed, well-organized agriculturalists in an earlier period. The suffering of slum dwellers, dispossessed peasants, unemployed men and women in cities, victims of war and of economic exploitation, and their occasionally well-orchestrated rebellions or alternative projects seeking autonomy from globalized capitalism, are the trueborn children of globalization, just as the cell phone and the Internet, the proliferation of international NGOs (nongovernmental organizations), the cheap tropical holiday, and the growth of transnational soccer fandom are results of globalization. The ambiguities and paradoxes of globalization are not going away, simply because they are constitutive of globalization—a fundamentally contradictory phenomenon, which constitutes the very fabric in which you and I live, in an overheated world where cooling may be patchy and partial, but sometimes sufficiently effective to allow us to retain personal autonomy and a real influence on our destiny.

Bibliography

Aas, Katja Franko (2007) Analyzing a World in Motion: Global Flows Meet the "Criminology of the Other." *Theoretical Criminology*, 11 (2): 283–303.

Adger, W. Neil, Irene Lorenzoni, and Karen O'Brien, eds. (2009) *Adapting to Climate Change: Thresholds, Values, Governance*. Cambridge: Cambridge University Press.

Aguiar, José Carlos G. (2012) "They Come from China": Pirate CDs in Mexico in Transnational Perspective. In *Globalization From Below: The World's Other Economy*, eds. Gordon Mathews, Gustavo Lins Ribeiro, and Carlos Alba Vega, pp. 36–53. London: Routledge.

Ali, Tariq (2002) *The Clash of Fundamentalisms: Crusades, Jihads and Modernity*. London: Verso.

Amin, Samir (1980) *Class and Nation: Historically and in the Current Crisis*. London: Heinemann.

Amin, Samir, Giovanni Arrighi, Andre Gunder Frank, and Immanuel Wallerstein (1982) *Dynamics of the World Economy*. New York: Monthly Review Press.

Amselle, Jean-Loup (2001) *Branchements. Anthropologie de l'universalité des cultures*. Paris: Flammarion.

Anderson, Benedict (1991 [1983]) *Imagined Communities: Reflections on the Origin and Spread of Nationalism*. London: Verso.

Anderson, Benedict (1992) *Long Distance Nationalism: World Capitalism and the Rise of Identity Politics*. Amsterdam: CASA.

Anderson, Benedict (2006) *Under Three Flags: Anarchism and the Anti-colonial Imagination*. London: Verso.

Anderson, Walter Truett (1999) *The Future of the Self: Inventing the Postmodern Person*. London: Jeremy Tarcher.

Appadurai, Arjun (1990) Being in the World: Globalization and Localization. In *Global Culture*, ed. Mike Featherstone, pp. 295–310. London: Sage.

Appadurai, Arjun (1996) *Modernity at Large*. Minneapolis: University of Minnesota Press.

Appadurai, Arjun, ed. (2003) *Globalization*. Durham, NC: Duke University Press.

Appadurai, Arjun (2013) *The Future as Cultural Fact: Essays on the Global Condition*. New York: Verso.

Appiah, Kwame Anthony (2003) Citizens of the World. In *Globalizing Rights*, ed. Matthew J. Gibney, pp. 189–233. Oxford: Oxford University Press.

Appiah, Kwame Anthony (2006) *Cosmopolitanism: Ethics in a World of Strangers*. London: Allen Lane.

ATTAC (n.d) Overview. http://www.attac.org/node/3727. Accessed October 6, 2013.

Augé, Marc (1992) *Non-lieux: Introduction à une anthropologie de la surmodernité*. Paris: Seuil.

Barber, Benjamin (1995) *Jihad versus McWorld: How Globalism and Tribalism are Reshaping the World*. New York: Ballantine.

Barkan, Elliott R., Hasia Diner, and Alan M. Kraut, eds. (2008) *From Arrival to Incorporation: Migrants to the US in a Global Era*. New York: New York University Press.

Barloewen, Constantin von (2003) *Anthropologie de la mondialisation*. Paris: Syrtes.

Bauman, Zygmunt (1999) *Globalization—The Human Consequences*. New York: Columbia University Press.

Bauman, Zygmunt (2000) *Liquid Modernity*. Cambridge: Polity.

Bayart, Jean-François (2003) The Paradoxical Invention of Economic Modernity. In *Globalization*, ed. Arjun Appadurai, pp. 307–34. Durham, NC: Duke University Press.

Beck, Ulrich (1992 [1986]) *Risk Society: Towards a New Modernity*. London: Sage.

Beck, Ulrich (1999) *World Risk Society*. Cambridge: Polity.

Beck, Ulrich (2005) *Power in the Global Age: A New Global Political Economy*, translated by Kathleen Cross. Cambridge: Polity.

Bell, Daniel (1973) *The Coming of Post-industrial Society: A Venture in Social Forecasting*. New York: Basic Books.

Berger, Peter, Birgitte Berger, and Hansfried Kellner (1973) *The Homeless Mind: Modernization and Consciousness*. New York: Random House.

Bergson, Henri (2001 [1889]) *Sur les données immédiates de la conscience*. Paris: PUF.

Beyer, Peter (2006) *Religions in Global Society*. London: Routledge.

Billionaires for Bush (2004) About the Billionaires. http://billionairesforbush.com/about.php. Accessed October 6, 2013.

Bolton, Matthew, Emily Welty, Meghana Nayak, and Christopher Malone (2013) Introduction: We Had a Front Row Seat to a Downtown Revolution. In *Occupying Political Science: The Occupy Wall Street Movement from New York to the World*, eds. Emily Welty, Matthew Bolton, Meghana Nayak, and Christopher Malone, pp. 1–24. London: Palgrave Macmillan.

Bourdieu, Pierre (1996) *Sur la télévision*. Paris: Raisons d'agir.

Bringsværd, Tor Åge (1988) The Man Who Collected the First of September, 1973. In *The Book of Fantasy*, eds. Jorge Luis Borges, Adolfo Bioy Cesares, and Silvina Ocampo, pp. 77–81, translated by Oddrun Grønvik. London: Viking.

British Council (2009) English. http://www.britishcouncil.org/english. Accessed September 9, 2009.

Carling, Jørgen (2008) The Determinants of Migrant Remittances. *Oxford Review of Economic Policy*, 24 (3): 582–99.

Carmel, Emma, Alfio Cerami, and Tehdoros Papadopoulos, eds. (2012) *Migration and Welfare in the New Europe: Social Protection and the Challenges of Integration*. Bristol: Policy.

Castells, Manuel (1996) *The Rise of the Network Society*. Oxford: Blackwell.

Castells, Manuel (1998) *End of Millennium*. Oxford: Blackwell.

Castells, Manuel (2009) *Communication Power*. Oxford: Oxford University Press.

Castles, Stephen, and Alasdair Davidson (2000) *Citizenship and Migration: Globalization and the Politics of Belonging*. London: Palgrave Macmillan.

Castles, Stephen, and Mark J. Miller (2009) *The Age of Migration: International Population Movements in the Modern World*, 4th edition. London: Palgrave Macmillan.

Chanda, Nayan (2007) *Bound Together: How Traders, Preachers, Adventurers, and Warriors Shaped Globalization*. New Haven: Yale University Press.

Chase-Dunn, Christopher, and Thomas Hall (1997) *Rise and Demise: Comparing World-Systems*. Boulder, CO: Westview.

Chua, Amy (2003) *World on Fire: How Exporting Free Market Democracy Breeds Ethnic Hatred and Global Instability*. London: Heinemann.

Cohen, Daniel (2006) *Globalization and its Enemies*. Boston: MIT Press.

Cohen, Robin (1997) *Global Diasporas*. London: Routledge.

Comaroff, John L., and Jean Comaroff (2009) *Ethnicity, Inc.* Chicago: University of Chicago Press.

Congress of the United States (2005) *Remittances: International Payments by Migrants*. Washington, DC: CBO.

Cowan, Jane, Marie-Bénédicte Dembour, and Richard Ashby Wilson, eds. (2001) *Culture and Rights: Anthropological Perspectives*. Cambridge: Cambridge University Press.

Croucher, Sheila (2004) *Globalization and Belonging: The Politics of Identity in a Changing World*. Lanham, MD: Rowman & Littlefield.

Crystal, David (2000) *Language Death*. Cambridge: Cambridge University Press.

Dahl, Robert A. (2000) Can International Organizations be Democratic: A Skeptic's View. In *The Global Transformations Reader*, eds. D. Held and A. McGrew, pp. 530–41. Cambridge: Polity.

David, Paul A. (1992) Heroes, Herds and Hysteresis in Technological History: "The Battle of the Systems" Reconsidered. *Industrial and Corporate Change*, 1: 129–80.

David, Paul A. (2007) Path Dependence: A Foundational Concept for Historical Social Science. *Cliometrica*, 1 (2): 91–114.

Davis, Mike (2006) *Planet of Slums*. London: Verso.

Della Porta, Donatella, and Mario Diani (2006) *Social Movements: An Introduction*. Basingstoke: Wiley.

Diamond, Jared (1998) *Guns, Germs and Steel: A Short History of Everybody for the Last 13,000 Years*. London: Random House.

Drummond, Lee (1980) The Cultural Continuum: A Theory of Intersystems. *Man*, 15 (2): 352–74.

Ensor, Jonathan, and Rachel Berger (2009) Community-Based Adaptation and Culture in Theory and Practice. In *Adapting to Climate Change: Thresholds, Values, Governance*, eds. W. Neil Adger, Irene Lorenzoni, and Karen O'Brien, pp. 227–39. Cambridge: Cambridge University Press.

Eriksen, Thomas Hylland (1998) *Common Denominators: Ethnicity, Nation-Building and Compromise in Mauritius*. Oxford: Berg.

Eriksen, Thomas Hylland (2001a) *Bak fiendebildet: Politisk islam og verden etter 11. september* (Behind the Enemy Image: Political Islam and the World after 11 September). Oslo: Cappelen.

Eriksen, Thomas Hylland (2001b) Between Universalism and Relativism: A Critique of the UNESCO Concept of Culture. In *Culture and Rights: Anthropological Perspectives*, eds. J. Cowan, M. B. Dembour, and R. A. Wilson, pp. 127–48. Cambridge: Cambridge University Press.

Eriksen, Thomas Hylland (2001c) *Tyranny of the Moment: Fast and Slow Time in the Information Age*. London: Pluto.

Eriksen, Thomas Hylland, ed. (2003) *Globalisation—Studies in Anthropology*. London: Pluto.

Eriksen, Thomas Hylland (2004) Traditionalism and Neoliberalism: The Norwegian Folk Dress in the 21st Century. In *Properties of Culture—Culture as Property*, ed. E. Kasten, pp. 267–86. Berlin: Dietrich Reimer Verlag.

Eriksen, Thomas Hylland (2007a) Creolization in Anthropological Theory and in Mauritius. In *Creolization: History, Ethnography, Theory*, ed. Charles Stewart, pp. 153–77. Walnut Creek, CA: Left Coast Press.

Eriksen, Thomas Hylland (2007b) Nationalism and the Internet. *Nations and Nationalism*, 13 (1): 1–18.

Eriksen, Thomas Hylland (2010) *Ethnicity and Nationalism: Anthropological Perspectives*, 3rd edition. London: Pluto.

Eriksen, Thomas Hylland (2013, in press) The Cartoon Controversy and the Possibility of Cosmopolitanism. In *We The Cosmopolitans*, eds. Alexandra Hall and Lisette Josephides. Oxford: Berghahn.

Eriksen, Thomas Hylland, Ellen Bal, and Oscar Salemink, eds. (2010) *A World of Insecurity: The Anthropology of Human Security*. London: Pluto.

Escobar, Arturo (1992) Imagining a Post-development Era. *Social Text*, 31: 20–56.

Escobar, Arturo (2008) *Territories of Difference: Place, Movement, Life, Redes.* Durham, NC: Duke University Press.

Fabian, Johannes (1983) *Time and the Other: How Anthropology Makes Its Object.* New York: Columbia University Press.

Fanon, Frantz (1986 [1952]) *Black Skin, White Masks.* London: Pluto.

Featherstone, Mike, ed. (1990) *Global Culture.* London: Sage.

Feld, Steven (2003) A Sweet Lullaby for World Music. In *Globalization*, ed. Arjun Appadurai, pp. 189–216. Durham, NC: Duke University Press.

Ferguson, James (1999) *Expectations of Modernity: Myth and Meanings of Urban Life on the Zambian Copperbelt.* Berkeley: University of California Press.

Fernandez-Armesto, Felipe (1995) *Millennium: A History of the Last Thousand Years.* New York: Prentice-Hall.

Fernandez-Armesto, Felipe (2000) *Civilizations.* London: Macmillan.

Flannery, Tim (2006) *The Weather Makers: The History and Future Impact of Climate Change.* London: Penguin.

Flemmen, Anne Britt, and Britt Kramvig (2008) Møter: Sammenstøt av verdier i samisk-norske hverdagsliv (Encounters: Collisions of Values in Sami–Norwegian Everyday Lives). In *Verdier* (Values), eds. Oddbjørn Leirvik and Åse Røthing, pp. 101–19. Oslo: Universitetsforlaget.

Fox, Jonathan (1999) Clash of Civilizations or Clash of Religions: Which is a More Important Determinant of Ethnic Conflict? *Ethnicities*, 1 (3): 295–366.

Frank, Andre Gunder (1975) *On Capitalist Underdevelopment.* Oxford: Oxford University Press.

Frank, Andre Gunder (1998) *ReORIENT: Global Economy in the Asian Age.* Berkeley: University of California Press.

Franklin, Adrian (2004) Tourism as an Ordering: Towards a New Ontology of Tourism. *Tourist Studies*, 4: 277–301.

Friedman, Jonathan (1990) Being in the World: Globalization and Localization. In *Global Culture*, ed. Mike Featherstone, pp. 311–28. London: Sage.

Friedman, Jonathan (1994) *Global Identity and Cultural Process.* London: Sage.

Friedman, Thomas (2005) *The World Is Flat: A Brief History of the Globalized World in the 21st Century.* London: Allen Lane.

Fuglerud, Øivind (1999) *Life on the Outside.* London: Pluto.

Furedi, Frank (2002) *Culture of Fear*, 2nd edition. London: Continuum.

Gellner, Ernest (1983) *Nations and Nationalism.* Oxford: Blackwell.

Gellner, Ernest (1990) *Plough, Sword, Book.* Chicago: University of Chicago Press.

Gibson, William (1984) *Neuromancer.* New York: Ace.

Giddens, Anthony (1985) *The Nation-State and Violence.* Cambridge: Polity.

Giddens, Anthony (1990) *The Consequences of Modernity.* Cambridge: Polity.

Giddens, Anthony (1991) *Modernity and Self-Identity.* Cambridge: Polity.

Giddens, Anthony (1999) *Runaway World: How Globalization is Reshaping our Lives.* London: Profile.

Gilpin, Robert (2002) *The Challenge of Global Capitalism: The World Economy in the 21st Century.* Princeton, NJ: Princeton University Press.

Giulianotti, Richard, and Roland Robertson (2004) The Globalization of Football: A Study in the Glocalization of the "Serious Life." *The British Journal of Sociology*, 55 (4): 545–68.

Gluckman, Max (1952) *Rituals of Rebellion in South-East Africa.* Manchester: Manchester University Press 1954.

Godelier, Maurice (2009) *In and Out of the West: Reconstructing Anthropology.* London: Verso.

Goodale, Mark (2009) *Surrendering to Utopia: An Anthropology of Human Rights*. Stanford, CA: Stanford University Press.

Goody, Jack (1977) *The Domestication of the Savage Mind*. Cambridge: Cambridge University Press.

Goody, Jack (2010) *The Eurasian Miracle*. Cambridge: Polity.

Graeber, David (2001) The Globalization Movement: Some Points of Clarification. *Items and Issues*, 2 (3–4): 12–14.

Gray, John (1998) *False Dawn: The Delusions of Global Capitalism*. London: Granta.

Gray, John (2003) *Al-Qaeda and What It Means to be Modern*. London: Faber.

Gray, John (2005) The World is Round. *New York Review of Books*, December 18: 20–23.

Green, Sarah, and Anna Malm (2013) *Borderwork: A Visual Journey Through Peripheral Frontier Regions*. Helsinki: Ja Silti.

Hall, Thomas D., and James V. Fenelon (2004) The Futures of Indigenous Peoples: 9–11 and the Trajectory of Indigenous Survival and Resistance. *Journal of World-Systems Research*, 10 (1):153–97.

Halliday, Fred (2000) Global Governance: Prospects and Problems. In *The Global Transformations Reader*, eds. D. Held and A. McGrew, pp. 483–89. Cambridge: Polity.

Hann, Chris, and Keith Hart (2011) *Economic Anthropology*. Cambridge: Polity.

Hannerz, Ulf (1987) The World in Creolization. *Africa*, 57: 546–59.

Hannerz, Ulf (1989) Notes on the Global Ecumene. *Public Culture*, 1: 66–75.

Hannerz, Ulf (1990) Cosmopolitans and Locals in World Culture. In *Global Culture*, ed. Mike Featherstone, pp. 237–53. London: Sage.

Hannerz, Ulf (1992) *Cultural Complexity: The Social Organization of Meaning*. New York: Columbia University Press.

Hannerz, Ulf (1996) *Transnational Connections*. London: Routledge.

Hardt, Michael, and Antonio Negri (2000) *Empire*. Cambridge, MA: Harvard University Press.

Hart, Keith (1973) Informal Income Opportunities and Urban Employment in Ghana. *Journal of Modern African Studies*, 11: 61–89.

Hart, Keith (2013) Manifesto for a Human Economy. The Memory Bank. http://thememory bank.co.uk/2013/01/20/object-methods-and-principles-of-human-economy/. Accessed August 10, 2013.

Hart, Keith, Jean-Louis Laville, and Antonio David Cattani, eds. (2010) *The Human Economy*. Cambridge: Polity.

Harris, Nigel (2002) *Thinking the Unthinkable: The Immigrant Myth Exposed*. London: I. B. Tauris.

Harris, Olivia (1995) Knowing the Past: The Antinomies of Loss in Highland Bolivia. In *Counterworks: Managing Diverse Knowledges*, ed. R. Fardon, pp. 105–23. London: Routledge.

Harvey, David (1989) *The Condition of Postmodernity*. Oxford: Blackwell.

Harvey, David (2005) *A Short History of Neoliberalism*. Oxford: Oxford University Press.

Hassan, Robert, and Ronald E. Purser, eds. (2007) *24/7: Time and Temporality in the Network Society*. Stanford, CA: Stanford Business Books.

Haugerud, Angelique (2013) *No Billionaire Left Behind: Satirical Activism in America*. Stanford, CA: Stanford University Press.

Held, David, Anthony Barnett, and Caspar Henderson (2005) *Debating Globalization*. Cambridge: Polity.

Held, David, and Anthony McGrew (2000) The Great Globalization Debate: An Introduction. In *The Global Transformations Reader*, eds. D. Held and A. McGrew, pp. 1–50. Cambridge: Polity.

Held, David, Anthony McGrew, David Goldblatt, and Jonathan Perraton (1999) *Global Transformations*. Cambridge: Polity.

Hemer, Oscar, and Thomas Tufte, eds. (2005) *Media & Glocal Change: Rethinking Communication for Development*. Buenos Aires: CLACSO.

Hirst, Paul, and Grahame Thompson (1999) *Globalization in Question*, 2nd edition. Cambridge: Polity.

Honoré, Carl (2005) *In Praise of Slow: How a Worldwide Movement is Challenging the Cult of Speed*. London: Orion.

Horst, Heather A. (2006) The Blessings and Burdens of Communication: Cell Phones in Jamaican Transnational Social Fields. *Global Networks*, 6: 143–59.

Huntington, Samuel (1996) *The Clash of Civilizations: Remaking of the World Order*. New York: Simon & Schuster.

Huyssen, Andreas (2003) Present Pasts: Media, Politics, Amnesia. In *Globalization*, ed. Arjun Appadurai, pp. 57–77. Durham, NC: Duke University Press.

International Organization for Migration (2013) World Migration Report 2013: Migrant Well-Being and Development. http://www.iom.int/cms/wmr2013. Accessed October 6, 2013.

Internet World Stats (2013) Usage and Population Statistics. http://www.internetworld stats.com. Accessed October 6, 2013.

Kang, Susan (2013) Demands Belong to the 99%? The Conflict Over Demands, Issues, and Goals in OWS. In *Occupying Political Science: The Occupy Wall Street Movement from New York to the World*, eds. Emily Welty et al., pp. 59–88. London: Palgrave Macmillan.

Kant, Immanuel (2001 [1795]) To Eternal Peace. In *Basic Writings of Kant*, pp. 433–77. New York: Modern Library.

Kasten, Erich, ed. (2004) *Properties of Culture—Culture as Property*. Berlin: Dietrich Reimer Verlag.

Kearney, Michael (1995) The Local and the Global: The Anthropology of Globalization and Transnationalism. *Annual Review of Anthropology*, 24: 547–65.

Keys, David (1999) *Catastrophe: An Investigation into the Origins of the Modern World*. London: Century.

Kiely, Ray (2005) *The Clash of Globalisations: Neo-liberalism, the Third Way and "Anti-globalisation."* Amsterdam: Brill Academic Press.

Klein, Naomi (1998) *No Logo: No Space, No Choice, No Jobs*. London: Picador.

Lanquar, Robert (2011) *Tourism in the Mediterranean: Scenarios Up To 2030*. Brussels: MEDPRO Report No. 1/July 2011.

Lash, Scott, and John Urry (1993) *Economies of Signs and Space*. London: Sage.

Latour, Bruno (1993) *We Have Never Been Modern*. Cambridge, MA: Harvard University Press.

Leitch, Alison (2003) Slow Food and the Politics of Pork Fat: Italian Food and European Identity. *Ethnos*, 68 (4): 437–62.

Levinson, Marc (2006) *The Box: How the Shipping Container Made the World Smaller and the World Economy Bigger*. Princeton, NJ: Princeton University Press.

Lévi-Strauss, Claude (1966 [1962]) *The Savage Mind*. Chicago: University of Chicago Press.

Lévi-Strauss, Claude (1989 [1955]) *Tristes Tropiques*. London: Picador.

Levitt, Peggy (2001) *The Transnational Villagers*. Berkeley: University of California Press.

Lewellen, Ted C. (2002) *The Anthropology of Globalization*. Westport, CT: Bergin & Garvey.

Liebowitz, Stan J., and Stephen E. Margolis (2013) The Troubled Path of the Lock-In Movement. *Journal of Competition Law and Economics*, 9 (1): 125–52.

Lien, Marianne E. (2007) Weeding Tasmanian Bush; Biomigration and Landscape Imagery. In *Holding Worlds Together: Ethnographies of Knowing and Belonging*, eds. M. E. Lien and M. Melhuus. Oxford: Berghahn.

Lien, Marianne E., and Marit Melhuus, eds. (2007) *Holding Worlds Together: Ethnographies of Knowing and Belonging*. Oxford: Berghahn.

Löfgren, Orvar (1999) *On Holiday: A History of Vacationing*. Berkeley: University of California Press.

Lovelock, James (2006) *The Revenge of Gaia: Why the Earth Is Fighting Back—and How We Can Still Save Humanity*. London: Allen Lane.

Luhmann, Niklas (1995) *Social Systems*. Stanford, CA: Stanford University Press.

Maeckelbergh, Marianne (2009) *The Will of the Many: How the Alterglobalisation Movement is Changing the Face of Democracy*. London: Pluto.

Malinowski, Bronislaw (1984 [1922]) *Argonauts of the Western Pacific*. Prospect Heights, IL: Waveland.

Marcus, George (1998) *Ethnography Through Thick and Thin*. Princeton, NJ: Princeton University Press.

Marling, William H. (2006) *How "American" is Globalization?* Baltimore: Johns Hopkins University Press.

Martin, Bill (1998) *Listening to the Future: The Time of Progressive Rock 1968–1978*. Chicago: Open Court.

Martin, Keir (2013) *The Death of the Big Man and the Rise of the Big Shots: Custom and Conflict in New Britain*. Oxford: Berghahn.

Mathews, Gordon (2012) Neoliberalism and Globalization from Below in Chungking Mansions, Hong Kong. In *Globalization From Below: The World's Other Economy*, eds. Gordon Mathews, Gustavo Lins Ribeiro, and Carlos Alba Vega, pp. 69–85. London: Routledge.

Mathews, Gordon, Gustavo Lins Ribeiro, and Carlos Alba Vega, eds. (2012) *Globalization from Below: The World's Other Economy*. London: Routledge.

Mayer-Schönberger, Viktor, and Kenneth Cukier (2013) *Big Data: A Revolution That Will Transform How We Live, Work and Think*. London: John Murray.

McAlpine, Rachel (2006) From Plain English to Global English. http://www.webpage content.com/arc_archive/139/5. Accessed on October 6, 2013.

McGovern, Patrick (2002) Globalization or Internationalization? Foreign Footballers in the English League, 1946–95. *Sociology*, 36 (1): 23–42.

McLuhan, Marshall (1994 [1964]) *Understanding Media: The Extensions of Man*. London: Routledge.

McNeill, William (1977) *Plagues and Peoples*. New York: Anchor.

Meyer, John W., Aaron Benavot, Yua-Kyung Cha, David H. Kamens, and Suk-Ying Wong (1992) *School Knowledge for the Masses*. London: Falmer.

Miller, Daniel (2011) *Tales from Facebook*. Cambridge: Polity.

Mittelman, James (2001) Globalization: Captors and Captives. In *Capturing Globalization*, eds. J. H. Mittelman and N. Othman, pp. 1–17. London: Routledge.

Monbiot, George (2003) *The Age of Consent: A Manifesto for a New World Order*. London: Flamingo.

Morris, Ian (2010) *Why the West Rules—For Now: The Patterns of History, and What They Reveal About the Future*. New York: Farrar, Straus, & Giroux.

Morley, David (2000) *Home Territories: Media, Mobility and Identity*. London: Routledge.

Naipaul, V. S. (1961) *A House for Mr Biswas*. London: Andre Deutsch.

Naipaul, V. S. (1981) *Among the Believers*. London: Andre Deutsch.

Naipaul, V. S. (1987) *The Enigma of Arrival*. London: Viking.

Naipaul, V. S. (1998) *Beyond Belief: Islamic Excursions Among the Converted People*. New York: Vintage.

Netcraft (2013) October 2013 Web Survey. http://news.netcraft.com. Accessed October 6, 2013.

Ngugi wa Thiong'o (1986) *Decolonising the Mind*. London: Heinemann.

Nuttall, Mark (2009) Living in a World of Movement: Human Resilience to Environmental Instability in Greenland. In *Anthropology and Climate Change: From Encounters to Actions*, eds. Susan A. Crate and Mark Nuttall, pp. 292–310. Walnut Creek, CA: Left Coast Press.

Olwig, Karen Fog (2003) Global Place and Place-Identities: Lessons from Caribbean Research. In *Globalisation—Studies in Anthropology*, ed. T. H. Eriksen, pp. 58–77. London: Pluto.

Orlove, Ben (2009) The Past, the Present and Some Possible Futures of Adaptation. In *Adapting to Climate Change: Thresholds, Values, Governance*, eds. W. Neil Adger, Irene Lorenzoni, and Karen O'Brien, pp. 131–63. Cambridge: Cambridge University Press.

Pálsson, Gísli (2013) Academics, Speak out Against Global Neoliberalism! Interview by Lorenz Khazaleh, Overheating research project. http://www.sv.uio.no/sai/english/research/projects/overheating/news/palsson.html. Accessed August 15, 2013.

Papastergiadis, Nikos (2000) *The Turbulence of Migration*. Cambridge: Cambridge University Press.

Petrini, Carlo (2007) *Slow Food Nation: Why Our Food Should Be Good, Clean, and Fair*. Portland, OR: Rizzoli Ex Libris.

Pleyers, Geoffrey (2010) Alter-Globalization. In *The Human Economy*, eds. Keith Hart, Jean-Louis Laville, and Antonio David Cattani, pp. 63–74. Cambridge: Polity.

Pliez, Olivier (2012) Following the New Silk Road Between Yiwu and Cairo. In *Globalization From Below: The World's Other Economy*, eds. Gordon Mathews, Gustavo Lins Ribeiro, and Carlos Alba Vega, pp. 19–35. London: Routledge.

Polanyi, Karl (1957 [1944]). *The Great Transformation: The Political and Economic Origins of our Time*. Boston, MA: Beacon.

Proulx, Craig (2010) Aboriginal Hip Hoppers: Representin' Aboriginality in Cosmopolitan Worlds. In *Indigenous Cosmopolitans: Transnational and Transcultural Indigeneity in the Twenty-First Century*, ed. Maximilian C. Forte, pp. 39–62. New York: Peter Lang.

Putnam, Robert (2000) *Bowling Alone: The Collapse and Revival of American Community*. New York: Simon & Schuster.

Riccio, Bruno (1999) Senegalese Transmigrants and the Construction of Immigration in Emilia-Romagna, Italy. D. Phil. thesis, University of Sussex.

Ritzer, George (1993) *The McDonaldization of Society: An Investigation into the Changing Character of Contemporary Social Life*. Newbury Park, CA: Pine Forge Press.

Ritzer, George (2004) *The Globalization of Nothing*. London: Sage.

Robertson, Roland (1992) *Globalization: Social Theory and Global Culture*. London: Sage.

Rodgers, Dennis (2004) "Disembedding" the City: Crime, Insecurity and Spatial Organization in Managua, Nicaragua. *Environment and Urbanization*, 16 (2): 113–23.

Rodrik, Dani (2011) *The Globalization Paradox: Why Global Markets, States, and Democracy Can't Coexist*. Oxford: Oxford University Press.

Rose, Flemming (2006) Why I Published those Cartoons. *Washington Post*, February 19.

Rosenau, James (1990) *Turbulence in World Politics: A Theory of Change and Continuity*. Princeton, NJ: Princeton University Press.

Rostow, Walt (1960) *The Stages of Economic Growth: A Non-Communist Manifesto*. Cambridge: Cambridge University Press.

Rushdie, Salman (1980) *Midnight's Children*. London: Jonathan Cape.

Rushdie, Salman (1988) *The Satanic Verses*. London: Viking.

Rushdie, Salman (1991) *Imaginary Homelands*. London: Granta.

Rushdie, Salman (2001) *Fury*. New York: Random House.

Sahlins, Marshall D. (1972) *Stone Age Economics*. Chicago: Aldine.

Sahlins, Marshall D. (1994) Goodbye to Tristes Tropes: Ethnography in the Context of Modern World History. In *Assessing Cultural Anthropology*, ed. Robert Borofsky, pp. 377–94. New York: McGraw-Hill.

Said, Edward (1978) *Orientalism*. New York: Vintage.

Sassen, Saskia (1998) *Globalization and Its Discontents*. New York: The New Press.

Sassen, Saskia (2003) Spatialities and Temporalities of the Global: Elements for a Theorization. In *Globalization*, ed. Arjun Appadurai, pp. 260–78. Durham, NC: Duke University Press.

Sassen, Saskia (2006) *Territory, Authority, Rights: From Medieval to Global Assemblages*. Princeton, NJ: Princeton University Press.

Sauper, Hubert (2004) *Darwin's Nightmare*. Documentary film.

Schiller, Nina Glick, Linda Basch, and Cristina Blanc-Szanton, eds. (1992) *Towards a Transnational Perspective on Migration: Race, Class, Ethnicity, and Nationalism Reconsidered*. New York: New York Academy of Sciences.

Scholte, Jan Aart (2005) *Globalization: A Critical Introduction*, 2nd edition. London: Palgrave.

Scholte, Jan Aart (2011) *Building Global Democracy? Civil Society and Accountable Global Governance*. Cambridge: Cambridge University Press.

Scott, James (2010) *The Art of Not Being Governed: An Anarchist History of Upland South Asia*. New Haven: Yale University Press.

Sennett, Richard (1997) *The Corrosion of Character: Personal Consequences of Work in the New Capitalism*. New York: W.W. Norton.

Sinding-Larsen, Henrik (1991) Computers, Musical Notation and the Externalisation of Knowledge: Towards a Comparative Study in the History of Information Technology. In *Understanding the Artificial: On the Future Shape of Artificial Intelligence*, ed. Massimo Negrotti, pp. 101–25. London: Springer-Verlag.

Smith, A. D. (1991) *National Identity*. Harmondworth: Penguin.

Soros, George (2002) *George Soros on Globalization*. Oxford: Public Affairs.

Standing, Guy (2011) *The Precariat: The New Dangerous Class*. London: Bloomsbury Academic.

Steger, Manfred (2008) *The Rise of the Global Imaginary: Political Ideologies from the French Revolution to the Global War on Terror*. Oxford: Oxford University Press.

Steger, Manfred (2009) *Globalization: A Very Short Introduction*. Oxford: Oxford University Press.

Stewart, Charles, ed. (2007) *Creolization: History, Ethnography, Theory*. Walnut Creek, CA: Left Coast Press.

Stiglitz, Joseph (2002) *Globalization and its Discontents*. London: Allen Lane.

Strange, Susan (1986) *Casino Capitalism*. Mancester: Manchester University Press.

Tambs-Lyche, Harald (1980) *London Patidars*. London: Routledge.

Tett, Gillian (2010) *Fools' Gold: How Unrestrained Greed Corrupted a Dream, Shattered Global Markets and Unleashed a Catastrophe*. London: Abacus.

Thrift, Nigel (1999) The Place of Complexity. *Theory, Culture and Society*, 16: 31–70.

Tilly, Charles (1984) *Big Structures, Large Processes, Huge Comparisons*. New York: Russel Sage.

Tsing, Anna Lowenhaupt (2005) *Friction: An Ethnography of Global Connection*. Princeton, NJ: Princeton University Press.

Tsing, Anna Lowenhaupt (2012) On Nonscalability: The Living World is not Amenable to Precision-Nested Scales. *Common Knowledge*, 18 (3): 505–24.

UNESCO (1995) *Our Creative Diversity*. Paris: UNESCO.

UNESCO (n.d.) Index Translationum. http://www.unesco.org/xtrans. Accessed October 6, 2013.

Urry, John (1990) *The Tourist Gaze: Leisure and Travel in Contemporary Societies*. London: Sage.

Urry, John (2000) *Sociology Beyond Societies*. Cambridge: Polity.

Urry, John (2003) *Global Complexity*. Cambridge: Polity.

Van Doorn, Judith (2002) *Migration, Remittances and Development*. Geneva: ILO.

Vertovec, Steven (2004) Cheap Calls: The Social Clue of Migrant Transnationalism. *Global Networks*, 4: 219–24.

Vertovec, Steven (2007) Super-diversity and its Implications. *Ethnic and Racial Studies*, 30 (6): 1024–54.

Vertovec, Steven (2010) Towards Post-multiculturalism? Changing Conditions, Communities and Contexts of Diversity. *International Social Science Journal*, 61: 83–95.

Virilio, Paul (1996) *Cybermonde: le politique du pire*. Paris: Philippe Petit.

Virilio, Paul (2000) *The Information Bomb*. London: Verso.

Wallerstein, Immanuel (1974–79) *The Modern World-System* (3 vols). New York: Academic Press.

Wallerstein, Immanuel (2004) *World-Systems Analysis: An Introduction*. Durham, NC: Duke University Press.

Williams, Raymond (1976) *Keywords*. London: Fontana.

Wilson, Godfrey (1941) *An Essay on the Economics of Detribalization in North Rhodesia*. Manchester: Manchester University Press.

Wilson, Richard A., ed. (1997) *Human Rights, Culture and Context*. London: Pluto.

Wilson, Richard A., ed. (2005) *Human Rights in the "War on Terror."* Cambridge: Cambridge University Press.

Wimmer, Andreas, and Nina Glick Schiller (2002) Methodological Nationalism and Beyond: Nation-State Building, Migration and the Social Sciences. *Global Networks*, 2 (4): 301–34.

Wisner, Ben, Piers Blaikie, Terry Cannon, and Ian Davis (2004) *At Risk: Natural Hazards, People's Vulnerability and Disasters*, revised edition. London: Routledge.

Wolf, Eric (1982) *Europe and the People without History*. Berkeley: University of California Press.

Yang, Yang (2012) African Traders in Guangzhou: Routes, Reasons, Profits, Dreams. In *Globalization From Below: The World's Other Economy*, eds. Gordon Mathews, Gustavo Lins Ribeiro, and Carlos Alba Vega, pp. 154–70. London: Routledge.

Index

CPSIA information can be obtained
at www.ICGtesting.com
Printed in the USA
LVHW060026020320
648621LV00008B/24

9 780